International Organizations and the Implementation of the Responsibility to Protect

This book seeks to understand the obligation of the international com implement the principles of the Responsibility to Protect (R2P).

With a focus on the humanitarian crisis in Syria, the volume examines what formal responsibility and actual capability international institutions have to protect and prevent civilians from systematic mass atrocities and presents an analysis of several prominent international organizations (IOs). Each chapter focuses on a specific organization and explores its formal responsibilities and how these pertain to the obligations of the R2P. Existing capabilities and actual abilities to address the challenges of R2P are analyzed by looking at these issues before, during, and after the occurrence of the humanitarian crisis in Syria.

With the UN not fully engaged in the Syrian conflict, the systematic human rights abuses have engendered greater attention on other organizations. This volume argues that if the UN Security Council's inactions result in an abdication of responsibilities under the UN Charter, there should not only be a discussion of how the UN must alter its approach, but also an examination of whether there are alternative R2P paths for other IOs to take in the name of international peace and human security.

This book will be of much interest to students of R2P, humanitarian intervention, international organizations, Middle Eastern politics and security studies.

Daniel Silander is Associate Professor in political science at Linnaeus University, Sweden.

Don Wallace is Professor of criminal justice at the University of Central Missouri, USA.

Global Politics and the Responsibility to Protect
Series Editors:
Alex J. Bellamy
Griffith University
Sara E. Davies
Griffith University
and
Monica Serrano
The City University of New York

The aim of this book series is to gather the best new thinking about the Responsibility to Protect into a core set of volumes that provides a definitive account of the principle, its implementation, and its role in crises, that reflects a plurality of views and regional perspectives.

Global Politics and the Responsibility to Protect
From words to deeds
Alex J. Bellamy

The Responsibility to Protect
Norms, laws and international politics
Ramesh Thakur

Humanitarian Intervention and the Responsibility to Protect
Security and human rights
Cristina G. Badescu

Sri Lanka and the Responsibility to Protect
Politics, ethnicity, genocide
Damien Kingsbury

International Responsibility and Grave Humanitarian Crises
Collective provision for human security
Hannes Peltonen

Global Justice, Kant and the Responsibility to Protect
A provisional duty
Heather M. Roff

UN Emergency Peace Service and the Responsibility to Protect
Annie Herro

International Organizations and the Implementation of the Responsibility to Protect
The humanitarian crisis in Syria
Edited by Daniel Silander and Don Wallace

Moral Responsibility, Statecraft, and Humanitarian Intervention
The US response to Rwanda, Darfur, and Libya
Cathinka Vik

International Organizations and the Implementation of the Responsibility to Protect

The humanitarian crisis in Syria

Edited by Daniel Silander and Don Wallace

Routledge
Taylor & Francis Group
LONDON AND NEW YORK

First published 2015
by Routledge

2 Park Square, Milton Park, Abingdon, Oxon OX14 4RN
711 Third Avenue, New York, NY 10017, USA

Routledge is an imprint of the Taylor & Francis Group, an informa business

First issued in paperback 2016

British Library Cataloguing-in-Publication Data
A catalogue record for this book is available from the British Library

Library of Congress Cataloging-in-Publication Data
International organizations and the implementation of the responsibility to protect : the humanitarian crisis in Syria / edited by Daniel Silander and Don Wallace.
pages cm. – (Global politics and the responsibility to protect)
Includes bibliographical references and index.
ISBN 978-1-138-89126-5 (hardback : alk. paper) –
ISBN 978-1-315-70964-2 (ebook : alk. paper)
1. International agencies–Syria. 2. Humanitarian assistance–Syria.
I. Silander, Daniel, 1972– II. Wallace, Don, 1932–
JZ5335.I68 2015
956.9104'2–dc23 2014046575

ISBN: 978-1-138-89126-5 (hbk)
ISBN: 978-1-138-72935-3 (pbk)

Typeset in Times New Roman
by Wearset Ltd, Boldon, Tyne and Wear

To the parents in humanitarian crises, subject to incomprehensible loss

Contents

Contributors

John Janzekovic is a lecturer of politics and international relations at the University of the Sunshine Coast, Australia. He earned his PhD in Political Science from the University of the Sunshine Coast, focusing on international politics, international law and human security.

Stephen Marr is a senior lecturer of peace and conflict studies at Malmö University, Sweden. He received his PhD in Political Science from the University of Florida, specializing in comparative politics, political theory and African studies.

Craig McLean is a senior lecturer in the Department of Social Sciences at the University of Northumbria, UK. He earned a PhD in Politics and International Relations from the University of Newcastle. His main interests are in the areas of European politics, the European Union and homeland security from a transatlantic perspective.

Niall Guy Michelsen is an associate professor of political science and public affairs and the director of the international studies BA at Western Carolina University in the US. He earned a PhD in Political Science at the University of North Carolina, Chapel Hill.

Melinda Negrón-Gonzales is an assistant professor and program coordinator of the Politics and Society Program at the University of New Hampshire-Manchester. She was awarded a PhD in Political Science from the University of Florida. One focus of her research explores the diffusion and impact of international norms, especially involving the Responsibility to Protect (R2P).

Martin Nilsson is a senior lecturer of political science at Linnaeus University, Sweden. He earned a PhD in Political Science from the School of Social Sciences at Växjö University, Sweden and has conducted research on European organizations, democratization and politics in Latin America and Europe.

Alan Patterson is a former soldier and UK civil servant. He studied at the University of Newcastle Upon Tyne, UK, where he completed a Master's degree in European Union public policy, followed by a doctoral research program, after which he was awarded a PhD on the UK government's handling of risk regulation.

Daniel Silander is an associate professor of political science and earned his PhD in Political Science from the School of Social Sciences at Växjö University, Sweden. He conducts research on international politics, democracy and democratization, human security, and humanitarian interventions. He has also published on the role of European organizations in democracy-building and peace-building processes.

Don Wallace is a professor of criminal justice at the University of Central Missouri, where he teaches and has published on counter-terrorism and civil liberties, the death penalty and international human rights. He has an LL.M. in International Law from the University of Missouri-Kansas City in addition to a J.D. from the University of Nebraska.

1 Introduction

Daniel Silander and Don Wallace

> Millions of human beings remain at the mercy of civil wars, insurgencies, state repression and state collapse. This is a stark and undeniable reality, and it is at the heart of all the issues with which this Commission has been wrestling. What is at stake here is not making the world safe for big powers, or trampling over the sovereign rights of small ones, but delivering practical protection for ordinary people, at risk of their lives, because their states are unwilling or unable to protect them.
>
> (International Commission on Intervention and State Sovereignty, 2001, p. 11).

In the fall of 2013, it appeared to the world that some form of armed intervention by the United States (US) and like-minded Western powers in the Syrian conflict was inevitable. This intervention, coming on the heels of a reluctant acknowledgement by the US that chemical weapons had been used by the Syrian government on its own people, would be to alleviate their suffering. However, the intervention did not occur. Using its significant influence over the country, Russia was able to convince the Syrian government to accept an unenthusiastic offer by the US to enter negotiations to remove the chemical weapons.

Today, although the efforts to remove these weapons are occurring, the Syrian government has the upper hand in the conflict. The war-weary Syrian public stumbles through a country that has been ravaged by civil war. In December 2013, the United Nations Secretary-General Ban Ki-moon raised his estimate on the death toll in Syria's civil war to more than 100,000, up from an estimate of nearly 93,000 just over a month earlier (Lederer, 2013). The Oxford Research Group estimated that, by the end of August 2013, 11,420 children aged 17 years and younger had been recorded killed in the Syrian conflict, out of a total of 113,735 civilians and combatants killed (Salama and Dardagan, 2013). In late March 2014, the United Nations (UN) stressed that around 150,000 people had been killed and that more than 40 percent of the population had become refugees or displaced persons (Nyheter, 2014). In September 2013, the Office of the UN High Commissioner for Refugees announced that violence in the country has created more than two million refugees, with a further 4.2 million people displaced inside Syria (UN Agency, 2013). The Western powers have avoided intervening in a desperate situation that appears can only be alleviated by a significant military effort with humanitarian goals. In early December 2013 the UN

High Commissioner for Human Rights linked President Bashar al-Assad of Syria to war crimes and crimes against humanity for the first time, citing evidence collected by her panel of investigators over the course of the 33-month-old conflict in Syria (Cumming-Bruce, 2013). The Commissioner repeated her demand that the situation in Syria be referred to the International Criminal Court (ICC).

The top UN official in charge of coordinating the destruction of Syria's chemical weapons stockpile confirmed that the country's ability to produce those munitions had been rendered inoperable since a joint mission with the Organisation for the Prohibition of Chemical Weapons (OPCW) began work in October of 2013. However, the official, Sigrid Kaag, said at the organization's annual meeting of member-states in The Hague, "the most complex and challenging work still lies ahead," referring to the safe disposal of the weapons. According to a UN Security Council (UNSC) resolution, they had to be destroyed by mid-2014 (Cumming-Bruce, 2013).

While the UN has become more engaged with the conflict in Syria, through its respective organizations, this has come at a glacial pace in a situation that has been ongoing since March 2011. Although the UN is the leading global authority for safeguarding international peace and security, numerous other international crises have at times portrayed the UN as unwilling or unable to safeguard the security of individuals across the world. Despite the basic principles of the UN Charter, interventions have often been flawed and absolutely unable to act to save lives. Although the UN can claim legality and legitimacy, as an intergovernmental organization, the organization has often, such as in Syria, acted too little and too late, with millions of people remaining in harm's way.

In the post-Cold War era, scholars have begun to acknowledge the escalating international challenge in addressing failing and failed states. These scholars have demonstrated how such states have failed in the core functions of statehood, resulting in domestic chaos and threatening international peace. At times, human security has been challenged due to neglect or deliberate disregard of the affected peoples' safety (Rummel, 1994, pp. 2–15). Examples of failing states in a list dating back to the 1990s include: Chad, Darfur, the Democratic Republic of Congo, East Timor, Ethiopia, Kosovo, Libya, Nigeria, Rwanda, Sierra Leone, Somalia, Sudan, Uganda, and the former Yugoslavia, among others. All of these crises have triggered international, academic, and political attention on the obligation and legitimacy of the international community to protect human rights with or without a UNSC mandate (Janzekovic and Silander, 2013, pp. 20–27).

Scholarly studies have identified only weak consistency in UN interventions, although the UN Charter sets out conditions for UN interventions in the name of international peace and security, the response has been selective. While Rwanda and Darfur were crises that led to accusations of the international community doing too little, too late; the intervention in Kosovo and perhaps also Libya met with criticism on actions that were taken to be too much, too fast. With the increasing number of crises and UN operations, the operations have also become increasingly complex, due to the nature of civil wars. Peacekeeping operations have developed into a mix of peacekeeping, peacemaking, and peace enforcement, thus providing severe pressure on the UN's ability and capacity to act. While the world may sit out another crisis while blaming the UN for not intervening and protecting human security, another possibility for the world community is to acknowledge the universality of human rights and the corresponding universal obligation to intercede in situations as desperate as that in Syria. In 2005, the UN World Summit formally acknowledged the principle of Responsibility to Protect (R2P). In paragraphs 138 and 139, its 2005 UN Outcome Document stressed the universal responsibilities of states and international organizations to promote and protect human security. Over the last several years, R2P has arguably become an important international principle. Based on the previous atrocities in Rwanda and the former Yugoslavia, the UNSC decided to apply R2P for the first time in Darfur and explicitly thereafter in Libya.

R2P addresses third-party actions to prevent violent behavior, prevent the escalation of ongoing violence, and prevent violence from re-emerging. The international principle of R2P also addresses how an absolute notion of state sovereignty conflicts with an obligation to safeguard citizens. If this obligation is not met by the state, there is a legitimate justification for humanitarian intervention to protect human security and prevent the escalation of human security abuses. Ignoring human security is therefore not an option; the UN Charter and R2P, with numerous conventions, treaties and protocols, address the legal and legitimate obligations of the international community to act. Though there does not yet exist an affirmative duty to implement the R2P doctrine (Rose, 2014), it can serve as a responsive principle for how the international community could act to protect human rights.

This book seeks to understand the obligation of the international community, through international organizations (IOs), to protect the inhabitants in these situations. The overall question for this book is: *What formal responsibility and actual capability do international organizations have to protect and prevent civilians from systematic mass atrocities?* The responsibility of these organizations to engage in the implementation of R2P is discussed in the next section of this chapter. It discusses the responsibilities and capabilities these organizations have in implementing the R2P principle, in partnership with each other and/or the UN.

The above question will be developed in the international context of the developing civil war in Syria, in which more than 150,000 people have been killed, millions have become refugees or displaced persons, millions are starving and a generation of children and young adults have been deprived their basic right to physical and psychological well-being. While the UN has not been fully engaged in Syria, the systematic human rights abuses in Syria have engendered greater attention to the abilities and capabilities of other IOs. If the UNSC's inactions result in breaches of the UN Charter, there should not only be a discussion on how the UN must alter its approach and how powerful member-states of the UNSC must be held accountable, but also an examination of whether there are alternative paths for other IOs to take in the name of international peace and human security.

International Organizations and R2P

The obligations of international organizations in the responsibility-to-protect paradigm are the focus of this book. An understanding is sought of the structure of these organizations, their authority and the roles they can and do play in situations involving failing or overreaching states that lead to massive humanitarian crises. In 2001, a report by the International Commission on Intervention and States Sovereignty (ICISS) triggered an international debate on human and state security. It set out the responsibility of the international community when state authorities fail or are unwilling to safeguard their people from mass atrocities (ICISS, 2001). The report argued for the protection of basic human security and the intervention by the international community when states fail to protect their own people. The report defined the international community as consisting of sovereign states but also included international, regional, and non-governmental organizations (ICISS, 2001, ¶¶3.6, 6.31).

One often overlooked dimension of this report was the responsibility of IOs to be engaged in the implementation of R2P and how these organizations could be crucial for turning a principle into action in international politics. In the 2005 UN General Assembly's (UNGA) World Summit Outcome Document, one section linked the notion of R2P to regional organizations and referred to Chapter VIII of the UN Charter, to further emphasize the importance of regional organizations on R2P. For example, paragraph 139 linked the UN implementation of R2P to other partners by emphasizing "relevant regional organizations" (UNGA, 2005, ¶¶138–139) as potential partners that might assist in the collective action needed to implement UNSC measures endorsing R2P.

Since the formation of the UN in 1945, this organization has shared its responsibility for providing peace and security with regional entities. Chapter VIII of the UN Charter directly addresses the following:

> [N]othing in the present Charter precludes the existence of regional arrangements or agencies for dealing with such matters relating to the maintenance of international peace and security as are appropriate for regional action provided that such arrangements or agencies and their activities are consistent with Purposes and Principles of the United Nations.
>
> (UN Charter, Article 52)

Article 52 of the UN Charter continues and emphasizes the responsibility of regional entities to assist the UN and for them to "make every effort to achieve pacific settlement of local disputes through such regional arrangements or by such regional agencies *before* referring them to the UNSC." It is important to acknowledge the word *before* in this sentence, as it implies an acceptance of the independent authority for regional organizations to protect and prevent the escalation of violence. Although the UN Charter explicitly sets out these responsibilities, it was first in a post-Cold War context that regional responsibilities to assist the UN were again highlighted in the security debate. The former UN Secretary-General, Boutros Boutros-Ghali, addressed in 1992 the importance of burden-sharing to assist the UN in its activities to promote peace (Boutros-Ghali, 1992). The idea of a "regional–global security partnership" (United Nations Security Council, 2007) was further discussed as post-Cold War crises emerged, such as that in Kosovo in 1999, in Darfur in 2006, in the Republic of Congo in 2008, and in Libya in 2010, and which engaged regional organizations, such as the North Atlantic Treaty Organization (NATO), the African Union (AU) and the European Union (EU).

The systematic atrocities taking place in these and other situations have triggered a debate on how to share responsibilities to prevent such future crises and, if necessary, how to conduct interventions, legal in their methods and legitimate in their goals, to protect civilians in harm's way. While the more authoritative UN Outcome Document stressed the importance of UN authority behind all regional actions in the name of R2P, the ICISS Report emphasized the many problems embedded in the UNSC structures and the UN's periodic inability to act according to the objectives set out in the UN Charter. Therefore, the ICISS Report would allow for the opportunity for regional engagement to implement R2P when the UN fails to deliver assistance according to the Charter and it would also enable regional actions to be endorsed *ex post facto* by the UNSC. However, the regional–global security partnership has come under scrutiny regarding the issue of burden-sharing (ICISS, 2001, ¶6.35). While current practice continues to be framed by the UN and its ultimate authority to legalize and legitimize international actions in international politics, the ICISS Report stressed the importance of regional organizations acting when the UNSC fails to deliver on R2P challenges (i.e., when mass atrocities are foreseen, are happening, or have occurred) (ICISS, 2001).

However, the UN Outcome Document and the ICISS Report would agree on the long-term process that contextualizes R2P. In both documents, the R2P principle is about both protection and prevention. In other words, acting in the name of R2P implies assisting societies that are under stress before crises and conflicts break out and then safeguarding people from mass atrocities, limiting the scope of mass atrocities when they occur and rebuilding societies after atrocities have occurred. Although most R2P debates in international politics have focused on military interventions to halt ongoing mass atrocities, R2P is much broader in its scope, highlighting the responsibilities of the international community to prevent and protect civilians from human-security abuses (UNGA, 2005, ¶138).

The UN Outcome Document and the ICISS agree on a broadened understanding of R2P. R2P encompasses the prevention, the protection, and the rebuilding phases; or, as Gareth Evans has argued, R2P is about prevention, reaction, and reconstruction and any actions in the name of R2P are multifaceted, including political/diplomatic–, economic/social–, constitutional/legal– and security-related tools. While the preventative and rebuilding stages of R2P embed a large scope of tools, the reaction stage is much more limited, covering only specific political and diplomatic measures in peacekeeping, peace enforcement and economic actions, as well as emergent military measures (Evans, 2008).

The notion of a multilayered R2P, including prevention, protection, and post-reconstruction, opens up the opportunity for a wide range of international organizations to be involved in implementing R2P when necessary. It addresses the increased leverage that the UNSC may have on R2P challenges when acknowledging the regional–global security partnership that is potentially provided by existing IOs, as well as their different capabilities. In this framework, this book provides a platform that explores the responsibilities and capabilities of a wide range of international organizations on R2P for the crisis in Syria in a context of debates about regional–global security partnerships between these entities and the UN.

Structure of the text

This book seeks to understand the obligation of the international community, through IOs, to protect the inhabitants of failing and failed states in humanitarian crises by focusing on the responsibility of these organizations to help implement the Responsibility to Protect (R2P) in the crisis in Syria. Again, the overall question for this book is: *What formal responsibility and actual capability do international organizations have to protect and prevent civilians from systematic mass atrocities?* The examination of this question will include analyses of several prominent IOs and several chapters will each examine a specific organization. These chapters will explore an organization's formal responsibilities and how they pertain to the obligations of R2P. The existing capabilities for implementing R2P and the actual abilities to address the challenges of R2P will also be examined, as will the challenges before, during, and after the occurrence of a humanitarian crisis. Each chapter then applies its examination to the case of Syria. Additionally, there is a chapter focusing on Syria that will present the reader with an understanding of the current humanitarian crisis due to the internal conflict in this country. Another chapter will provide the reader with an understanding of the general concept of the responsibility to protect and the burden that is placed on the role of IOs to engage in this responsibility, particularly in relation to the situation of failing/failed states.

This book will combine assessments of the structures and roles of important IOs in situations that call for R2P, with a focus on the developing humanitarian crisis in Syria. This innovative combination of tasks will provide the reader with an assessment of these organizations' roles as they confront a challenging obligation in the context of a current and ongoing humanitarian crisis. This book is structured in three parts. The first part, Chapters 1–3, sets out the aim of the study, focusing on the role projected for IOs in the UN Outcome Document and the ICISS on R2P, the notion of R2P as a principle in international politics and the nature of failing states in general and Syria in particular. The first part addresses the failing states as black holes in international politics that present major challenges to international security, order and human security, and provides a means with which to understand IOs in relation to R2P challenges. It provides a descriptive analysis of key concepts that underscore the themes of the book with discussion on R2P as a principle in international relations and the guiding role of the UNSC. The discussion proceeds to identify the role that is projected for IOs by the UN in its 2005 Outcome document and by the report of the ICISS regarding R2P. A context is provided for this discussion on R2P, with an elaboration of the causes and consequences of failing states. One chapter is devoted to the current situation in Syria; it places the civil war in historical context and provides information on the participants. Additionally, there is a discussion of the threat of the conflict that is posed for international security.

The second part of the book, which consists of Chapters 4–11, focuses on several IOs and their capacities for recognizing the responsibility to protect based on the 2005 UN document. Each organization is explored by discussing its formal responsibilities in relation to R2P, its existing capabilities for implementing R2P and its actual abilities to address R2P challenges before, during, and after mass human rights violations have occurred. The organizations in focus are the International Criminal Court (ICC), the Organisation for the Prohibition of Chemical Weapons (OPCW), the Organization for Islamic Cooperation (OIC), the League of Arab States (LAS), the Gulf Cooperation Council (GCC), the North Atlantic Treaty Organization (NATO), the Group of Eight (G8), and the Organization for Security and Co-operation in Europe (OSCE).

The third and final part of the book, Chapter 12, summarizes this analysis of the responsibilities, and capabilities for the collective group of IOs included in this study on R2P. Also examined are what every individual organization should and must do better in the future in order to avoid another atrocity like the one in Syria and, if not avoided, how to intervene in a coherent, principle-based manner.

What are the possibilities and problems identified within the international community and within each IO to address R2P obligations set out in the UN Outcome Document? Why have the mass atrocities in Rwanda in 1994, in which it was obvious that the international community did too little and too late, been followed by failures to prevent further atrocities elsewhere in the world? Why did the international community not prevent the atrocities in Syria from happening or at least protect civilians from the civil war and the systematic murders? After all of these efforts, why has there been no systematic response from IOs to situations so desperate that they cry out for the various entities of the international community to meet their obligations under the R2P principle?

References

Boutros-Ghali, B. (1992, June 17). Report of the Secretary-General–An agenda for peace. *Preventive diplomacy, peacemaking and peacekeeping*. United Nations General Assembly. (UN Doc. No. A/47/277-S/24111).

Cumming-Bruce, N. (2013, December 3). Top UN rights official links Assad to crimes in Syria. *New York Times*. p. A8.

Evans, G. (2008). *The responsibility to protect: Ending mass atrocity crimes once and for all*. Washington DC: Brookings Institution Press.

International Commission on Intervention and State Sovereignty. (2001). *Report on the responsibility to protect*. Retrieved from: http://responsibilitytoprotect.org/ICISS%20 Report.pdf (accessed April 5, 2014).

Janzekovic, J. and Silander, D. (2013). *Responsibility to protect and prevent: Principles, promises and practicalities*. London: Anthem Press.

Lederer, Edith M. (2013, December 12). Death toll in Syria rises to 100,000, UN Chief Ban Ki-Moon says. *The World Post*. Retrieved from: www.huffingtonpost.com/2013/07/25/death-toll-syria-100000_n_3652448.html (accessed April 5, 2014).

Nyheter, Dagen (2014, March 21). Syrien i skuggan av krim. Dagen Nyheter. p. 4 (Stockholm).

Rose, Steven J. (2014). Moving forward with the responsibility to protect: Using political inertia to protect civilians. *Boston College International and Comparative Law Review*, 37, 209–240.

Rummel, R. (1994). *Death by government*. New Brunswick, NJ: Transactions Publishers.

Salama, Hana and Dardagan, Hamit (2013, November 24). *Stolen futures: The hidden toll of child casualties in Syria*. Oxford Research Group. Retrieved from: www.oxfordresearchgroup.org.uk/publications/briefing_papers_and_reports/stolen_futures (accessed April 5, 2014).

United Nations. (1945). *Charter of the United Nations*. New York: United Nations.

UN Agency. (2013, September 3). Number of Syrian refugees tops 2 million, with "more on the way," *UN News Centre*. Retrieved from: www.un.org/apps/news/story.asp?NewsID=45757#.UqnBU-AmWRI (accessed April 5, 2014).

UN General Assembly. (2005). *UN world summit outcome document*. (UN Doc. No. A/RES/60/1). Retrieved from: www.un.org/womenwatch/ods/A-RES-60-1-E.pdf (accessed April 17, 2014).

UN Security Council. (2007, March 23). *The UN and regional organizations – Update report*, No. 3. Retrieved from www.securitycouncilreport.org/atf/cf/{65BFCF9B-6D27-4E9C-8CD3-F6E4FF96FF9}/Update%20Report%2023%20Mar%202007_ROs.pdf (accessed April 5, 2014).

2 The United Nations, international organizations and responsibility to protect

Don Wallace and Daniel Silander

This book is about the roles and capacities of international organizations (IOs) in international crises, such as the ongoing tragedy in Syria. This chapter addresses the principle of the Responsibility to Protect (R2P) in international politics. It sets out the nature of the R2P principle and how it emphasizes human security as a requirement to state security; R2P highlights the sovereignty of human beings and how state sovereignty is derived from the people. State sovereignty implies the obligation of each government to protect its people and to promote state functions that are necessary to promote good lives. R2P is a new international principle that may transform international politics (see Bellamy and Wheeler, 2005; Finnemore and Sikkink, 1998; Knight and Egerton, 2012; Stahn, 2007). It has evolved due to the new post-Cold War era, but also because many state governments, IOs, global bodies, and individual leaders have spoken out on protecting and promoting human security. Although state sovereignty and non-intervention are leading norms in international politics and sovereign states continue to be core units in international relations, R2P promotes human security and human rights to such an extent that it has become a reference point or a guiding principle that is essential in all international discussions on security and human rights (Brunnée and Toope, 2006; Janzekovic and Silander, 2013).

The supreme authority of the United Nations

Security has always been an essentially contested concept (Gallie, 1956; Peoples and Vaughan-Williams, 2010). The end of the Cold War opened up a long and intensive debate on what constitutes the security construct (Gaddis, 2007; Walker, 1995). The contemporary notion of security has been vigorously debated, although a common definition refers to security as the alleviation of threats to cherished values (Collins, 2007; Williams, 2008). "Traditionally, the state has been the thing to be secured, what is known as the referent object" (Collins, 2007, p. 2). The scholarly debates on international security have addressed state security in terms of state survival and state military capacity. International politics consists of states as key actors with the objective of surviving in an anarchic setting. Seeking power has been the ultimate national interest, as power is the capacity to influence other states. The scholarly debate has assumed that states have different levels of power, which makes some states more vulnerable than others. Due to the chaotic setting, without a universal supreme power, states are part of a hierarchical order of polarity that may be altered through alliances, although self-help capacity always remains crucial (Bull, 1977; Mansfield, 1993; Morgenthau, 1978; Waltz, 1979).

The state security approach was based on the Peace of Westphalia of 1648, when the modern international state order was created. It approached the international order by defining state internal sovereignty in terms of territorial claims, centralized authority, and external state sovereignty under a non-intervention principle (Spruyt, 2000; Waltz, 2001). The contemporary international order has been based on the state sovereignty norm and the principle of non-intervention (Onuf, 1971), as institutionalized in the United Nations (UN) Charter (1945). Article 2(1) of the UN Charter affirms, "The Organization is based on the principle of the sovereign equality of its entire Members." Article 2(4) also states that "All Members shall refrain in their international relations from the threat or use of force against the territorial integrity or political independence of any state" and Article 2(7) articulates the sovereignty norm in international relations by prohibiting international interventions into state matters:

> Nothing contained in the present Charter shall authorize the United Nations to intervene in matters which are essentially within the domestic jurisdiction of any state or shall require the Members to submit such matters to settlement under the present Charter.

The UN Charter highlights how the aforementioned articles on the principles of state sovereignty and non-intervention are central to the assumptions of the role of the UN as it was originally conceived. In Article 1 of the UN Charter, these purposes rest on the assumption of the need to resolve disputes between states: "To maintain international peace and security" and to settle "international disputes or situations which might lead to a breach of the peace." There are two exceptions to the principle of non-intervention declared in the Charter. First, there is a limitation on the States' exclusive right to use force where Article 39 sets out the right of the UN Security Council (UNSC) to use force to protect international peace and stability. The UN Charter sets out the responsibility of the UNSC to provide remedies for threats to peace in international relations. Such remedies may be recommendations in Chapter VII to the involved parties, as stated in Article 39; the use of economic and diplomatic tools, as set out in Articles 41 and 42; or the deployment of armed forces, as stated as a possibility in Article 43. Second in Chapter VII, Article 51 sets out a restriction on the right of self-defense, allowing for a limiting role by the UNSC:

> Nothing in the present Charter shall impair the inherent right of individual or collective self-defence if an armed attack occurs against a Member of the United Nations, until the Security Council has taken measures necessary to maintain international peace and security.

Thus, the same article re-emphasizes the supreme role of the UNSC to uphold peace and security and how individual states are obliged to follow the principles of state sovereignty and non-intervention. The state sovereignty norm and the principle of non-intervention guided the international community throughout the Cold War period. The traditional state sovereignty norm and the non-intervention principle were perceived to organize international order, protect each state's national interests and safeguard the citizens of the state (Moore, 1995). However, the UN has also addressed the promotion and protection of universal human rights and liberties. The UN Charter consists of broad references to human rights, which have been described as being "scattered, terse, even cryptic" (Steiner *et al.* 2008, p. 135). The Charter observes that the primary function of the UN is to maintain international peace and security (see UN Charter, Article 1(1)). Yet, the Charter refers to the need to promote and encourage respect for human rights in the context of achieving the goal of international peace and security. Though the inclusion of references to human rights in the Charter has been seen to be radical for its time, there is no comprehensive system placed in this document for the protection of human rights (Smith, 2010). Thus, at most the affirmative obligation within the ascribed purposes of the UN in Article 1 is to "achieve international cooperation … in promoting and encouraging respect for human rights and for fundamental freedoms for all …"

It is also the responsibility of the UN General Assembly to promote human rights and freedoms (see UN Charter, Article 13). With this authority, there has been considerable development by the UN of human rights. To that end, the UN has been instrumental in the institutionalized progress made on human rights in the Universal Declaration of Human Rights, the Geneva Conventions, the 1948 Convention on the Prevention and Punishment of the Crime of Genocide, and the two 1966 Covenants on Economic, Social and Cultural Rights and on Civil and Political rights (see Janzekovic and Silander, 2013).

The end of the Cold War resulted in changed international perceptions regarding the concept of security (for a lengthy discussion on state vs. human security, see Janzekoivc and Silander, 2013); there was a shift from concern for security of the state to that of the individual. The notion of human security has embedded within it a critical perspective on what previously had been a state-oriented approach to security. Now, human security advocates argue that the referents for security are individuals (Collins, 2007, pp. 6–7). That individuals were the main referent point for security implied that human security was the endpoint and state security was, but a means to reach these security goals. The notion of human security also involved reinvigorating the various treaties and conventions that had been approved by state governments, but had become somewhat dormant. These treaties and conventions were aimed at protecting individuals from abuse by state governments, and by non-state actors (Kerr, 2007, pp. 93–94).

The recent Secretaries-General of the UN, Javier Perez de Cuellar (1982–91), Boutros Boutros-Ghali (1992–96), Kofi A. Annan (1997–2006) and Ban Ki-moon (2007–current), have all argued for a reorientation of UN security consideration by addressing human security (Boutros-Ghali, 1995). In 1994, the

Human Development Report and the United Nations Development Programme (UNDP) established several areas to be considered in order to safeguard human security and welfare (UN Development Programme, 1994, pp. 22–23). Based on the importance of protecting and promoting human security, as conceptualized in the 1994 UN Development Plan, Kofi Annan stressed a solution to human security abuses in the importance of humanitarian intervention to halt atrocities and safeguard civilians. It was time for the international community to accept that humanitarian interventions had to be launched in situations such as in Rwanda. In a provocative question he asked, "if humanitarian intervention is, indeed, an unacceptable assault on sovereignty, how should we respond to a Rwanda, to a Srebrenica—to gross and systematic violations of human rights that offend every precept of our common humanity?" (International Commission on Intervention and State Sovereignty, 2001, p. 2).

In the early 2000s, the UN repeatedly stressed the importance of both state and human security. The UN General Assembly in the 2005 World Summit Outcome statement confirmed that:

> We acknowledge that peace and security, development and human rights are the pillars of the United Nations system and the foundations for collective security and well-being. We recognize that development, peace and security and human rights are interlinked and mutually reinforcing.
>
> (UN General Assembly, 2000, §9)

A better and more secure world has to address challenges in four areas: development, peace and collective security, human rights and the rule of law, and the strengthening of the UN (UN General Assembly, 2000).

The UN and Syria

To varying degrees, the major constituent elements of the UN have been involved from shortly after the beginning of the protracted humanitarian crisis in Syria. The UNSC has primary, though discretionary, responsibility for responding to humanitarian crises when there is a threat to international peace and security. The UN General Assembly (UNGA) has significant authority to consider human rights issues and has provided numerous resolutions regarding Syria. The UN Human Rights Council (UNHRC) has utilized its special procedures mechanisms to investigate the continuing tragedy in Syria.

UN Security Council

Under the Charter the primary responsibility for international peace and security in the UN system is with the UNSC, because this body can make certain mandatory decisions, such as sanctions determinations, that all UN member-states are required to undertake. However, due to recurring vetoes by two permanent UNSC members, Russia and China, the UN has failed to impose sanctions, let alone authorize a humanitarian intervention, against the al-Assad regime in Syria (Golumbic and Ruff, 2013). On August 3, 2011, the UNSC formally first addressed the situation in Syria when it issued a presidential statement, calling upon the "Syrian authorities to fully respect human rights and to comply with their obligations under applicable international law" (UN Security Council President, 2011). However the concern over the "use of force against civilians by the Syrian authorities" was cabined in the stated affirmation of Syrian "sovereignty, independence, and territorial integrity" (UN Security Council President, 2011; see also Marauhn, 2013, pp. 415–416). A second presidential statement on March 21, 2012, was successful only after two prior draft resolutions had been vetoed by China and Russia. This second presidential statement expresses the support of the UNSC for the six-point proposal submitted to the Syrian authorities by Joint Special Envoy for the UN and the League of Arab States (LAS), Kofi Annan (UN Security Council President, 2012a). This proposal sought both a cessation of hostilities and a political solution. A third presidential statement was issued on April 5, 2012 and called upon all parties to cease armed violence and announced an intention to authorize a mechanism to monitor the end of violence (UN Security Council President, 2012b).

Within a few days, the UNSC adopted its first resolution, Resolution 2042, on the situation in Syria (UN Security Council, 2012a). This resolution included an endorsement of Kofi Annan's six-point proposal and the UNSC's expressed intention to establish a supervisory mission in Syria to monitor a cessation of the armed conflict. Resolution 2043 was adopted on April 21, 2012 (UN Security Council, 2012b), to establish the UN Supervision Mission for Syria (UNSMIS) with 300 observers that would monitor the cessation of violence and implement Kofi Annan's plan. Nearly from the first day of its operations onwards, UNSMIS has been confronted with tremendous difficulties stemming from the violence that would not abate. Kofi Annan resigned from the mission, in part due to disagreements among the permanent UNSC members on the best approach to take in a worsening situation (Bernstein, 2012). A draft resolution, which would have required compliance by the Syrian government with Resolution 2043 or face sanctions, as authorized under Article 41 of the UN Charter, was vetoed by China and Russia on July 19, 2012. The Secretary-General announced that he and the LAS had agreed upon Lakhdar Brahimi for Annan's replacement as Joint Envoy on August 17 (Nanda, 2013). This impasse in the UNSC was effectively formalized under the terms of Resolution 2059 (UN Security Council, 2012c), which brought the mission to an end on August 19, 2012, a date that largely marked the end of UNSC efforts to resolve the conflict in Syria. Subsequent attempts have been met with similar vetoes (Marauhn, 2013) and action by the UNSC has been limited to managing the conflict, not ending it.

In 2013 the UNSC was forced to address the issue of chemical weapons. In Resolution 2118 (UN Security Council, 2013) the UNSC condemned any use of chemical weapons in Syria and required it to work with the Organisation for the Prohibition of Chemical Weapons (OPCW) to eliminate the stockpile under Chapter VII of the Charter. In 2014, the increasing concern on access by the

Syrian people to humanitarian assistance resulted in Resolution 2139 on February 22 (UN Security Council, 2014a), which demanded that the Syrian authorities provide unhindered access for UN humanitarian assistance. Lakhdar Brahimi relinquished his post as UN Special Envoy to Syria on May 31, 2014. UN Secretary-General Ban Ki-moon Tuesday announced the envoy's resignation, terming it a "tragedy for the Syrian people" and a "failure" for the UN, leaving the international community "hopelessly divided" over how to end more than three years of bloodshed in Syria (Ki-moon, 2014). On July 14, 2014, Resolution 2165 (UN Security Council, 2014b) demanded that the Syrian authorities open access to all parts of the country for humanitarian assistance and called for a UN monitoring mechanism with the consent of the relevant neighboring countries of Syria for the distribution of humanitarian relief, allowing direct humanitarian access across four border crossings not controlled by the Syrian government.

UN General Assembly

While the UNSC has been plagued by an inability to act to resolve the crisis, the UNGA has already played a very important role in this crisis. On November 22, 2011, the UNGA passed a resolution condemning the Syrian government for not upholding its responsibility to protect Syrian civilians. The UNGA, on December 19, 2011, adopted a resolution, Resolution 66/176, that condemned the violence in Syria and called for the full implementation of the LAS's November 2011 Plan of Action and called upon Syria to comply with the UN Human Rights Council resolutions S-16/1 and S-17/1, which included cooperating with an independent international commission of inquiry (UN General Assembly, 2011). Three months later, in Resolution 66/253A, the UNGA again condemned the violence by all parties in Syria, endorsed the LAS's January 22 declaration on a Syrian political transition and requested the Secretary-General to appoint a special envoy for Syria (UN General Assembly, 2012a). The target audience shifted in the August 3, 2012 Resolution 66/253B from Syria to the UNSC where the UNGA deplored its failure to act on Syria, when on July 19 another UNSC resolution calling for sanctions on Damascus had been vetoed by China and Russia, and called for a political transition in that country (UN General Assembly, 2012b). A subsequent UNGA resolution, 67/262, condemned the Syrian government's indiscriminate violence against civilian populations and welcomed the establishment of the National Coalition for Syrian Revolutionary and Opposition Forces as a provisional entity needed for a political transition (UN General Assembly, 2013a). At the end of 2013, Resolution 68/182 condemned human rights violations in Syria and urged the UNSC to take measures to end human rights violations (UN General Assembly, 2013b).

UN Human Rights Council

The most activist organ of the UN with the Syrian crisis has been the UN Human Rights Council (UNHRC) (Marauhn, 2013). Within weeks of the government crackdown on protesters that triggered the unrest in Syria, on April 29, 2011, the UNHRC was addressing the situation in Syria. In its Resolution S-16/1, the UNHRC condemned the lethal violence against the protesters and requested an investigative mission to Syria, with preliminary findings expected in June and a follow-up report in September of 2011 (UN Human Rights Council, 2011a). Based upon the initial report, the UNHRC, on August 22, 2011, adopted Resolution S-17/1 and decided to dispatch an independent international commission of inquiry to investigate all alleged violations of international human rights law in Syria that had occurred since March 2011 and to identify those responsible with a view of ensuring that perpetrators of violations would be held accountable (UN Human Rights Council, 2011b). The Commission began its work immediately and has presented several comprehensive reports. These reports have formed the basis for further resolutions adopted by the UNHRC. In these subsequent resolutions, the UNHRC has consistently called for an end to the violence and for a peaceful resolution, while stressing the importance of its fact-finding mission and the need to hold the perpetrators of human rights violations accountable (Marauhn, 2013). In March of 2014, the UNHRC adopted Resolution 25/L.7 to extend the mandate of the Commission of Inquiry for another year (UN Human Rights Council, 2014).

The failing states syndrome

Up until the 1990s, the UN had too often taken for granted that sovereign states were the protector and not the abuser of human security (Piiparinen, 2010, p. 129). The UN Charter was founded on the idea that all participating governments at the founding meeting in San Francisco of 1945 were "in good and due form" (UN Charter, Preamble) and were therefore able to agree to and protect the principles and purposes of the Charter. Traditionally, international peace operations had been occupied with overseeing peace treaties between states or controlling territorial disputes between state governments in situations where official state acceptance was necessary for the UN to act. Since the 1990s, however, the nature of the scholarly debate (Buzan, 1983; Buzan, Wæver and Wilde, 1998; Mayall, 1991) and the UN humanitarian missions has changed (Bellamy, 2009; Bellamy *et al.*, 2010; Piiparinen 2010). UN missions have a complex set of objectives—to keep peace, make peace, or enforce peace; these missions have also been implemented in security and political contexts where the regime may have been the most serious challenge to peace (UN General Assembly, 2000). The number of UN missions has escalated and these missions have become complex in nature, facing intra-state wars between multiple armed factions, often ethnically- or culturally-based and with massive manipulation by elites of the masses (Thakur, 2006; Hampson and Malone, 2002; Helman and Ratner, 1992–93).

There have been discussions concerning international engagement to avoid failing states (Chauvet and Collier, 2008; Newman, 2010). The increasing number of internal conflicts is partly due to what the scholarly debate has labeled the "failing states syndrome" (Rotberg, 2002, 2004; Zartman, 1995; Fund for Peace, 2014). Up until the 1990s, the international community had too often assumed sovereign states were behaving responsibly towards the well-being of individuals. However, this approach not only caused enormous humanitarian suffering due to brutalizing regime violence against civilians, but also an inhumane international order in which people were allowed to be tortured, raped and killed under the shield of state sovereignty and non-intervention (Zartman, 1995). During the twentieth century, about 262 million people were killed in internal conflicts, six times higher than the total number of causalities from state-to-state wars (International Commission on Intervention and State Sovereignty, 2001). The statistics have been followed by a growing interest in security and the reorientation from a focus on state security to one that enshrines human security (Hampson and Malone, 2002; Rummel, 1994; Jackson, 1990):

> [I]n terms of international law, a tendency to broaden the definition of what may constitute a threat to international security according to the UN Charter is clearly discernible over recent decades … the inclusion of 'failed states' and ethnic conflicts in the definition of international security threats point to such a normative change, which also entails a broadening of the legitimacy of the use of force.
>
> (del Sarto, 2006, p. 508)

Numerous states have fundamental difficulties in upholding the rule of law and societal order, as well as providing safety to their people (Rotberg, 2004). Failing or failed states are unable to provide the core functions that have been embedded in the sovereignty norm. These regimes may have misused their power against their own people, being shielded by the notions of sovereignty and non-intervention. Instead of serving their people, numerous regimes have been unable to provide core duties, but also were the sole perpetrator in human insecurity within the state as well as beyond state territory (Jackson, 1990). *First*, the failing states syndrome portrays such a state as failing to provide its people with basic socio-economic services. It has included the failure to promote economic growth and social development, leaving citizens without the basic socio-economic conditions needed to secure basic rights and to avoid human suffering (Eizenstat *et al.*, 2005; Jackson, 2001; Rustow, 1999). *Second*, the failing states syndrome also consists of states failing to provide security to prevent mass atrocities against civilians. The inability to centralize authority and monopolize the use of violence has resulted in the misuse of power by official security forces, activities from paramilitary groups and/or pure mobs. *Third*, the failing states syndrome has finally included the failure to be a legitimate regime by the refusal or inability to represent the aspirations of the people (Janzekovic and Silander, 2013).

The recognition of this phenomenon of failed states has also examined the destabilizing effects that failing states have had on neighboring states, leading to the re-examination of external sovereignty and the principle of non-intervention

(Helman and Ratner, 1992–93; Newman, 2010). As the sovereignty norm embeds territorial control, centralized authority, and law and order to provide for stable and peaceful international relations, failing states are unable to uphold law and order internally, with external consequences. The destabilizing spillover effects that come from these internal incapacities may very well challenge other neighboring states and the international order at large. When failing and failed states become the immediate threat to other states' sovereignty and territorial integrity, due to domestic incapacities, the sovereignty of such a state is problematic (Wade, 2005). The growing concern for the failing states syndrome in international politics is fundamentally rooted in the structures of the Westphalian order, in that state security is to be underscored by state sovereignty and non-intervention and human security is at best relegated to a secondary concern. Individual states are expected to consist of a centralized authority that ensures a rule of law, provides for its people and respects the territorial integrity of other states. On the contrary, failing and failed states result in anarchy and human despair within their territory, as well as generate destabilizing effects on other states as dysfunctional black holes in the international landscape (Kaldor, 2007).

R2P as a principle in international politics

The failing state syndrome has resulted in the international community's response of humanitarian interventions (Murphy, 1996, pp. 282–295; Milliken and Krause, 2002, pp. 753–774; Krasner, 1999, pp. 3–43, 43–73; Krasner, 2001). As stated by advocates for human security, "[i]t is acknowledged that sovereignty implies a dual responsibility: externally—to respect the sovereignty of other states and internally—to respect the dignity and basic rights of all the people within the state" (International Commission on Intervention and State Sovereignty, 2001, ¶135).

The model of humanitarian intervention, in turn, has evolved into a focus on the sovereignty obligations of the failing state and the international community. The R2P was officially developed after the atrocities within Rwanda in 1994 (Abbott, C., 2005; Welsh and Sharma, 2012). The escalation of violence in Rwanda (Vaccaro, 1996) was due to the unwillingness of the French government to engage a former colonial entity at the same time as other major powers—the US and China—refused to label the mass slaughter in Rwanda as a genocide in order to avoid being legally required to intervene. While the American refusal to engage was due to its failed intervention in Somalia in 1992, the Chinese government argued in favor of inviolate state sovereignty and continued to refuse to engage in another state's domestic purview. While the international community was unwilling to halt the ongoing civil war, likely over 800,000 civilians (History Place, 1999) were murdered; moreover, the civil war destabilized the region, with local wars taken place in neighboring Zaire. Despite the legal and moral obligations of the international community to prevent the genocide from happening, the men, women and children were left to die due to the aggressive nationalism and the manipulation of ethnic politics between Hutus and Tutsis

(Grünfeld and Huijboom, 2007). The genocide in Rwanda sparked an international debate on the legal and moral duties of the international community to engage a situation when a sovereign state is part of genocide or is unable and/or unwilling to stop genocide from happening. The Rwanda crisis was followed by atrocities and/or systematic human rights violations in Bosnia in 1995 and in Kosovo in 1999.

The civil wars in the Balkans in 1991–95 had caused regional instability and grave human rights abuses in Bosnia and Croatia (Janzekovic, 2006; Rogel, 2004; Blitz, 2006; Cordial and Rosandhaug, 2008; Crnobrnja, 1996). Peace was finally settled after the Dayton Peace Agreement in 1995, but civil war broke out again in 1998–99 in Kosovo. In 1998, Serbian forces attacked Kosovo Albanians in an attempt to stop any Albanian efforts to seek independence or greater autonomy. As the UNSC was unable to reach an agreement (UN Security Council, 1999; UN Security Council, 1998), the North Atlantic Treaty Organization (NATO) decided to interfere militarily to stop what was argued could become ethnic cleansing (NATO, 1999). Based on UN Resolution 1199, which set out an ultimatum to Serbia to stop using military force in Kosovo, NATO implemented an air war forcing Serbian troops to withdraw from Kosovo in favor of a UN interim regime (Bieber and Daskalovski, 2003; Henriksen, 2007; Krieger, 2001).

The humanitarian crises in Rwanda and Kosovo exemplified the inability or unwillingness of the UNSC to act to protect civilians from regime violence (Abbott, 2005; Boutros-Ghali, 1992; Hehir, 2008). While some saw the international community doing too little too late in Rwanda, implying the illegality and illegitimacy of standing aside and doing nothing, others also argued that NATO's actions in Kosovo were too much and too soon; the goal was perhaps legitimate but the means were likely illegal (Independent International Commission, 2000; Independent International Commission, 2001; Molony, 2004). The perceived clash of norms between state security and non-intervention, on the one hand, and human security and humanitarian intervention, on the other, was once again raised in the debate (Wheeler and Bellamy, 2001; Wheeler, 2000; Hehir; 2012).

The atrocities of the 1990s, against which the UNSC did very little, were acknowledged by the UN Secretary-General Kofi Annan in September 1999. The Secretary-General stressed the importance of acknowledging human security to the UN General Assembly. He argued that individuals are sovereign and that state sovereignty is derived from the people: "State sovereignty, in its most basic sense, is being redefined … states are now widely understood to be instruments at the service of their peoples and not vice versa" (UN Meetings Coverage and Press Release, 1999). His statement was a way of emphasizing the moral obligations to act against atrocities and potential genocide when the UNSC was unable or unwilling to do so. His statement appeared in the context of the NATO intervention in Kosovo, which occurred without a UNSC mandate. Kofi Annan clearly argued for a new interpretation of state sovereignty. The Charter, he argued, necessitates that the international community protect and prevent civilians from harm and emphasized three important freedoms embedded in the UN

Charter: freedom from want and from fear, and to live in dignity (Annan, 2000). The UN Charter also addresses that the role the UNSC is to "investigate any dispute, or any situation which might lead to international friction or give rise to a dispute," (UN Charter, Article 34) which might in the long run jeopardize international peace and security.

A year after Annan's outspoken declaration, Canada's Foreign Minister Lloyd Axworthy and the Canadian government decided to organize the International Commission on Intervention and State Sovereignty (ICISS) as a platform for seeking international consensus on issues of state sovereignty, human security and humanitarian intervention. ICISS met for the first time on November 5–6, 2000, in Ottawa, Canada, which was followed by meetings in major cities around the world (International Commission on Intervention and State Sovereignty, 2001). The overall objective of the ICISS was to promote consensus on when and how humanitarian interventions were to be applied.

ICISS launched a report on R2P, which echoed Kofi Annan's previous statement by observing that when states fail to protect their people and prevent them from harm's way by not providing security and safety, it becomes the international community's role to intervene and safeguard civilians (International Commission on Intervention and State Sovereignty, 2001).

The ICISS Report sets out obligations for the international community to protect human security when sovereign states fail to protect their own people. The ICISS Report highlights three fundamental responsibilities embedded in R2P: first, the responsibility to address the causes of civilian insecurity; second, the responsibility to react to crises involving human despair with appropriate measures and third, the responsibility to rebuild societies in need through recovery, reconstruction and reconciliation (International Commission on Intervention and State Sovereignty, 2001). At times, these responsibilities may require military intervention by the international community. The ICISS Report also acknowledged that such interventions should be extraordinary and only in times when civilians are in great danger. It approached R2P by referring to the just cause threshold in the dangers of "large-scale of loss of life" and "large-scale ethnic cleansing." It also highlighted the precautionary principles to be considered before an intervention is launched. These principles are the (i) right intention to intervene; (ii) intervening as a last resort, (iii) using proportional means when intervening; and, (iv) having reasonable prospects to succeed when intervening (International Commission on Intervention and State Sovereignty, 2001, pp. xiii, 35–37).

The ICISS report did not accept what state security advocates had referred to as a clash of norms in the UN Charter. By referring to the UN Charter and the embedded notions of both state and human security, the ICISS report highlighted how state security in "peaceful and friendly relations among nations" required human security in "higher standards of living, full employment and conditions of economic and social progress and development," "solutions of international economic, social, health and related problems" as well as "universal respect for and observance of human rights and fundamental freedoms for all" (UN Charter,

Chapter IX). The report also stressed how Chapter IX, Article 5, addressed the pledge of member-states to take actions to ensure these human security issues (UN Charter, Chapter IX).

By referring to the disagreements within the UNSC to protect civilians, both in Rwanda in 1994 and in Kosovo in 1998–99, the ICISS Report argued for the need for an international metric on how and when humanitarian interventions are to be taken. The ICISS Report verified the supreme role of the UNSC as the appropriate body to authorize military intervention for human protection purposes. However, the ICISS Report also stressed that, although all authorization to intervene should be sought from the UNSC and that the UNSC in those cases has to deal promptly with such requests, the report questioned the ability of the UNSC to uphold the obligations set out in the UN Charter. If the UNSC fails to deliver security and protection in clearly identifiable humanitarian situations, the idea of the UN as a security provider and human rights protector would not only be in danger, it would also open up selective and biased responses from individual states, coalitions of states or IOs to act upon the failure of the UN. Such actions could very well be based on other reasons than humanitarian ones, could be highly selective and unjust, and could lead to international anarchy in which state sovereignty is always challenged (International Commission on Intervention and State Sovereignty, 2001).

The report suggested several major changes in how to authorize R2P. *First*, the permanent members of the UNSC would pledge to not use their veto power if no vital national interests are involved and when there is majority support for humanitarian action. *Second*, the report also highlighted that, if the UNSC rejects a proposal of humanitarian intervention or fails to address the issue in a timely manner, the General Assembly should have the possibility to decide. *Third and finally*, regional and sub-regional organizations should be able to assist the UNSC in protecting human security based on Chapter VIII of the Charter (International Commission on Intervention and State Sovereignty, 2001).

The ICISS Report on R2P resulted in lengthy political discussions within the UNGA. The unsolved issues after the report seemed to concern not just who will implement R2P in necessary cases, but also when humanitarian military intervention is justifiable in relation to state sovereignty. Every member-state acknowledged the importance of avoiding genocide, such as in Rwanda, but also the need to set out clear-cut principles for when to intervene militarily in order to avoid future debates like the one on NATO in Kosovo. In November 2003, the challenges of intra-state wars, systematic human rights abuses and potential genocide were raised at the UN Secretary-General–initiated High-Level Panel on Threats, Challenges and Change (UN Report of the Secretary-General's High-level Panel, 2004, pp. 56–57). This panel focused on how to build international security in the twenty-first century through protection and prevention mechanisms. One particular mission was to explore how to develop a transparent and effective relationship between the UNGA and the UNSC in order to seek international peace and order. The report developed by the UN High-Level Panel in 2004—*A More Secure World: Our Shared Responsibility*—re-emphasized the main content of the previous ICISS report by stating how state sovereignty embedded R2P and how the international community had to react when states failed to protect citizens (Kerr, 2007, p. 101). This High-Level Panel endorsed the "emerging norm" of a collective international responsibility to protect (High-level Panel, 2004, ¶203). Since this High-Level Panel report, the obligatory scope of R2P principles has become the subject of intense debate within the international community (Bell, 2014).

In September 2005, at the UN World Summit in New York, nearly all of the 198 states consented to the proposition that, although the principle of non-intervention is important to the structure of international security, it does not provide a permanent shield to international intervention when atrocities appear. However, despite such consensus, R2P provoked debate and a clash of interests, While major states, such as Argentina, Australia, Canada, Chile, all of the European Union member-states, Japan, Mexico, New Zealand, Peru, Rwanda, Singapore, South Africa, and Tanzania, stressed their support of R2P as a new international principle, other powerful states, such as Brazil, China, Cuba, Egypt, India, Iran, Malaysia, Pakistan, Russia, Syria, the US, and Venezuela, questioned different aspects of the proposal. They were critical of the challenges to state sovereignty and how R2P could be misused to interfere in state politics, as well as how R2P would be implemented. Some major powers also refused to set out limitations as to when they were allowed to use force in the name of state security (Janzekovic and Silander, 2013).

One major disagreement existed over what role the UNSC was supposed to have on implementing R2P. While the ICISS Report suggested a non-veto authority among UNSC member-states, if a major part of the General Assembly addressed the principle of R2P, China, Russia and the US agreed on their right to use their veto in all security-related issues (China voiced difficulty with part of this resolution (Baodong, 2011). The outcome of the debate on R2P was quite far from what the ICISS Report and Kofi Annan had earlier offered.

However, in Paragraphs 138 and 139 of the Outcome Statement of the UN World Summit, R2P was viewed as an emerging international principle on the responsibility of the international community to protect civilians from atrocities. In 2006, UNSC Resolution 1674 reaffirmed Paragraphs 138 and 139 on the responsibility to protect civilians from atrocities. Paragraph 138 states clearly that "Each individual State has the responsibility to protect its people from genocide, war crimes, ethnic cleansing and crimes against humanity;" it is also stated in Paragraph 139 that "The international community, through the United Nations, also has the responsibility to use appropriate diplomatic, humanitarian and other peaceful means, in accordance with Chapters VI and VIII of the Charter to help to protect populations ..." (UN General Assembly (2000, ¶138–139). In Paragraph 139, the UN also assures that it is ready to take action "in a timely and decisive manner" (UN General Assembly, 2000, p. 30). It requires, however, that there be a general consensus reached within the UNSC on R2P. In addition, even if such an agreement can be found, the five member-states also need to agree on how and by whom R2P is to be implemented (Peltonen, 2012).

The direct application of R2P since 2005 has been very limited and highly selective. The UN formally endorsed R2P in 2006 when the United Nations Mission in Sudan (UNMIS) included peacekeepers for Darfur (UN Security Council, 2006). R2P was also referred to in 2011–12 in Libya when the UNSC moved for the protection of civilians against the Gaddafi regime (UN News Centre, 2011; UN Security Council, 2011). In the last two decades or so, the UN has initiated humanitarian interventions in Liberia (1990–97), Somalia (1992–93), Bosnia (1992–95), Eastern Zaire (1994–96), Haiti (1994–97), Sierra Leone (1997–present) and East Timor (1999–present) (for more information on ethnic conflicts (Bangura, 2007). However, despite these UN efforts, the UN has also failed to intervene (Holzgrefe and Keohane, 2003) effectively to protect civilians in other places, such as in the ongoing civil war in Syria (Hashemi and Postel, 2013).

The legal basis of R2P

In the years following the ICISS's aspirational report, national governments have engaged in a contentious debate on the meaning of R2P. The concepts that have emerged from this process differ significantly from the principle in its form as presented by the ICISS. The debates in the UN system have produced no real consensus on the propriety of the principle, other than that it remains a principle and not yet developed into a binding legal obligation (Mohamed, 2012). As R2P is not enshrined in a formal treaty, for it to be considered a norm of international law, it will need to be accepted within customary international law (Hingst, 2013), which will be evidenced by State practice and *opinio juris* (Dickinson, 2013). Thus, though there may be a norm extending for some time and accepted by the international community, that allows collective intervention to respond to serious human rights abuses (Teson, 2000; Gassama, 2013), it is at most arguable that there is a norm, which, instead, obligates nations or international organizations to intervene in such situations of mass atrocities. However, as a set of principles that serve to limit the legal norms of sovereignty and non-intervention, it is clear that as observed by the world's leading powers in their declarations both individually (France has included R2P in its intervention guidelines, see Gramyk, 2014) and through the UNSC, that sovereignty entails a legal duty to protect civilian populations and where states fail in this regard, they cannot presume some sovereign right to a guarantee of non-intervention, which include the use of force (Brooks, 2013). To qualify as a legal norm, the concept of R2P has been criticized as being too amorphous, thus the development of concrete and objective criteria for undertaking international action will be a continuing goal of R2P advocates (Hingst, 2013).

There are juristic underpinnings of the R2P that can be traced to the general State responsibility concept, established by the International Court of Justice (ICJ) in the *Corfu Channel Case* in 1949. This judgment recognized international obligations of states towards individuals. Additionally, the ICJ in *Barcelona Traction* recognized a distinction between obligations owed to particular states and those owed to "the international community as a whole" and for the latter, "all States can be held to have a legal interest in their protection." The ICJ referred to this interest as obligations *erga omnes*. In the *Barcelona Traction* decision, the ICJ enumerated a few of the precipitating acts that result in this obligation: aggression, genocide, slavery and racial discrimination (Weiss, 2002).

Subsequently, in the 2001 International Law Commission's (ILC) Draft Articles on the Responsibility of States for Internationally Wrongful acts (ILC Draft Articles), which provides a platform for codification of the legal obligations of State responsibility for acts that attain the international community's attention, the UN acknowledged the importance of State responsibility. Under the ILC Draft Articles States have an obligation to respect human rights to the extent of not causing or tolerating mass atrocities upon their populations, otherwise such would constitute an internationally wrongful act (Saechao, 2007). The ILC Draft Articles have importance for nations considering their obligations under R2P for taking measures through IOs or for NGOs to do so. Article 54 of the Draft Articles on the Responsibility of States for Internationally Wrongful acts deals with measures taken by entities other than the injured state, more colloquially known as "collective countermeasures" (Bederman, 2002). Article 54 provides the essential basis for the language of Article 48, paragraph 1, which allows standing for states to take countermeasures, where the breached obligation "is owed to a group of States … and is established for the protection of a collective interest of the group; or … is owed to the international community as a whole." Article 48's broad reference to the international community demonstrates a broad concern that includes IOs, thus, the concept of international community relevant for article 48 does not consist exclusively of States and includes other non-governmental and governmental entities, for example the UN, the European Union (EU) and the International Committee of the Red Cross (Crawford, 2001). Here it has been observed that the reference in Article 48 to the "international community as a whole," conforms to the view that the international community today consists of actors in addition to the traditional constituency of nation-states (Weiss, 2002). The additional provision in Article 48(2) considers that a state invoking the responsibility of another state may ask not only for the cessation of the act and assurances that it will not recur, but also for reparation of the interest of the beneficiaries of the obligation that has been breached. Seemingly this Article could extend these reparations to individuals who have suffered from human rights violations (Bederman, 2002). Thus, these Draft Articles delineate an international obligation of states to take action in situations that would qualify as R2P. As such these actions are not explicitly dependent on UNSC permission.

Of some concern is that these specific consequences envisioned for an act that results in mass atrocities appear to be rather limited in the language of Article 48(2) when compared to the possible sanctions enumerated by the ICISS Report (Payandeh, 2010). These ICISS sanctions cover a range of options for military, economic and political/diplomatic sanctions that fall short of a military intervention (International Commission on Intervention and State Sovereignty. 2001, Articles 4.7–.9). While the ICISS Report took the view that the authority to legalize a military intervention should be concentrated in the UNSC, it did not limit other sanctions to the UN framework or to injured states. It would appear that the juristic developments in collective countermeasures would lend more than modest support to a robust use, which is not reliant on authorization by the UNSC, of non-military measures by an international community that includes intergovernmental and non-governmental organizations.

The role projected for international organizations

The potential role of IOs regarding R2P has received considerable interest since the 2010 crisis in Libya and the ongoing civil war in Syria. The UNSC decision on Resolution 1970 (UN Security Council, 2011a) was aimed at stopping the Libyan regime and Colonel Gaddafi from using violence against the Libyan people (For more analysis on the UNSC on Libya, see Janzekovic and Silander, 2013). The resolution included an arms embargo, the freezing of regime assets abroad and a travel ban for many key members of the regime. More importantly, Resolution 1970 was a direct result of the support from four IOs involving member-states of NATO, the EU, the African Union (AU) and the League of Arab States (LAS). Over time, all of these organizations agreed on the necessity of launching international measures against the Libyan regime in the name of R2P. In addition, as the civil war continued and Colonel Gaddafi's regime seemed to take no measures to halt the war, these organizations also argued in favor of measures that led to Resolution 1973 (UN Security Council, 2011b). Resolution 1973 re-stressed the requirements set out in the previous resolution, but added a no-fly zone against Gaddafi forces. The activities of NATO and its core member-states—France, the UK and the US—were a direct effect of the many IOs that continued to condemn the Libyan regime. Resolution 1973 called for regional support for the actions of various IOs. Appendix II of UN Resolution 1973 stressed the "condemnation by the League of Arab States, the African Union and the Secretary-General of the Organization of the Islamic Conference of the serious violations of human rights and international humanitarian law …" (UN Security Council, 2011b).

The Libya crisis addressed the importance of engaging IOs in the name of R2P in the context of its greatest challenge to national sovereignty, which is armed intervention. Many states and spokespersons within the UN have acknowledged that IOs often have greater insights into regional problems than individual states, have greater capacities to act upon R2P challenges as a coalition of governments and may be perceived to act more legitimately than individual regimes. The role of IOs on R2P was also mentioned both by the UN Outcome Document of 2005 and the ICISS Report on R2P. Both documents addressed IOs as legal and legitimate collaborators to the UN to protect civilians from mass atrocities.

The UN World Summit on R2P and international organizations

The UN World Summit of 2005 stressed the idea of using IOs as partners of the UN with the potential of developing working relationships (UN General Assembly,

2005). Its UN Outcome Document mentioned regional organizations in two paragraphs. Paragraph 139 referred explicitly to "relevant regional organizations." (UN General Assembly, 2005). It addressed the responsibilities of organizations as inherent in the UN Charter. Chapter VIII of the UN Charter outlines how "[n]othing in the present Charter precludes the existence of regional arrangements or agencies for dealing with such matters relating to the maintenance of international peace and security as are appropriate for regional action...." (UN Charter, Article 52). Although the UN Outcome Document addressed the importance of regional organizations to the UN's structures and policies, it also admonished that the UN is the superior authority on R2P challenges. It clearly argued that R2P issues must be addressed through the UN system. It re-emphasized that the use of military force must be authorized by the UNSC, as the intergovernmental entity that decides on matters of international peace and security. It acknowledged the potential role of regional organizations, as set out in the UN Charter, Chapter VIII on Regional Arrangements, but re-emphasized the superior role of the UN in such partnerships.

In this context, it must be observed that the UN Summit Outcome did not address whether the UN is the only international actor that can exercise the responsibility to protect, or merely the preferred actor (Bannon, 2006). The 2005 World Summit Report's omission in considering possible non-UN interventions by members of the international community stems from its purpose being to articulate guidelines by which the UN will take on its responsibilities. The premise of the concept of R2P, which rejects a claim of national sovereignty when a nation allows or commits mass atrocities against its own people, should delegitimize an objection on sovereignty grounds to coercive measures taken to intervene to protect these populations (Bannon, 2006).

> [S]ince respect for human rights is a State obligation under customary international law, it is a logical inference that States have an international responsibility not to allow violations of human rights to occur in their territories. Otherwise, they have committed an internationally wrongful act. Therefore, international human rights law has challenged the traditional understanding of State sovereignty by reinforcing a concept of sovereignty that imposes on States the responsibility to protect human rights.
>
> (Saechao, 2007, p. 674)

A critical question can be presented regarding what can and should be done by members of the international community should the UN fail to fulfill its responsibilities. The 2005 World Summit supports only non-UN action for a narrow range of conditions. *First*, the Report is itself limited to UN or non-UN action for only a small set of extreme human rights atrocities. *Second*, the agreement implies some preferences of interventions, in that good-faith UN action takes precedence over unilateralism by non-UN international actors and peaceful action is preferred over violent means. *Third and finally*, the agreement limits the scope of any intervention to that of protection of a nation's citizens from suffering of mass atrocities (Bannon, 2006).

The ICISS Report on R2P and international organizations

Although the ICISS report lacks the stature of the formal agreement of UN World Summit document, it is relevant to this discussion of the evolution of R2P principles and to developing a fuller understanding of the more limited set of principles that were adopted in the latter document. For those states that earlier adopted the ICISS Report this document can continue to serve as a normative baseline for R2P. The ICISS report called upon the international community to protect and prevent civilian suffering in an event of state failure. The report explicitly set out that IOs are an essential part of the international community and are therefore entitled to act and react in situations of atrocities (International Commission on Intervention and State Sovereignty, 2001). The ICISS report challenged the role of the UNSC and the UN Summit Outcome in 2005 in several ways. *First*, the report maintained a critical perspective of the UN that it has, at times, failed to uphold its duties to provide for international security and peace and that civilians have suffered due to such failures. It argued that there have been repeated situations in which the UN "[has rejected] a proposal or [failed] to deal with it in a reasonable time" (International Commission on Intervention and State Sovereignty, 2001, ¶6.35). *Second*, the ICISS report also stressed the need to reform the UN's procedures regarding the UNSC veto. It argued that the international community is better represented by the UNGA and that the General Assembly should have a greater voice on R2P (International Commission on Intervention and State Sovereignty, 2001, ¶¶6.29 and 6.30). The report emphasized the need to let the General Assembly establish a "Uniting for Peace" procedure during emergency special sessions. This procedure was developed in the 1950s to address crises when the UNSC was unwilling or unable to reach a decision (International Commission on Intervention and State Sovereignty, 2001, p. 53). *Third*, the report addressed the importance of regional actions on R2P challenges as a more efficient and timely procedure than the UN. Based on Chapter VIII of the UN Charter, the report stresses how regional organizations should be able to intervene in a situation. The ICISS Report also called upon IOs to be ready to act in the name of R2P even without a UNSC decision. It asked for "greater involvement by regional actors with intimate local knowledge" (International Commission on Intervention and State Sovereignty, 2001, p. 22).

Both documents on international organizations

Despite existing differences in the UN Summit Outcome and the ICISS reports, it is interesting to see how a UN–regional partnership is visualized in both documents. The ICISS report and the UN Summit Outcome address the need for regional organizations to take action on R2P. While the ICISS document sets out a more independent role for regional organizations, the UN Summit Outcome statement addresses the UNSC as the superior authority to decide on regional actions. The UN Summit Outcome report observes the responsibility of the international community for assisting states to exercise their responsibility to their populations, but also a more direct responsibility of the international community to help protect populations (UN General Assembly, 2005, ¶¶138–139). However, this broad responsibility to protect populations must be exercised according to the structures of the Charter. For appropriate diplomatic, humanitarian and other peaceful means, in accordance with Chapters VI and VIII, it is here where collective responsibility is recognized. It is only vaguely stated in the UN Summit Outcome report (Payandeh, 2010) that collective military action may be taken through the UNSC in cooperation with relevant regional organizations, should peaceful means be inadequate and national authorities manifestly fail to protect their populations from mass atrocities, this will be taken under Chapter VII on a case-by-case basis (UN General Assembly, 2005, ¶139).

The ICISS report suggested a greater role of regional organizations. Though acknowledging that the strict letter of the UN Charter requires action by regional organizations to be subject to prior authorization from the UNSC, such a role would be to react to R2P challenges in the event of the UNSC's failure or unwillingness to act, but as recent cases illustrate for the ICISS Report, notably Liberia and Sierra Leone, approval might be obtained after the event (International Commission on Intervention and State Sovereignty, 2001, p. 54). The ICISS Report cogently observed that realities on the ground might overwhelm a reluctance to act without UNSC authorization, in that if the UNSC fails to discharge its responsibility in egregious situations, then it is "unrealistic to expect that concerned states will rule out other means and forms of action to meet the gravity and urgency of these situations" (International Commission on Intervention and State Sovereignty, 2001, p. 55).

Non-military measures by IOs

There are interventions that can be far more instrumental in addressing R2P obligations than the use of military force at the height of a humanitarian crisis. After the 2005 World Summit approved R2P, the UN Secretariat began the process of incorporating the Summit Outcome into policy. The new UN Secretary-General, Ban Ki-moon, produced the 2009 report, "Implementing the Responsibility to Protect: Report of the Secretary-General," which was the first document from the UN Secretariat since the adoption of R2P by the World Summit in 2005. This document sought to clarify the commitments set forth in paragraphs 138 and 139 of the World Summit Outcome Document eventually to turn R2P into a practicable norm (Cribbs, 2013).

With regard to the operationalization of the R2P, the Secretary-General outlined a three-pillar approach for advancing the agenda of the World Summit Outcome Document. The first pillar consists of the protection responsibilities of the state for its own population from serious mass atrocities. Importantly for this discussion on the role of IOs, the second pillar entails the assistance and capacity building responsibility of the international community to support the state in its efforts to comply with its first pillar responsibilities. The third pillar considers the timely and decisive response by the international community should a state not live up to its responsibility to protect its people from mass atrocities (Payandeh, 2010).

Under Pillar Two, forms of assistance measures were delineated that IOs, as members of the international community, could enlist to help states to meet their obligations under R2P. These include encouraging states to meet their responsibilities through "confidential or public suasion, education, training and/or assistance," helping states with capacity-building, which would include "the civilian capacities of regional and sub-regional organizations to prevent crimes and violations," and assisting states "under stress before crises and conflicts break out" (Marks and Cooper, 2010, p. 98)

One widely accepted aspect of R2P is the responsibility of the international community to react to serious crimes with measures that fall below the threshold of an intervention that involves the use of armed force. When serious human rights violations occur, other states are allowed to react to this harm, as part of the obligation of R2P for the international community, through diplomatic, political or economic sanctions. Even the rather restrictive World Summit Outcome document acknowledges the international community's responsibility to use appropriate diplomatic, humanitarian, and other peaceful means through the auspices of the UN Charter. They may also implement economic, diplomatic, or political sanctions that can be imposed by the UNSC under Chapter VII of the UN Charter (Payandeh, 2010). Within this context, the question arises regarding what measures, outside UN auspices, the international community may resort to in order to fulfill their responsibility to protect.

Conclusion

The growing interest in a UN–regional partnership on R2P opens up questions regarding what regional organizations could do in the event of circumstances demanding an R2P response. We may approach this question by discussing the capacities and abilities of regional organizations. While the capacity of an organization refers to the resources and know-how to be used militarily, economically, politically and technologically, the ability refers to the possibility and/or willingness of a regional organization to act. Many regional organizations have great capacity to act upon R2P. However, great capacity to act does not necessarily mean an ability to do so. The ability to react upon R2P challenges may very well be undermined or troubled by consensus in decision-making procedures, the national interests of one or more member-states or by an organizational policy not to interfere in state affairs. This has been addressed above in the discussion concerning the selective responses by the UNSC on human security and is approached for IOs in the upcoming chapter. As long as the UNSC allows events like Rwanda and Syria to happen, there will be a continued debate on the suggestions set out in the ICISS report on independent regional organizations' actions in the name of R2P.

The advent of the R2P principle has symbolized a transformative change in international politics. It has implied a greater attention to human security in the world. It has also questioned the state sovereignty norm and the principle of non-intervention when failing and/or failed states misuse their power against their people. Enlightenment era political philosophers, present-day state leaders, Secretaries-General of the UN and scholars have argued that state sovereignty is derived from the people (Matheson, 2001). If states fail to implement necessary policies to provide socio-economic services, security and/or representation, it might be the legal and moral duty of the international community to safeguard civilians that are at most risk from resulting atrocities. The failing states syndrome is a global challenge that requires greater attention from the international community.

R2P encompasses two broad dimensions of responsibility. Beyond the responsibility of the state to protect its own people from mass atrocities, there is the responsibility of the international community to prevent and react to atrocity crimes and to help the affected nation to rebuild from the effects of these massive human rights violations. Thus, the questions raised for the array of IOs should consider the operational tasks expected and permitted under the accepted notions of R2P and the scope of their independence to act outside the purview of the UN. Both the UN Outcome Summit and the ICISS reports address the potential role of IOs to assist the UN on R2P challenges. These two documents have different approaches to a UN–regional partnership. The ICISS Report argues for a stronger position for regional organizations to take action in the event of UN failure. While the UN Summit Outcome establishes the UN as the exclusive authority with the possibility to decentralize power to regional organizations in order to take action, the ICISS Report argues in favor of regional interventions ex ante UN resolutions to safeguard human security. The proposal in this report is a direct effect of previous selective and failed responses by the UN. The idea of a UN–regional partnership on R2P and how it could look requires a deeper discussion on the capacities and practical abilities of IOs on R2P in international politics.

References

Abbott, C. (2005). Rights and responsibilities: Resolving the dilemma of humanitarian intervention. *Journal of Humanitarian Assistance*, 7, 1–8.

Annan, K. (2000). *"We the Peoples:" The Role of the United Nations in the 21st Century*. Retrieved from: www.un.org/en/events/pastevents/pdfs/We_The_Peoples.pdf (accessed July 13, 2014).

Bangura, A. (2007). Politicized ethnicities versus tribal ethnicities: Examples from Liberia, Rwanda and Sierra Leone. In Santosh C. Saha. (ed.). *The Politics Ethnicity and National Identity*, (pp. 121–138). New York: Peter Lang Publishing.

Bannon, A. L. (2006). The responsibility to protect: The UN world summit and the question of unilateralism. *Yale Law Journal*, 115, 1157–1165.

Baodong, L. (2011). *Statement by H.E. Ambassador Li Baodong, Permanent Representative of China to the United Nations, at the Security Council meeting on the situation in Libya*. Retrieved from: www.china-un.org/eng/hyyfy/t824183.htm (accessed July 13, 2014).

Bederman, D. J. (2002). Counterintuiting countermeasures. *American Journal of International Law*, 96, 817–832.

Bell, A. M. (2014). Using force against the "weapons of the weak": Examining a chemical-biological weapons usage criterion for unilateral humanitarian intervention under the responsibility to protect. *Cardozo Journal of International and Comparative Law*, 22, 261–320.

Bellamy, A. (2009). *Responsibility to protect: The global effort to end mass atrocities*. Cambridge UK: Polity Press.

Bellamy, A. and Wheeler, J. (2005). Humanitarian Intervention in World Politics. In J. Baylis and S. Smith (eds.). *Globalization of world politics*: *An introduction to international relations* (pp. 555–573). 3rd ed. New York: Oxford University Press.

Bellamy, A., Williams, P. and Griffin, S. (2010). *Understanding peacekeeping*. 2nd Edition. Cambridge, UK: Polity Press, Blackwell Pub.

Bernstein, S. (2012). The responsibility to protect after Libya: Humanitarian prevention as customary international law. *Brooklyn Journal of International Law*, 38, 305–342.

Bieber, F. and Daskalovski, C. (2003). *Understanding the war in Kosovo*. London; Portland, OR.: Frank Cass.

Blitz, B. (2006). *War and change in the Balkans: Nationalism, conflict and cooperation*. New York: Cambridge University Press.

Boutros-Ghali, B. (1992). *An agenda for peace, United Nations*. New York. Retrieved from: www.un.org/Docs/SG/agpeace.html (accessed July 13, 2014).

Boutros-Ghali, B. (1995). *An agenda for development 1995: With related UN documents*. New York: United Nations.

Brooks, R. (2013). Lessons for international law from the Arab spring. *American University International Law Review*, 28, 713–732.

Brunnée, J. and Toope, S. (2006). Norms, institutions and UN reform: The responsibility to protect. *Journal of International Law and International Relations*, 2, 121–137.

Bull, H. (1977). *The anarchical society: A study or order in world politics*. New York: Columbia University Press.

Buzan, B. (1983). *People, states and fear: The national security problem in international relations*. Brighton, UK: Wheatsheaf.

Buzan, B., Wæver, O. and Wilde, J. (1998). *Security: A new framework for analysis*. Boulder, CO: Lynne Rienner.

Chauvet, L. and Collier, P. (2008). What are the preconditions for turnarounds in failing states? *Conflict Management and Peace Science*, 25(4). 332–348.

Collins, A. (2007). Introduction: What is security studies? In A. Collins (ed.), *Contemporary Security Studies* (pp. 1–10). Oxford and New York: Oxford University Press.

Cordial, M. and Rosandhaug, K. (2008). *Post-conflict property restitution: The Approach in Kosovo and lessons learned for future international practice*. Leiden: Koninklijke Brill NV.

Crawford, J. (2001). Historical background and development of codification. Articles on Responsibility of States for Internationally Wrongful Acts. *Audiovisual Library of International Law*. Retrieved from: http://legal.un.org/avl/ha/rsiwa/rsiwa.html (accessed July 13, 2014).

Cribbs, M. (2013). *Expanding the responsibility to protect: Saving populations from HIV/AIDS*. Temple Law Review, 85, 879–919.

Crnobrnja, M. (1996). *The Yugoslav drama*. London: I. B. Tauris & Co Ltd.

del Sarto, R. A. (2006). Security and democracy: A reprise. *European Security*, 15(4). 507–518.

Dickinson, R. (2013). Responsibility to protect: Arab spring perspectives. *Buffalo Human Rights Law Review*, 20, 91–123.

Eizenstat, S. E., Porter, J. E. and Weinstein, J. M. (2005). Rebuilding weak states, *Foreign Affairs*, 84(1), 134–147.

Finnemore, M. and Sikkink, K. (1998). International norm dynamics and political change, *International Organization*, 52(4), 887–917.

Fund for Peace. (2014). *The failed states index 2013*. Retrieved from: http://ffp.statesindex.org/rankings-2013-sortable (accessed July 13, 2014).

Gaddis, J. (2007). *The cold war: A new history*. London: Penguin Books.

Gallie, W. B. (1956). *Essentially contested concepts*. Proceedings of the Aristotelian Society, 56, 167–198.

Gassama, I. J. (2013). Dealing with the world as it is: Reimagining collective international responsibility. Washington University *Global Studies Law Review*, 12, 695–753.

Golumbic, C. E. and Ruff III, R. S. (2013). Who do I call for an EU sanctions exemption?: Why the EU economic sanctions regime should centralize licensing. *Georgetown Journal of International Law*, 44, 1007–1053.

Gramyk, E. (2014). Increased Franco-British military cooperation: The impetus, its results, and the impact on international humanitarian intervention. *San Diego International Law Journal*, 15, 377–423.

Grünfeld, F. and Huijboom, A. (2007). *The failure to prevent genocide in Rwanda: The role of bystanders*. Leiden: Martinus Nijhoff.

Hampson, F. and Malone, D. (2002). Improving the UN's capacity for conflict prevention, *International Peacekeeping*, 9(1) 77–98.

Hashemi, N. and Postel, D. (2013). *The Syria dilemma*. Cambridge, MA: The MIT Press.

Hehir, A. (2008). *Humanitarian intervention after Kosovo: Iraq, Darfur and the record of global civil society*. Houndmills, Basingstoke: Palgrave Macmillan.

Hehir, A. (2012). *The responsibility to protect: Rhetoric, reality and the future of humanitarian intervention*. Basingstoke: Palgrave Macmillan.

Helman, G. and Ratner, S. (1992–1993). Saving failed states. *Foreign Policy Analysis*, 89, 3–20.

Henriksen, D. (2007). *NATO's gamble: Combining diplomacy and airpower in the Kosovo Crisis 1998–1999*. Annapolis: Naval Institute Press.

Hingst, Z. D. A. (2013). Libya and the responsibility to protect: Building block or roadblock? *Transnational Law & Contemporary Problems*, 22, 227–265.

History Place (1999). *The history place: Genocide in the 20th century*. Retrieved from: www.historyplace.com/worldhistory/genocide/rwanda.htm (accessed July 13, 2014).

Holzgrefe, J. and Keohane, R. (2003). *Humanitarian intervention: Ethical, legal and political dilemmas* (pp. 205–216). New York: Cambridge University Press.

Independent International Commission on Kosovo (2000). *The Kosovo Report: Conflict, International Response, Lessons Learned*. Oxford, UK: Oxford University Press.

Independent International Commission (2001). *The Follow-up of the Kosovo report: Why conditional independence?* Stockholm: Palme International Centre and Global Reporting.

International Commission on Intervention and State Sovereignty (2001). *Report on the Responsibility to Protect*. Retrieved from: http://responsibilitytoprotect.org/ICISS%20Report.pdf (accessed July 13, 2014).

Jackson, R. (2001). The state and internal conflict, *Australian Journal of International Affairs*, 55(1). 65–81.

Jackson, R. (1990). *Quasi-states: Sovereignty, international relations and the third world.* Cambridge: Cambridge University Press.

Janzekovic, J. (2006). *The use of force in humanitarian intervention: Morality and practicalities*. Hampshire: Ashgate.

Janzekovic, J. and Silander, D. (2013). *Responsibility to protect and prevent: Principles, promises and practicalities*. London: Anthem Press.

Kaldor, M. (2007). *New and old wars: Organized violence in a global era.* Stanford: Stanford University Press.

Kerr, P. (2007). Human security. In Alan Collins (ed.). *Contemporary Security Studies*, pp. 91–108. Oxford and New York: Oxford University Press.

Ki-moon, B. (2014, May 13). *Transcript of press briefing with the Secretary-General and Lakhdar Brahimi*, Joint Special Representative for Syria. Retrieved from: www.un.org/sg/offthecuff/index.asp?nid=3414 (accessed July 13, 2014).

Knight, W. A. and Egerton, F. (2012). *The Routledge handbook of the responsibility to protect*. New York: Routledge.

Krasner, S. (1999). *Sovereignty: Organized hypocrisy*. Princeton: Princeton University Press.

Krasner, S. (2001). Rethinking the sovereign state model. *Review of International Studies*, 27(5), 17–42.

Krieger, H. (2001). *The Kosovo conflict and international law: An analytical documentation 1974–1999*. Cambridge: Cambridge University Press.

Mansfield, E. D. (1993). Concentration, polarity and the distribution of power. *International Studies Quarterly*, 37, 105–128.

Marks, S. P. and Cooper, N. (2010). The responsibility to protect: Watershed or old wine in a new bottle? *Jindal Global Law Review*, 2, 86–130.

Marauhn, T. (2013). Sailing close to the wind: Human Rights Council fact-finding in situations of armed conflict – The case of Syria. *California Western International Law Journal*, 43, 401–459.

Matheson, M. (2001). United Nations governance of postconflict societies. *American Journal of International Law*, 95, 76–85.

Mayall, J. (1991). Non-intervention, self-determination and the "new world order." *International Affairs*, 67(3), 421–429.

Milliken, J. and Krause, K. (2002). State failure, collapse and reconstruction: Concepts, lessons and strategies. *Development and Change*, 33(5), 753–774.

Mohamed, S. (2012). Taking stock of the responsibility to protect. *Stanford Journal of International Law*, 48, 319–339.

Molony, S. (2004, August 4), Response to Rwanda "too little, too late". *News Africa*. Retrieved from: www.independent.ie/world-news/africa/response-to-rwanda-too-little-too-late-175164.html (accessed July 13, 2014).

Moore, M. (1995). UN peacekeeping: A glass half empty, half full. *Bulletin of the Atomic Scientists*, 51(2), 22–23.

Morgenthau, H. J. (1978). *Politics among nations* (5th ed.). New York: Knopf.

Murphy, S. (1996). *Humanitarian intervention: The United Nations in an evolving world order*. Philadelphia: University of Pennsylvania Press.

Nanda, V. P. (2013). The future under international law of the responsibility to protect after Libya and Syria. Michigan State University *Journal of International Law*, 21, 1–42.

NATO (1999, April 23), *Statement on Kosovo: Issued by the heads of state and government participating in the meeting of the North Atlantic Council in Washington, D.C. on*

23rd and 24th April 1999. Retrieved from: www.nato.int/docu/pr/1999/p99-062e.htm (accessed July 18, 2014).

Newman, E. (2010). Peacekeeping and peacebuilding as security in "failing" and "conflict-prone states," *Journal of Intervention and Statebuilding*, 4(3), 305–322.

Onuf, N. (1971). The principle of nonintervention, the United Nations and the international system. *International Organization*, 25(2), 209–227.

Payandeh, M. (2010). With great power comes great responsibility? The concept of the responsibility to protect within the process of international lawmaking. *Yale Journal of International Law*, 35, 469–516.

Peltonen, H. (2012). *International responsibility and grave humanitarian crises: Collective provision for human security*. (Global Politics and the Responsibility to Protect.) London: Routledge.

Peoples, C. and Vaughan-Williams, N. (2010). *Critical security studies: An introduction*. New York: Routledge.

Piiparinen, T. (2010). *The transformation of UN conflict management: Producing images of genocide from Rwanda to Darfur and beyond*. London; New York: Routledge.

Rogel, C. (1998). *The breakup in Yugoslavia and the war in Bosnia*. Westport: Greenwood Press.

Rogel, C. (2004). *The breakup of Yugoslavia and its aftermath*. Westport: Greenwood Press.

Rotberg, R. (2002). Failed states in a world of terror. *Foreign Affairs*, 81(4), 127–140.

Rotberg, R. (2004). *When states fail: Causes and consequences*. Princeton: Princeton University Press.

Rummel, R. (1994). *Death by government*. New Brunswick, N.J.: Transactions Publishers.

Rustow, Dankwart (1999). Transitions to democracy: Toward a dynamic model. In Lisa Anderson (ed.). *Transitions to Democracy* (pp. 14–40). New York: Columbia University Press.

Saechao, T. R. (2007). Natural disasters and the responsibility to protect: From chaos to clarity. *Brooklyn Journal of International Law*, 32, 663–707.

Smith, R. K. M. (2010). *International human rights*. Oxford, UK: Oxford University Press.

Spruyt, H. (2000). The end of empire and the extension of the Westphalian system: The normative basis of the modern state order. In James A. Caporaso. (ed.). *Continuity and change in the Westphalian order* (pp. 62–92). Malden: Blackwell Publishers, Inc.

Stahn, C. (2007). Responsibility to protect: Political rhetoric or emerging legal norm? *American Journal of International Law*, 101, 99–121.

Steiner, H., Alston, P. and Goodman, R. (2008). *International human rights in context: Law, politics, morals*. (3rd ed.). Oxford, UK: Oxford University Press.

Teson, F. R. (2000). Collective humanitarian intervention. *Michigan Journal of International Law*, 17, 323–371.

Thakur, R. (2006). *The United Nations, peace and security: From collective security to the responsibility to protect*. Cambridge, UK: New York: Cambridge University Press;

UN Development Programme (1994). *United Nations human development report 1994*. New York: Oxford University Press. Retrieved from: http://hdr.undp.org/en/media/hdr_1994_en_contents.pdf (accessed August 1, 2014).

UN General Assembly (2000). *Millennium declaration* (U.N. Doc A/RES/55/2). Retrieved from: www.un.org/en/ga/search/view_doc.asp?symbol=A/RES/55/2 (accessed August 1, 2014).

UN General Assembly (2005). *UN world summit outcome document.* (U.N. Doc A/RES/60/1). Retrieved from: www.un.org/womenwatch/ods/A-RES-60-1-E.pdf (accessed August 1, 2014).
UN General Assembly (2011, December 19). *Situation of human rights in the Syrian Arab Republic: Resolution adopted by the General Assembly on 19 December 2011* (U.N. Doc A/RES/66/176). Retrieved from: http://daccess-dds-ny.un.org/doc/UNDOC/GEN/N11/469/38/PDF/N1146938.pdf?OpenElement (accessed August 1, 2014).
UN General Assembly (2012a, February 21). *The situation in the Syrian Arab Republic: Resolution adopted by the General Assembly* (U.N. Doc A/RES/66/253 A). Retrieved from: www.refworld.org/docid/5013f0002.html (accessed August 1, 2014).
UN General Assembly (2012b, August 7). *The situation in the Syrian Arab Republic: Resolution adopted by the General Assembly* (U.N. Doc A/RES/66/253 B). Retrieved from: www.securitycouncilreport.org/atf/cf/%7B65BFCF9B-6D27-4E9C-8CD3-CF6E4FF96FF9%7D/a_res_66_253_b.pdf (accessed August 1, 2014).
UN General Assembly (2013a, June 4). *The situation in the Syrian Arab Republic: Resolution adopted by the General Assembly* (U.N. Doc A/RES/67/262). Retrieved from: www.securitycouncilreport.org/atf/cf/%7B65BFCF9B-6D27-4E9C-8CD3-CF6E4FF96FF9%7D/a_res_67_262.pdf. (accessed August 1, 2014).
UN General Assembly (2013b, December 18). *The situation in the Syrian Arab Republic: Resolution adopted by the General Assembly* (U.N. Doc A/RES/68/182). Retrieved from: www.securitycouncilreport.org/atf/cf/%7B65BFCF9B-6D27-4E9C-8CD3-CF6E4FF96FF9%7D/a_res_68_182.pdf. (accessed August 1, 2014).
UN Human Rights Council (2011a, April 29). *The current human rights situation in the Syrian Arab Republic in the context of recent events: Resolution adopted by the Human Rights Council* (U.N. Doc A/HRC/RES/S-16/1). Retrieved from: www.securitycouncilreport.org/atf/cf/%7B65BFCF9B-6D27-4E9C-8CD3-CF6E4FF96FF9%7D/Syria%20AHRC%20RES%20S-16%201.pdf. (accessed August 1, 2014).
UN Human Rights Council (2011b, August 23). *Situation of human rights in the Syrian Arab Republic: Resolution adopted by the Human Rights Council* (U.N. Doc A/HRC/RES/S-17/1). Retrieved from: www.ohchr.org/documents/hrbodies/hrcouncil/coisyria/ress17_1.pdf (accessed August 1, 2014).
UN Human Rights Council (2014, March 21). *Human rights situations that require the Council's attention* (U.N. Doc A/HRC/25/L.7). Retrieved from: www.securitycouncilreport.org/atf/cf/%7B65BFCF9B-6D27-4E9C-8CD3-CF6E4FF96FF9%7D/a_hrc_25_l7.pdf (accessed August 1, 2014).
UN Meetings Coverage and Press Release (1999, September 20). *Implications of international response to events in Rwanda, Kosovo examined by Secretary-General, in address to General Assembly* (GA/9595). Retrieved from: www.un.org/News/Press/docs/1999/19990920.ga9595.html (accessed August 1, 2014).
UN News Centre (2011, March 18) *Libya: Ban welcomes Security Council authorization of measures to protect civilians*, Retrieved from: www.un.org/apps/news/story.asp?NewsID=37809&Cr=libya&Cr1#.VEQPwijFkgY (accessed August 1, 2014).
High-level Panel (2004). *UN Report of the Secretary-General's high-level panel on threats challenges and change. A more secure world: Our shared responsibility*. pp. 56–57. Retrieved from: www.un.org/en/peacebuilding/pdf/historical/hlp_more_secure_world.pdf (accessed August 1, 2014).
UN Security Council President (2011, August 3). *Statement by the President of the Security Council* (U.N. Doc S/PRST/2011/16). Retrieved from: http://daccess-dds-ny.un.org/doc/UNDOC/GEN/N11/442/75/PDF/N1144275.pdf?OpenElement (accessed August 1, 2014).

UN Security Council President (2012b, April 5). *Statement by the President of the Security Council* (U.N. Doc S/PRST/2012/10). Retrieved from: www.un.org/en/ga/search/view_doc.asp?symbol=S/PRST/2012/10 (accessed August 1, 2014).

UN Security Council President (2012a, March 21). *Statement by the President of the Security Council* (U.N. Doc S/PRST/2012/6). Retrieved from: www.un.org/en/ga/search/view_doc.asp?symbol=S/PRST/2012/6&referer=www.un.org/en/sc/documents/statements/2012.shtml&Lang=E (accessed August 1, 2014).

UN Security Council (1998), *Resolution 1160* (U.N. Doc. S/RES/1160). Retrieved from: www.sipri.org/databases/embargoes/un_arms_embargoes/yugoslavia/yugoslavia-1998/1160 (accessed August 1, 2014).

UN Security Council (1999). *3989th Meeting* (U.N. Doc. S/PV.3989). Retrieved from: www.securitycouncilreport.org/atf/cf/%7B65BFCF9B-6D27-4E9C-8CD3-CF6E4FF96FF9%7D/kos%20SPV3989.pdf (accessed August 1, 2014).

UN Security Council (2006, August 31). *Resolution 1706* (U.N. Doc. S/RES/1706). Retrieved from: http://daccess-dds-ny.un.org/doc/UNDOC/GEN/N06/484/64/PDF/N0648464.pdf?OpenElement. (accessed August 1, 2014).

UN Security Council (2011a, February 26). *Resolution 1970* (U.N. Doc. S/RES/1970). Retrieved from: www.un.org/en/ga/search/view_doc.asp?symbol=S/RES/1970(2011) (accessed August 1, 2014).

UN Security Council (2011b, March 17) *Resolution 1973* (U.N. Doc. S/RES/1973). Retrieved from: http://daccess-dds-ny.un.org/doc/UNDOC/GEN/N11/268/39/PDF/N1126839.pdf?OpenElement (accessed August 1, 2014).

UN Security Council (2012a, April 12). *Resolution 2042* (U.N. Doc. S/RES/2042). Retrieved from: www.refworld.org/docid/4fbe14782.html (accessed August 1, 2014).

UN Security Council (2012b, April 21). *Resolution 2043* (U.N. Doc. S/RES/2043). Retrieved from: www.refworld.org/docid/4fbe13972.html (accessed August 1, 2014).

UN Security Council (2012c, July 20). *Resolution 2059* (U.N. Doc. S/RES/2059). Retrieved from: www.refworld.org/docid/50508cf32.html (accessed August 1, 2014).

UN Security Council (2013, September 27). *Resolution 2118* (U.N. Doc. S/RES/2118). Retrieved from: www.refworld.org/docid/524d3540707.html (accessed August 1, 2014).

UN Security Council (2014a, February 22). *Resolution 2139* (U.N. Doc. S/RES/2139). Retrieved from: www.refworld.org/docid/530c948e4.html (accessed August 1, 2014).

UN Security Council (2014b, July 14, 22). *Resolution 2165* (U.N. Doc. S/RES/2165). Retrieved from: www.refworld.org/docid/53c66b974.html (accessed August 1, 2014).

Vaccaro, M. (1996). The politics of genocide – Peacekeeping and disaster relief in Rwanda. In W. J. Durch (ed.). *UN Peacekeeping, American Policy and the Uncivil wars of the 1990s* (pp. 367–409). New York: St Martin's Press.

Wade, R. H. (2005). Failing states and cumulative causation in the world system. *International Political Science Review*, 26(1), 17–36.

Walker, M. (1995). *The cold war: A history*. New York: Henry Holt & Company Inc.

Waltz, K. (1979). *Theory of international politics*. Reading, MA: Addison-Wesley.

Waltz, K. (2001). *Man, the state and war: A theoretical analysis*. New York: Columbia University Press.

Welsh, J. and Sharma, S. (2012). Policy Brief: Operationalizing the Responsibility to Prevent. *Oxford Institute for Ethics, Law and Armed Conflict*. Retrieved from: www.oxfordmartin.ox.ac.uk/downloads/briefings/201204ELACResponsibility-to-Prevent.pdf (accessed August 1, 2014).

Wheeler, J. and Bellamy, A. (2001). Humanitarian intervention in world politics. In John Baylis and Steve Smith (eds.). *The globalization of world politics: An introduction to international relations* (pp. 522–539). Oxford, UK: Oxford University Press.
Wheeler, N. (2000). *Saving strangers: Humanitarian intervention in international society.* Oxford, UK: Oxford University Press.
Williams, P. D. (2008). Security studies: an introduction. In Paul D. Williams (ed.). *Security studies: an introduction* (pp. 1–12). London: Routledge.
Zartman, W. (1995). *Collapsed state: The disintegration and restoration of legitimate authority.* Boulder, CO: Lynne Rienner.

3 Contextualizing conflict

Trends and challenges in the Syrian Civil War[1]

Stephen Marr

On August 20, 2012, United States (US) President Barack Obama made a surprise appearance at the White House's daily press briefing. The ensuing Q and A ranged widely over topics important to what was becoming an increasingly contentious presidential race. In the waning moments of the press conference, NBC White House Correspondent Chuck Todd interjected a final question about the civil war in Syria and whether the situation warranted American military intervention. Obama's response highlighted the US's humanitarian efforts in the conflict while noting that the time for military intervention on behalf of the opposition or the people of Syria had not yet come. In his final remarks before departing he struck a firmer tone, warning:

> We have been very clear to the Assad regime, but also to the other players on the ground, that a red line for us is if we start seeing a whole bunch of chemical weapons moving around or being utilized. This would change my calculus. This would change my equation.
>
> (Office of the Press Secretary, 2012)

Nearly one year later, this red line would be put to the test following the use of poison gas on civilian populations in the Damascus suburbs. Addressing the American people on September 10, 2013, from the East Wing of the White House, Obama explained the primary motivations behind his decision to seek Congressional approval—pending what were ultimately successful diplomatic efforts to rid Syria of its chemical weapons stockpiles—for limited airstrikes in Syria. Though acknowledging to a war-weary public that America was unable to "resolve someone else's civil war through force" the "situation [had now] profoundly changed" (CBS News, 2013b). He continued, "On August 21st these basic rules [of international law] were violated, along with our common sense of humanity." And indeed, in light of the brutality of the attack, in which approximately 1,400 people were asphyxiated, this point is in little dispute. Though evidence existed of chemical weapons being deployed on at least two previous occasions (CBS News, 2013a), the scale of this occurrence made it impossible to ignore (Hubbard *et al.*, 2013). The chemical "cocktail"—a mixture of sarin and other gases blended so as to complicate identification of the composition—that exploded over the suburb of Eastern Ghouta stood as the deadliest use of chemical weapons since Saddam Hussein killed thousands of Kurds in 1988 (Hubbard *et al.*, 2013). Despite the confusion at the time as to who was responsible (Polk, 2013; Hubbard and Saad, 2013), US Secretary of State of John Kerry went so far as to refer to the attacks as a "moral obscenity" (Gordon and Landler, 2013) while UK Prime Minister David Cameron struck a slightly more measured tone by calling them "morally indefensible" (BBC News, 2013a). Other commentators suggested that the gas shell detonated above Damascus might well become "Syria's Srebrenica," (Western, 2013) prompting fundamental change in the political "calculus" for intervention. This chapter notes this event not to apportion blame or re-litigate the arguments for American intervention presented at this stage, but rather to highlight one of the most dramatic and horrifying moments in a civil war full of them.

Looking back at the beginning of 2011 and the apex of turmoil wrought by the Arab Spring in Tunisia and Egypt, the idea that Syria would be wracked by uprisings similar to those happening elsewhere across the region seemed unlikely, at least on the surface. Certainly, President Bashar al-Assad seemed unconcerned about the possible impact of the Arab Spring within Syria, telling the *Wall Street Journal*, in an interview on January 31, 2011, that "if you have stagnant water, you will have pollution.... If you want to talk about Tunisia and Egypt, we are outside of this; at the end we are not Tunisians and we are not Egyptians" (*Wall Street Journal*, 2011). In the same conversation, Assad went on to elaborate that the secret of Syria's stability in comparison to its neighbors stemmed from the fact that there was no gap between the policies of the Syrian state and the "people's beliefs and interests" (*Wall Street Journal*, 2011). Despite the harmonious picture of state-society relations Assad gave in public, in private, he exercised prudence and commissioned a secret working group to study the likelihood of protests in Syria and how to best deal with them should they occur. One of the primary conclusions of the "special committee" was that the "fall of the Tunisian and Egyptian regimes had been the failure to crush the protests at the moment of their inception" (Hassan, 2011).

The possibility of an insurrection, in early 2011, seemed minimal. Although Assad's regime—both the military elite and the civil service—was dominated by minority Alawites, who comprised about 12 percent of Syria's population of 22 million (Heydemann, 2013), there was little evidence for cracks in the government's authority. First, ever since the coup that brought the Ba'ath party to power in 1963, the regime had not been shy in suppressing dissent and was willing to utilize violence when and where necessary. The brutality directed toward the Muslim Brotherhood in the 1982 uprising left a lasting imprint on the collective memory of the majority Sunni population as a reminder of the Ba'ath Party's willingness to do what it took to stay in power (Landis, 2012). In that incident the Syrian army leveled a substantial part of the city of Hama and killed anywhere between 10,000–25,000 people (*Guardian*, 2011).

Moreover, the Ba'ath Party-led government did well to placate the rural base on which it was founded. From the early 1960s into the 1990s dramatic leaps forward in education, public health, access to water and infrastructure development had a significant impact on the quality of life of rural-based citizens. For example, in 1963, only 2 percent of the rural population had access to electricity; by 1992 that figure increased to 95 percent (Hinnebusch, 2012, p. 96). Assad, who ascended to power in 2000 following the death of his father, sought to continue this trajectory of development based on the Chinese model of economic liberalization before democratization (Hinnebusch, 2012, p. 103). Although this policy rationale enabled Assad to dismiss the calls for political reform until the economy was adequately modernized, economic liberalization proved inordinately difficult for reasons internal and external to Syria. Externally, Assad faced the challenge of integration into a global community from which Syria was often isolated, while domestically; liberalization of the economy was often equated with increased corruption and crony capitalism. The failings of Assad's economic high-wire act were compounded by factors ranging from severe drought, escalating poverty, ineffective resource management and an ever-increasing population of unemployed young males. Given the structural fragility of Syrian economics and society, in 2011 the situation was far more combustible than Assad recognized or was willing to admit. In the early spring of 2011, a spark ignited in a most unlikely setting. Three years later more than 170,000 people are dead (Karam, 2014) and millions of individuals remain displaced for the near future.

The remainder of this chapter seeks to accomplish the following: first, it will present a concise narration of the current situation in Syria along with some discussion as to how this present moment arrived. Admittedly, a full presentation of the war in Syria is well beyond the scope of this chapter.[2] Instead, it will endeavor to offer a thumbnail sketch of events, key actors and interests at stake in the conflict. The latter half of the chapter provides a summation of some of the primary security dilemmas and challenges posed by the civil war in Syria that will need to be confronted by international organizations or states compelled to intervene and/or assist in the resolution of the war in Syria. This section is divided into two parts. One focuses on immediate concerns and is followed by another that emphasizes longer-term challenges. The chapter ends with a brief conclusion.

Syria: brief history of a civil war

If forced to choose a precise location to note the beginning of the conflict in Syria the obvious place to look would be Dar'a, a city dating back to 1400 BCE situated in the southwest corner of Syria near the Jordanian border. The specific moment would be the early March 2011 arrest and torture of a group of teenage boys caught spraying graffiti that mimicked protester chants in Tunisia and Egypt: "The people/want/to topple the regime" (McLeod, 2011) Of course, this was not the first time the security institutions of the state had responded with excessive, even brutal, force on those who dared to criticize the regime. What was different in this instance was that people in Dar'a and elsewhere in Syria sensed the "winds of change" across the Middle East and that this was their opportunity to demonstrate against state violence (Leenders and Heydemann, 2012, p. 141). Even so, Dar'a was perceived as too tribal, too "backwards" to pose much risk for widespread protest—so much so that Syrian authorities relocated police from Dar'a in order to place them in locations thought to be more susceptible to protest (Leenders and Heydemann, 2012, p. 142). This proved to be a consequential misjudgment as it provided space in which outraged relatives and neighbors could express their displeasure. Indeed, an irony of the situation in Dar'a is that it was in large part because of the dense "clan based or tribal social structures" of the city's residents that facilitated the sustained, ever increasing demonstrations against the regime (Leenders and Heydemann, 2012, p. 141). Predictably and perhaps in line with the conclusions of President Assad's "special committee" on how to deal with protests, the police reacted to them with violence[3] and matters escalated from there: by May there were tanks in the streets and so many people had been corralled by the police that they could barely fit into the city's local stadium (Leenders and Heydemann, 2012, pp. 142–143). By then, though, there was no going back—far more protesters were on streets across Syria than could fit in any one stadium. The death toll started to climb as well. In early June 2011, ten weeks into the protests, 1,100 people had been killed (*Guardian*, 2011).

As the pace of the protests accelerated so did the violence, both on the part of the state and on behalf of what were, at the beginning, still largely peaceful demonstrations in which a wide range of people and groups from regions across Syria participated. The trend, however, veered ever more towards violence. Indeed, one of the most ominous, if not striking, aspects of the Syrian situation was the speed and abruptness with which widespread peaceful, mostly moderate, protests morphed into a "thoroughly militarized, militantly Islamist armed movement wracked by internal fissures and factions, bereft of a coherent and effective political leadership and hard-pressed to respond to [what became] a reconsolidated regime backed by a stubbornly cohesive security apparatus" (Heydemann, 2013, p. 70). Despite the at-times rudderless and disorganized—more on that below—opposition, most observers possessed a guarded optimism that they would eventually prevail without a protracted conflict. As the rebels gained territory around the country, especially in the areas encircling Damascus, accompanied by the increasing international isolation of the Assad government, these feelings seemed reasonable enough. As the conflict settled well into 2014, the optimism felt a year into the conflict seems quite premature. Or, as one observer has called these predictions, "wishful thinking" (Landis, 2012, p. 72).

Staring into the bleak abyss that is 170,000 casualties, a third of whom are civilians, it seems reasonable to label the optimism as something far worse than "wishful thinking." Indeed, the US Department of State expressed the fatality rate in more individual terms during its 2013 review of the human rights situation in Syria by noting that every two hours during the preceding year a child was killed and a woman was killed every three hours (US Department of State, 2013). The toll of the conflict could be—and probably is—grimmer. In April

2014, for example, the UK based Syrian Observatory for Human Rights pegged the death toll at a figure closer to 220,000 dead, not accounting for the nearly 20,000 who remain missing and the 8,000 currently held in detention by the Syrian government (Reuters, 2014).[4] The human toll, however, goes far beyond the total casualty count. For example, consider the refugee crisis confronting surrounding countries. As of July 2014, UNICEF counted nearly 3 million Syrian refugees residing outside the country's borders (UNICEF, 2014). Within Syrian borders the situation is no better. An August 2014 UNHCR report estimates the number of internally displaced Syrians at over 6.5 million (UNHCR, 2014). The number of Syrians displaced by the conflict is equivalent to nearly 50 percent of the country's total population. In light of these catastrophic numbers, by the end of 2013 half of the Syrian population were estimated to require some sort of humanitarian assistance (Heydemann, 2013, p. 16).

What happened? How did the crisis arrive at this point, in which the early prognosis of a fairly quick resolution has been proven so dramatically off-base? Two points seem worth mentioning here. *First* is the strength of the Assad regime. *Second* is the overall weakness and factionalization of the opposition movement(s). In terms of state strength, Assad has been proven right that Syria is neither Egypt nor Tunisia. Despite being on the verge of a regime-ending knockout blow in the early days of the conflict, Assad's government has demonstrated a remarkable resiliency in its fight for survival. Even as control of state institutions falters—or has been largely lost in some areas of the country—Assad's government has managed to retain loyalty and control of the military, which has facilitated the rollback of opposition gains around Damascus and elsewhere. One of the primary reasons for this relative success can be attributed to the fact that the state has learned throughout the war. Thus, the government forces have managed to improve their tactics and capabilities as the conflict has unfolded. Part of the transformation is the result of technical and military support provided by both Iran and Hezbollah (Heydemann, 2013, pp. 63–64; Filkins, 2013b). For instance, the Syrian regime has been able to take advantage of internet surveillance technology developed by Iran during the "Green Revolution" in 2009 (Reuters, 2011). Maintaining control of the internet has given Assad a decisive advantage over the opposition that other authoritarian states, such as Egypt, lacked (Fischer and Keller, 2011). Consequently, the regime has been able to choke off a key means of organizational capability of regime opponents while affording them the opportunity to manage the narrative of the conflict in a way that places the regime in the best possible light. Coordinated efforts to "spin" the conflict on behalf of the Syrian government has produced online attacks directed toward the homepages of the US Department of the Treasury, ABC News, and Oprah Winfrey (Fischer and Keller, 2011), while for the past year Assad's family has been the focal point of an Instagram account designed to soften the face of the President and the first family for a domestic and international audience.[5] Assad's online presence depicting him as a calm, serious, even normal, leader is intended to serve a propaganda purpose. The images serve as a reminder to domestic and international observers that even as many of the institutions of the state collapse around him, Assad remains the serene centerpiece of the government; the last line of defense against an increasingly chaotic and brutal opposition.

Second, one of the ironies of the conflict's evolution is that the Syrian state and its supporters have become even more bound to Assad's survival, if only out of fear of what would happen should he be deposed. This skepticism of both the opposition's ability to govern or not embark on a violent cleansing of minorities or Ba'ath Party loyalists following its success is motivation enough to keep a significant portion of the population in support of Assad, or at the very least, to not actively oppose his rule. The significant point to make, then, is that the strength of the Assad government is to a large extent relative. The state derives a substantial portion of its (staying) power from the weakness and fragmentation of the opposition (Landis, 2012). Since the spring of 2011, the loose unity that characterized the initial stages of the protests has dissolved into a combustible, decentralized mixture of factions, competing interests, and ephemeral coalitions engaged in an escalation of violence with both the regime and each other. The Syrian National Coalition (SNC) was an early attempt at establishing a unified opposition voice. Dominated by Sunnis, the SNC demonstrated an inability to bring other minority groups into its fold, which so hampered its efforts to lead the opposition that just over a year after its founding, US Secretary of State Hillary Clinton proclaimed in November 2012 that it was no longer possible to consider the SNC "as the visible leader of the opposition" (BBC News, 2013b).

The case of the Free Syrian Army (FSA) is also indicative of the above trend. Two years after its founding in July 2011, the FSA counted upwards of 80,000 fighters among its organizational ranks (Heydemann, 2013a). These figures mask the fact that the FSA, whose leadership and logistical hubs are located outside Syrian territory have very little command authority over the militants and rebels ostensibly under its control. As William Polk notes, the FSA's "influence over the actual combatants inside of Syria derives from its ability to allocate money and arms and shared objectives; it does not command them" (Polk, 2013). Indeed, as of December 2013, the bewildering array of armed factions operating in Syria numbers somewhere in the range of 1,000 (BBC News, 2013c). These range from collections of relative moderates and supporters of Kurdish autonomy to more vicious and unpredictable jihadi groups such as ISIS (Islamic State of Iraq and Syria), Jabhat al-Nusra, and contingents of foreign fighters possessing varying motivations. Add to those numbers the criminal gangs and warlords with an interest in carving out small fiefdoms within Syria and it seems reasonable to conclude that the FSA's ability to promulgate even the idea of "shared objectives" is ever diminishing. Furthermore, as the growing capacity of a group like ISIS to finance itself; while at the same time demonstrating sophisticated governance capabilities (however brutal) of the territory it conquers, only increases the likelihood that the FSA will continue to be marginalized.

Neither the reconsolidation of Assad's grip on power nor the violent scramble for influence between the diverse arrays of anti-government forces bodes well for the future of Syria. As the death toll mounts, sectarian-driven violence becomes more pervasive and institutions disintegrate across much of the country, envisioning an end to the fighting is increasingly difficult. Protracted conflict is not only a problem for Syrians, but will be—and already is—a source of instability for the entire region. Be it Lebanon, the Kurds, Turkey, Iran, Israel, Iraq, not to mention the US, Russia, China, and now international jihadi networks, all have a stake in the outcome of Syria's civil war. Consequently, it is likely to lead to the increased regionalization of the conflict as "Syria's strategic position" in the Middle East "give[s] important (state and non-state) players in the region ample cause to view the Syrian revolution as directly affecting it core interests" (Heydemann, 2013b, p. 3). "Core interests," it goes without saying, often at odds with one another. Different actors supporting their favored proxies will feed the conflict and thus prolong it: No one can afford to lose. Were the "international paralysis" (Navi Pillay [who served as the UN High Commissioner for Human Rights] quoted in Cumming-Bruce, 2014), currently restraining international action in Syria to be overcome, the challenges opposing a successful intervention to stop the conflict would be as complex as they are numerous. Mustering the will to engage the conflict would need to be followed by a sustained effort. In the remaining pages this chapter will outline some of the immediate security challenges to be overcome in order to bring about the conclusion of the civil war.

Dilemmas of security and intervention in the Syrian Civil War

In light of the North Atlantic Treaty Organization (NATO)-led intervention in Libya, which prevented a slaughter of civilians and ultimately led to the demise of Colonel Gaddafi and the regime he led, international attention quickly shifted to the case of Syria in the summer of 2011 as the Syrian government pressed its assault against what were then still largely peaceful demonstrators. If sustained intervention was achievable in Libya, the question was asked, why not in Syria? The attempt to answer that question has resulted in a contentious, yet largely inconclusive debate that continues to the present. A significant part of the policy conversation has centered on the idea whether the US, the UN, regional powers, or the international community however defined—someone, anyone?—has an obligation to intervene in order to stop outright, or at least ameliorate, the mushrooming humanitarian catastrophe and violence produced by the civil war in Syria. According to the umbrella doctrine set down as the Responsibility to Protect (R2P), there are three types of actions that are legitimate in an intervention into another state: prevention, reaction, and post-intervention aid to help put things back together once the conflict is concluded (Nuruzzaman, 2013, p. 58). In the middle of 2011 into 2012 when the prevention of the worst atrocities might have still been possible there was no international consensus or appetite for sustained engagement in Syria. Both Russia and China were opposed to military action (Allison, 2013), the Obama administration had no interest in another Middle Eastern entanglement so soon after extricating the American military from Iraq, and key regional players were in disagreement as to what actions were needed, if any. Even as circumstances deteriorated into March 2012, then UN-Arab League envoy to Syria, Kofi Annan, publicly opposed military action:

> We have to be careful that we don't introduce a medicine that is worse than the disease.... The situation in the country is extremely serious for the Syrian people and the region, and I think we should not forget the possible impact of Syria on the region if there is any miscalculation.
>
> (Kofi Annan, quoted in Buckley, 2012)

Even though intervention is most effective when prevention is still possible (Abramowitz, 2013) the "complex combination of strategic, political and operational factors [that] coalesced" in Libya were absent in Syria (Morris, 2013, p. 1271). Indeed, given the optimism that the Assad regime would, sooner rather than later, collapse there was little incentive to muster an intervention and therefore "own" whatever turmoil would come afterwards. But as Assad surprised many by continuing to survive and the civilian situation became more dire, calls for intervention became more pronounced in the US and elsewhere. By this time however, "prevention" was no longer possible. Any "reaction" on behalf of Syrian civilians would necessarily be a much more substantial and dangerous endeavor as the conditions on the ground destabilized. Cognizant of the difficulties of intervening in a more complex environment the Obama administration purposely kept the crossing threshold of the "red line" blurry (Filkins, 2013a). Paraphrasing a senior White House official involved in the formulation of their Syrian policy, the reason for the ambiguity was to forestall the possibility of intervention for as long as it took: "[T]he cost of saving lives [in Syria] may simply be too high (Filkins, 2013a).

President Obama put the calculus of intervention in a slightly different way during an interview with the *New Republic* a few weeks after his second inauguration in late January 2013. Posing a series of rhetorical questions he asked,

> Can we make a difference in that situation? Would a military intervention have an impact? ... What would be the aftermath of our involvement on the ground? Could it trigger even worse violence or the use of chemical weapons? What offers the best prospect of a stable post-Assad regime?
>
> (Foer and Hughes, 2013)

The underlying message behind these questions is yet another more fundamental one: Will intervention work? For those opposed to military intervention being unable to answer the preceding question in the affirmative makes all other considerations irrelevant.

A cursory appraisal of the current situation in Syria provides insight into the immediate challenges confronting any potential intervention with the objective of bringing the conflict to a conclusion. Obtaining a positive answer to the question of "Will it work?" is not so easily accomplished. Highlighted here are three obstacles: deciding on whom to support, the factionalization and increasing militancy of the opposition and the profitability of the chaos for some of the parties involved. Given its fragmentation, speaking of Syria's opposition as a singular, monolithic force obscures reality more than it reflects it. As noted above, there are approximately 1,000 armed groups operating in Syria with varying capabilities and motivations. This diversity thus presents significant problems when it comes to even making the basic decision to intervene and how—for the sheer fact that being anti-Assad does not automatically make a group worthy of support. The contours of this debate have flared recently as neo-conservative analysts have come out of the post-Iraq woodwork and tried to make the case for forceful intervention in Syria. The calls for engagement often have an apocalyptic tinge, such as Anne-Marie Slaughter's assertion that failing to intervene means that the "world would see Syrian civilians rolling on the ground, foaming at the mouth, dying by the thousands while the United States stands by" (Filkins, 2013a). Former Secretary of State Hillary Clinton, brandishing her hawkish tendencies, recently argued that the US and her allies missed a chance to make a difference in the initial stages of the conflict by failing to "carefully vet, train and equip early on a core group of the developing Free Syrian Army" (Goldberg, 2014). The US needed to choose a side and vigorously support it; Clinton went on to say, because:

> [I]n a conflict like this, the hard men with guns are going to be more likely actors in any political transition than those on the outside just talking. And therefore [the U.S.] needed to figure out how to support them on the ground, better equip them, and we didn't have to go all the way, and I totally understand the cautions that we had to contend with, but we'll never know.
>
> (Goldberg, 2014)

But in the Syrian conflict, the ability to discern the right "hard men" to throw one's weight behind from everybody else has never been an obvious task and even if it were, there is no guarantee that arming one side over another would actually work. In what amounted to a competing interview given to *New York Times*' columnist Tom Friedman, President Obama expressed the rationale behind the countervailing "cautions" to which Clinton referred. Obama explained, the

> notion that arming the Syrian rebels would have made a difference has always been a fantasy. The idea that we could provide some light arms or even more sophisticated arms to what was essentially an opposition made up of former doctors, farmers, pharmacists and so forth and they were going to go be able to battle not only a well-armed state backed by Russia, backed by Iran, a battle-hardened Hezbollah, that was never in the cards.
>
> (Friedman, 2014)

A "Goldilocks" intervention of the sort described above, in which "the right quantity of weapons will be provided to just the right armed groups to create just the right level of threat" is much more likely to make things worse than it is to succeed (Heydemann, 2013b, p. 17). Part of the reason for this is that in Syria the challenge of intervention is made far more complicated by the fact that there is no obvious, Manichean distinction between the forces that need to be opposed and those who might be worth supporting. Choosing any course of action that favors one opposition group over the other inevitably opens a Pandora's box of unintended consequences in which the only controllable action is the initial decision to engage.

Furthermore, another related obstacle to a somewhat swift resolution to the conflict is the faulty assumption that all parties possess some self-interest in ending the fighting. As the conflict is increasingly instrumentalized it is apparent that the chaos engendered by the fighting can actually be quite profitable. Although, it is important to point out that Syria's black market economy has long been a significant portion of the country's economic output—some estimates have suggested that it often amounts to about one quarter of the annual economic output (Herbert, 2014, p. 70)—it has recently taken on a new significance. In the years of the civil war, as the Assad government's grip on the mechanisms of state and economy has been challenged, new actors—from Syrian tribes to jihadist militant groups to networks of foreign smugglers—have begun to carve out expanding footholds of economic power that were previously unavailable. The implications of an entrenched variation of the sort of warlordism seen elsewhere in West Africa, Somalia and more recently, in Afghanistan are potentially dire.[6] Once achieved, economic gains are not easily or willingly relinquished. Instead, what is more likely to occur is that these groups and their leaders are "able to leverage their economic resources into political influence, shaping the post-conflict trajectory of their state" (Herbert, 2014, p. 70). Over the longer term then the existence of sustained disorder has both economic and political uses.[7]

In the short term, however, competition for resources is likely to produce even more violent outcomes. These processes have worsened in the latter stages of the conflict as the opposition has realized that control of resources—oil, grain, water—is mandatory for survival in light of the dual facts that these basic necessities will be harder to come by within Syrian borders and that external benefactors outside Syria cannot be relied upon to consistently provide them (al Abdeh, 2013). One observer describes the scenario currently underway as "opposition-held Syria is Mad Max meets the Sopranos" (al Abdeh, 2013) as the struggle for resources is fought one wheat field, oil field or water well at a time. Reuters, for example, suggested in a May 2013 piece that every tribe now has a claim in at least one oil producing area and that the black market price of a barrel is over 50 dollars with mobile refineries capable of refining up to 200 barrels a day an increasingly common sight (Karouny, 2013). Or, to demonstrate the motivation behind opposing groups' willingness to confront one another over limited arable land consider that, as a result of the worst wheat harvest in a generation, food prices have skyrocketed nearly 300 percent compared to their pre-war prices (Pamuk and Saul, 2013). Out of the war-driven chaos opportunities previously absent are now there to be taken by anyone with enough muscle to do so. In an unfortunate bit of irony, the muscle aggregated from the same kinds of clan/tribal networks that gave early pro-democracy protests such force in places like Dar'a has now been put to work in the pursuit of resource control. At the moment, five "families" dominate the privatization of resources and the workings of the black market economy that includes basic livelihood staples to rackets organized around kidnapping, drugs and protection "services" (al Abdeh, 2013). Syria's "Mad Max" scenario means it is no longer entirely possible to disentangle the pursuit of funding in the service of a higher ideological goal with the pursuit of resources as an end in itself.

Such is the fluidity of the situation. As jihadist groups, such as ISIS, expand their reach across Syria and the region making obscene ransom demands to the tune of 132 million dollars for the safe return of American journalists along the way, it is becoming increasingly unclear that an Assad victory or an indefinite stalemate in the fighting is the worst possible outcome. To intervene on behalf of the opposition seems to mean more and more to be an intervention on behalf of jihadi groups with the stated intention to establish a new Middle Eastern caliphate. The ability to thus "vet" and select favored opposition groups has long diminished: already in the spring of 2013, the Chairman of the Joint Chiefs of Staff admitted to the Senate Armed Services Committee that "it is actually more confusing on the opposition side today than it was six months ago" (Filkins, 2013a). A year earlier, in 2012, General Dempsey had seen his advice for military intervention in Syria—seconded by C.I.A. Director David Petraeus, Hillary Clinton, and other key administrative figures—roundly rejected by the President.

Confusion is thus as common on the battlefields of Syria as it is thousands of miles away in Washington corridors. Intra-opposition violence has increased to the extent that there is now a civil war within the civil war as the dominant factions fight to further their own divergent objectives: FSA moderates continue their pursuit to overthrow the regime, independence-seeking Kurds try to assert their autonomy over a significant chunk of Syria now labeled "Western Kurdistan," the jihadists fight everybody who opposes their imposition of Islamic law (Doornbos and Moussa, 2013). The sectarian trajectory the violence has taken during the past few years only serves to accelerate the trend toward winner-take-all violence. In the words of one Syrian Kurd, "The Islamists are now our biggest enemy.... The Assad regime only oppressed us. The jihadists want to exterminate us" (Doornbos and Moussa, 2013). Unfortunately, given the recent history of sectarian violence in Syria a statement predicting possible annihilation such as the above is not necessarily an exaggeration. For example, following the siege of Homs, the population of Christians living in the city fell from around 80,000 to approximately 400 residents (Adams, 2012). At the same time, to eventually defeat the Assad regime, the FSA and the Kurds need jihadist groups such as al-Nusra or ISIS in order to effectively counter regime forces. Only the jihadists have the organizational capacity and technical proficiency to sustain the broad offensives needed to overrun the Syrian military and topple the Assad government (Hassan, 2013). Barring coordinated action between important regional actors, the hair-trigger stand-off between different segments of the opposition makes navigating the conflict difficult in the extreme for a would-be intervener seeking to ratchet down the violence. In the longer-term, the more entrenched the sectarian character of the fighting becomes suggests an even bleaker prognosis for resolution or stability. Syria's neighbor, Iraq, is an instructive example that demonstrates the difficulty of attaining peace after a sectarian conflict because this sort of "violence reifies ethnic identity and post-civil war politics is inevitably cast along ethnic lines" (Russell and Sambanis, 2014). The effort to undo the legacy of ethnic and religious conflict that has been produced by this civil war is to be an even more arduous, challenging, and time-consuming task than the already daunting task of trying to simply end it.

Conclusion

The preceding pages have sought to provide some sense of the scope and timeline of the Syrian conflict along with some of the immediate security challenges that need to be grappled with before any engagement with or resolution of the conflict will be successful. The difficulties are steep, yet not insurmountable—all wars have their end. At the same time, a focus solely on the problems of the present without consideration of the longer-term implications of the conflict, both for the people within and beyond Syria's borders, is deficient. In light of R2P's third pillar that calls for sustained post-conflict engagement, these final lines briefly outline some of the underlying problems in Syria that will need to be dealt with following the eventual cessation of fighting.

Although the beginning of the Syrian civil war is often placed in the protests held in the spring of 2011, at the height of the optimistic fervor of the Arab Spring, the seeds of dissent were perhaps sown years earlier. In the decade or two prior to the uprising, Syrian society had undergone transformative shifts in processes of demography (in terms of accelerated patterns of urbanization), socio-economic equality and resource allocation. The profound lifestyle changes wrought by these transformations were negatively compounded by government-led efforts at privatization—emulating the Chinese model as noted earlier—intended to spur the development of a modern and self-reliant economy. The unintended consequences of these (de)regulatory mandates have been a sharp increase in inequality throughout the country, the demise of livelihoods for most rural peasants unable to compete for government-sponsored agricultural subsidies and an unsustainable drive for groundwater that has in less than two decades exhausted an already meager reserve. Citizens were willing to forestall democracy in the name of development so long as they could fulfill basic needs, but once these conditions were no longer possible, stability was no longer guaranteed.[8]

Assuming the conclusion of the civil war, any post-conflict resolution process must necessarily deal with these socio-economic grievances that helped feed the uprising from the start. The presence of a rising warlord economy in Syria, in addition to the fact that a significant proportion of the 50 percent of Syria's population who are now displaced (Chulov, 2014) internally or as international refugees, will eventually make their way back to leveled homes and communities in disarray, the structural problems present in the beginning in 2011 will be far more intractable. Not only because of what will be a shattered formal economy, but also because of the fact that the sectarian lines drawn in the current fighting will shape the scramble for scarce resources going forward (Raleigh, 2011, p. 88). These significant challenges will be complicated by the fact that the post-conflict reconstruction of Syria will occur under conditions of what is expected to be persistent, long-term drought due to the escalating effects of climate change in the region. Analysts currently understand climate change to be a "threat multiplier" rather than a direct cause of conflict.[9] However, there is less understanding of how the effects of climate change impact post-conflict stability, particularly in a country that does come out from under sectarian violence and occupied by populations who already possess a strong sense of clan identity. Therefore, any semblance of a stable order in Syria after the fighting subsides will require that attention be paid not just to the immediate, television-friendly, goals such as the laying down of arms and political compromise, but also, and perhaps for a much longer stretch of time, to the protection of public access to an adequate system of water distribution. Lest we find ourselves observers to a bloody morass similar to what we bear witness to now in 2014, the challenge of stopping the current violence in Syria is great; the task of preventing a further conflagration in the future is likely to be even more daunting.

Notes

1 The author would like to thank the editors for their invitation to participate in this timely volume. A special mention of appreciation is reserved for research assistant extraordinaire, Jack Palmieri, who put in a great deal of effort and time in compiling much of the background material used in the text.

2 For those interested in a more comprehensive look at the situation in Syria *Perspectives on Terrorism* published an extensive bibliography of academic, policy and grey literature. Please see: Tinnes (2013).

3 In these early days of the protests and the accompanying police response there is some confusion as to whether the violence was intended or was more a consequence of trigger happy, uncoordinated crowd control on the part of the security forces. The International Crisis Group has a useful primer on the initial Syrian protests. See International Crisis Group (2011).

4 I should note here that as of this writing the UN released a figure that put the death toll at 191,369 covering a timeframe from the start of the conflict in March 2011 to April 2014. The UN's confirmed death toll increased by over 91,000 from the time of their previous announcement in July 2013. See: Heilprin (2014).

5 The somewhat disorienting propaganda photos can be viewed at: http://instagram.com/syrianpresidency.

6 Key texts on contemporary wars and warlord politics include: Kaldor (2013) and Reno (1999).

7 An instructive example of the logics of disorder from the African Context is (Chabal and Daloz, 1999).

8 For a deeper analysis of the socio-economic conditions present in Syria leading up to the civil war, see: Saleeby (2012), Marzouq (2011), and Kilcullen and Rosenblatt (2014).

9 For some of the current literature on climate change, conflict and/or Syria, please see: de Chatel (2014), Nordås and Gleditsch (2007), Erian, Katlan and Babah (2010), Werrell and Femia (2013), and Barnett and Adger (2007).

References

Abbas, H. (2011, October). The dynamics of the uprising in Syria. *Arab Reform Brief, 51, 2*. Retrieved from: www.arab-reform.net/sites/default/files/ARB_51_Syria_Oct_2011_ H-Abbas_En.pdf. (accessed July 5, 2014).

Abramowitz, M. (2013, September 6). Does the United States have a "responsibility to protect" the Syrian people? *Washington Post*. Retrieved from: www.washingtonpost.com/opinions/does-the-united-states-have-a-responsibility-to-protect-the-syrian-people/2013/09/06/5decf4c0-167d-11e3-be6e-dc6ae8a5b3a8_story.html (accessed July 7, 2014).

Adams, S. (2012, November 15). The world's next genocide. *New York Times*. Retrieved from: www.nytimes.com/2012/11/16/opinion/the-worlds-next-genocide.html (accessed July 28, 2014).

al Abdeh, M. (2013, November 21). Rebels Inc *Foreign Policy*. Retrieved from: www.foreignpolicy.com/articles/2013/11/21/rebels_inc (accessed July 7, 2014).

Allison, R. (2013). Russia and Syria: Explaining alignment with a regime in crisis, *International Affairs*, 89(4), 795–823.

Barnett, J. and Adger, N. (2007). Climate change, human security and violent conflict. *Political Geography*, 26(7), 639–655.

BBC News (2013a, August 27). *Syria: Cameron says Syrian use of chemical weapons "cannot stand."* Retrieved from: www.bbc.com/news/uk-23851292 (accessed July 3, 2014).

BBC News (2013b, October 17). *Syria crisis: Guide to armed and political opposition*. Retrieved from: www.bbc.com/news/world-middle-east-15798218 (accessed July 7, 2014).

BBC News (2013c, December 13). *Syria crisis: Guide to armed and political opposition*. Retrieved from: www.bbc.com/world-middle-east-24403003 (accessed July 4, 2014).

Buckley, C. A. (2012). Learning from Libya, acting in Syria. *Journal of Strategic Studies*, 5(2), 81–104.

CBS News (2013a, June 4). *France, Britain say sarin gas used in Syria*. Retrieved from: www.cbsnews.com/news/france-britain-say-sarin-gas-used-in-syria/ (accessed July 3, 2014).

CBS News (2013b, September 10). *Transcript: Obama's Remarks to the nation on Syria*. Retrieved from: www.cbsnews.com/news/transcript-obamas-address-to-the-nation-on-syria/ (accessed July 3, 2014).

Chabal, P. and Daloz, J. (1999). *Africa works: Disorder as political instrument* (African issues). Bloomington: Indiana University Press.

Chulov, M. (2014, May 5). Lebanon's refugee schools provide hope for Syria's lost generation. *Guardian*. Retrieved from: www.theguardian.com/world/2014/may/05/lebanon-refugee-schools-syria-lost-generation (accessed July 4, 2014).

Cumming-Bruce, N. (2014, August 22). U.N. raises estimate of dead in Syrian conflict to 191,000. *New York Times*. Retrieved from: www.nytimes.com/2014/08/23/world/middleeast/un-raises-estimate-of-dead-in-syrian-conflict-to-191000.html (accessed August 28, 2014).

de Chatel, F. (2014). The role of drought and climate change in the Syrian uprising: Untangling the triggers of the revolution. *Middle Eastern Studies*, 50(4), 521–535

Doornbos, H. and Moussa, J. (2013, August 28). The civil war within Syria's civil war. *Foreign Policy*. Retrieved from: www.foreignpolicy.com/articles/2013/08/28/the_civil_war_within_syria_s_civil_war_kurdish_fighters (accessed July 28, 2014).

Erian, W., Katlan, B. and Babah, O. (2010). *Drought vulnerability in the Arab region: Special case study: Syria, Global Assessment Report on Disaster Risk Reduction*. Retrieved from: www.preventionweb.net/english/hyogo/gar/2011/en/bgdocs/Erian_Katlan_&_Babah_2010.pdf (accessed July 16, 2014).

Filkins, D. (2013a, May 13). The thin red line. *New Yorker*. Retrieved from: www.newyorker.com/magazine/2013/05/13/the-thin-red-line-2 (accessed July 26, 2014).

Filkins, D. (2013b, September 30). The shadow commander. *New Yorker*. Retrieved from: www.newyorker.com/magazine/2013/09/30/the-shadow-commander (accessed July 26, 2014).

Fisher, M. and Keller, J. (2011, August 31). Syria's digital counter-revolutionaries. *Atlantic*. Retrieved from: www.theatlantic.com/international/archive/2011/08/syrias-digital-counter-revolutionaries/244382/ (accessed July 22, 2014).

Foer, F. and Hughes, C. (2013, January 27). *Barack Obama is not pleased*. New Republic. Retrieved from: www.newrepublic.com/article/112190/obama-interview-2013-sit-down-president (accessed July 23, 2014).

Friedman, T. L. (2014, August 8). Obama on the world. *New York Times*. Retrieved from: www.nytimes.com/2014/08/09/opinion/president-obama-thomas-l-friedman-iraq-and-world-affairs.html (accessed August 28, 2014).

Goldberg, J. (2014, August 10). Hillary Clinton: "Failure" to help Syrian rebels led to the rise of ISIS. *Atlantic*. Retrieved from: www.theatlantic.com/international/archive/2014/08/hillary-clinton-failure-to-help-syrian-rebels-led-to-the-rise-of-isis/375832/ (accessed August 28, 2014).

Gordon, M. R. and Landler, M. (2013, August 26). Kerry cites clear evidence of chemical weapon use in Syria. *New York Times*. Retrieved from: www.nytimes.com/2013/08/27/world/middleeast/syria-assad.html?pagewanted=all (accessed August 14, 2014).

Guardian (2011, February 3). Syrian forces kill at least 34 protesters at anti-government protest. Retrieved from: www.theguardian.com/world/2011/jun/03/syrian-forces-kill-34-protesters (accessed July 16, 2014).

Hassan, H. (2013, September 18). Rebel vs. rebel. *Foreign Policy*. Retrieved from: www.foreignpolicy.com/articles/2013/09/18/rebel_vs_rebel_syria_jihadists_groups. (accessed July 6, 2014).

Heilprin, J. (2014, August 22). Death toll from Syrian civil war tops 191,000, UN Reports. *Huffington Post*. Retrieved from: www.huffingtonpost.com/2014/08/22/syria-death-toll_n_5698848.html (accessed August 28, 2014).

Herbert, M. (2014). Partisans, profiteers, and criminals: Syria's illicit economy. *The Fletcher Forum of World Affairs*, 38(1), 69–86.

Heydemann, S. (2013a). Syria and the future of authoritarianism. *Journal of Democracy*, 24(4), 59–73.

Heydemann, S. (2013b, May). *Syria's uprising: Sectarianism, regionalisation, and state order in the Levant*, (FRIDE and HIVOS Working Paper no. 119). Retrieved from: http://fride.org/descarga/WP_119_Syria_Uprising.pdf (accessed July 12, 2014).

Hinnebusch, R. (2012). Syria: From "authoritarian upgrading" to revolution? *International Affairs*, 88(1), 95–113.

Hubbard, B. and Saad, H. (2013, August 21). Images of death in Syria, but no proof of chemical attack. *New York Times*. Retrieved from: www.nytimes.com/2013/08/22/world/middleeast/syria.html?pagewanted=all&_r=0

Hubbard, B., Mazzetti, M. and Landler, M. (2013, August 26). Blasts in the night, a smell, and a flood of Syrian victims. *New York Times*. Retrieved from: www.nytimes.com/2013/08/27/world/middleeast/blasts-in-the-night-a-smell-and-a-flood-of-syrian-victims.html?pagewanted=all&_r=0 (accessed July 28, 2014).

International Crisis Group (2011, July 13). Popular protests in North Africa and the Middle East (VII): The Syrian regime's slow-motion suicide. *Middle East/North Africa Report* (no. 109). Retrieved from: www.crisisgroup.org/en/publication-type/media-releases/2011/mena/the-syrian-regimes-slow-motion-suicide.aspx (accessed July 28, 2014).

Kaldor, M. (2013). *New and old sars: Organized violence in a global era*. London: John Wiley and Sons, 3rd edition.

Karam, Z. (2014, July 28). Syria suffers record death toll. *Huffington Post*. Retrieved from: www.huffingtonpost.com/2014/07/28/syria-death-toll_n_5626482.html (accessed July 13, 2014).

Karouny, M. (2013, May 10). In eastern Syria Oil smugglers benefit from chaos. *Reuters*. Retrieved from: http://uk.reuters.com/article/2013/05/10/uk-syria-crisis-oil-tribes-insight-idUKBRE94906Y20130510. (accessed July 13, 2014).

Kilcullen, D. and Rosenblatt, N. (2014). The rise of Syria's urban poor: Why the war for Syria's future will be fought over the country's new urban villages. *Prism*, 4, 33–42.

Landis, J. (2012). The Syrian uprising of 2011: Why the Assad regime is likely to survive to 2013. *Middle East Policy*, 19(1), 72–85.

Leenders, R. and Heydemann, S. (2012). Popular mobilization in Syria: Opportunity and threat, and the social networks of early risers. *Mediterranean Politics*, 17(2), 139–159.

Marzouq, N. (2011, August 28). The economic origins of Syria's uprising, *Al Akhbar* English. Retrieved from: http://english.al-akhbar.com/node/372

McLeod, H. (2011, April 19). Inside Deraa. Al Jazeera. Retrieved from: www.aljazeera.com/indepth/features/2011/04/201141918352728300.html

Morris, J. (2013). Libya and Syria: R2P and the spectre of the swinging pendulum. *International Affairs*, 89(5), 1265–1283.

Nordås, R. and Gleditsch, N. P. (2007). Climate Change and Conflict. *Political Geography*, 26, 627–638.

Nuruzzaman, M. (2013). The responsibility to protect' doctrine: Revived in Libya, Buried in Syria. *Insight Turkey*, 15(12), 57–66. Retrieved from: http://file.insightturkey.com/Files/Pdf/15_2_2013_nuruzzaman.pdf (accessed July 22, 2014).

Office of the Press Secretary (2012, August 20). *Remarks by the President to the White House press corps*. Retrieved from: www.whitehouse.gov/the-press-office/2012/08/20/remarks-president-white-house-press-corps (accessed July 22, 2014).

Pamuk, H. and Saul, J. (2013, September 5). Syria's economy goes underground as black market thrives. *Reuters*. Retrieved from: www.reuters.com/article/2013/09/05/us-syria-crisis-blackmarket-insight-idUSBRE98405I20130905 (accessed July 22, 2014).

Polk, W. (2013, September 2). Your labor day Syria reader, part 2. *Atlantic*. Retrieved from: www.theatlantic.com/international/archive/2013/09/your-labor-day-syria-reader-part-2-william-polk/279255. (accessed July 22, 2014).

Raleigh, C. (2011). The search for safety: The effects of conflict, poverty and ecological Influences on migration in the developing world. *Global Environmental Change*, 21, 82–86. Retrieved from: http://ejournal.narotama.ac.id/files/Global%20Environmental%20Change.pdf (accessed July 16, 2014).

Reno, W. (1999). *Warlord politics in African states*. Boulder: Lynne Rienner Publishing.

Reuters (2011, July 13). *Social media: A double-edged sword in Syria*. Retrieved from:

www.reuters.com/article/2011/07/13/us-syria-social-media-idUSTRE76C3DB20110713 (accessed July 16, 2014).

Reuters (2014, April 1). *Death toll in Syria's civil war above 150,000*. Retrieved from: http://news.yahoo.com/death-toll-syrias-civil-war-above-150-000-122633297.html (accessed August 30, 2014).

Russell, K. and Sambanis, N. (2014, June 24). Maliki isn't the problem. *Foreign Affairs*. Retrieved from: www.foreignaffairs.com/articles/141599/kevin-russell-and-nicholas-sambanis/maliki-isnt-the-problem (accessed August 30, 2014).

Saleeby, S. (2012, February 16). Sowing the seeds of dissent: Economic grievances and the Syrian social contract's unraveling. *Jadaliyya*. Retrieved from: www.jadaliyya.com/pages/index/4383/sowing-the-seeds-of-dissent_economic-grievances-an (accessed July 28, 2014).

Tinnes, J. (2013). Literature on the conflict in Syria (2011–November 2013). *Perspectives on Terrorism*, 7(6), 137–165.

UNHCR (2014, August 29). Needs soar as number of Syrian refugees tops 3 million, Retrieved from: www.unhcr.org/53ff76c99.html (accessed August 30, 2014).

UNICEF (2014). *Syria Crisis: Monthly Humanitarian Situation Report, June 13–July 14, 2014*. Retrieved from: http://reliefweb.int/report/syrian-arab-republic/syria-crisis-monthly-humanitarian-situation-report-13-june-14-july-2014 (accessed August 30, 2014).

US Department of State (2013). *Bureau of Democracy, Human Rights and Labor, Syria 2013 Human Rights Report*. Retrieved from: www.state.gov/documents/organization/220588.pdf (accessed July 28, 2014).

Wall Street Journal (2011, January 31), *Interview with Syrian President Bashar al-Assad.* Retrieved from: http://online.wsj.com/articles/SB10001424052748703833204576114712441122894 (accessed August 30, 2014).

Werrell, C. E. and Femia, F. (2013, February). *The Arab spring and climate change*. Center for American Progress, Stimson and The Center for Climate and Security. Retrieved from: www.Americanprogress.org/issues/security/report/2013/02/28/54579/the-arab-spring-and-climate-change/ (accessed July 28, 2014).

Western, J. (2013, August 21). *The Syrian chemical attack: Things fall apart, the centre cannot hold.* [The Duck of Minerva (blog)]. Retrieved from: www.whiteoliphaunt.com/duckofminerva/2013/08/the-syrian-chemical-attack-things-fall-apart-the-centre-cannot-hold.html (accessed July 16, 2014).

4 International Criminal Court (ICC)

Don Wallace

Due to the intransigence of some permanent members on the United Nations Security Council (UNSC), the International Criminal Court (ICC) has been, and unless the political circumstances remain unaltered will continue to be, unable to address the crisis in the Syrian Arab Republic (Syria). As they continue to veto UNSC resolutions regarding action on Syria, Russia and China will not consider the proposition of an investigation by the ICC into the mass atrocity crimes occurring in Syria (Lomeli, 2014). The ICC could play a significant role in the operationalization of the Responsibility to Protect (R2P) for Syria in that it could contribute to the third pillar of the approach to R2P outlined by the Report of the UN Secretary-General, for advancing the agenda of the 2005 World Summit Outcome Document (UN Secretary-General, 2009). The investigation and prosecution by the ICC of atrocity crimes committed in the ceaseless humanitarian crisis in Syria should be a substantive part of the R2P response by the international community.

The ICC, governed by the 1998 Rome Statute, is the first permanent, treaty-based, tribunal established with the intention of facilitating the end of the practice of impunity for the perpetrators of the most serious crimes confronting the international community. The Rome Statute, which secured for international criminal justice a permanent structure in international law, was signed by over 120 states in 1998. The United States (US) was one of seven countries voting against the Rome Statute. Two other permanent members of the UNSC, China and Russia, have not ratified the treaty. Yet, as of July 1, 2014, 139 countries are signatories and 122 are States Parties, having ratified or acceded to the Rome Statute of the ICC. Syria signed the treaty on November 29, 2000, but has not ratified this document.

The foundational propositions of the R2P and the ICC share a common objective of preventing and addressing mass atrocity crimes. Both strive to instill in governments and leaders the primary responsibility to prevent and address these concerns and provide that the international community will take on the obligations, should domestic remedies prove ineffectual. The ICC can be instrumental in furthering the goals of R2P in providing a tool to prevent egregious human rights violations and a mechanism for accountability. By contrast, though R2P is a principle of universal application, the ICC suffers from jurisdictional limitations and only through the cooperation of the UNSC can it reach mass atrocity crimes in nations, such as Syria, that are not party to its treaty. Thus, in its proffer of establishing a rule of law, the ICC must operate in a political reality that challenges its very legitimacy.

This chapter addresses these issues by briefly exploring the formal responsibilities of the ICC regarding R2P principles. There is a discussion of the existing capabilities for implementation of R2P, which is followed by a summation of the actual abilities to address R2P challenges and a focused view towards addressing the situation in Syria.

Formal responsibilities of the ICC

Now operative, the ICC has jurisdiction over war crimes, genocide and crimes against humanity. Through the jurisprudence developed with the establishment in the 1990s of the International Criminal Tribunal for the former-Yugoslavia (ICTY) and the International Criminal Tribunal for Rwanda (ICTR) and in hybrid and internationalized tribunals that have since been established to deal with mass atrocities in other locations, there is now a consistent body of case law that can be traced to the post-WWII efforts in Nuremberg. Standards have been established in this jurisprudence for the substantive definitions of international crimes and for the general principles for criminal liability of these mass atrocities (Defeis, 2011). While ICC investigations and prosecutions are only relatively recent developments and there are few convictions to date, there is now a developed body of international criminal law (Defeis, 2011). The ICC has jurisdiction only for crimes committed after the entry into force of the Rome Statute, which occurred on July 1, 2002 (Rome Statute of the ICC, Art. 11(1)). As of April 2014, 21 investigations in eight situations have been brought before the ICC (International Criminal Court, 2014).

Under the Rome Statute, the ICC Prosecutor can initiate an investigation on the basis of a referral from any State Party or from the UNSC. The Prosecutor also has authority to initiate investigations under the prosecutor's discretion (*proprio motu*), without such a prior referral, on the basis of information received from individuals or organizations concerning crimes that are within the jurisdiction of the ICC. In the case of a referral by a State Party or the Prosecutor's exercise of *proprio motu* authority, there is jurisdiction under the Rome Statute only when the State on the territory of which the conduct in question occurred, or the State of the accused, is a Party to the Statute (Rome Statute of the ICC, Art. 12(2)). Neither of these conditions applies to a non-member-state such as Syria. A state that is not a party to the Rome Statute may on its own accord, accept the exercise of jurisdiction by the ICC with respect to a specific crime in question (Rome Statute of the ICC, Art. 12(3)); without a change in its government, this is a seemingly unlikely event for Syria.

There remains the possibility of the UNSC referring a situation to the ICC, where states, in which the deeds were done or whose national who has allegedly committed the deed, are not parties to the Statute (Rome Statute of the ICC, Art. 13). This can happen without the consent of the governments of the country where the conflict occurs. For the three permanent members that have refused to ratify the Rome Statute, although they can vote on who will be subjected to the ICC, they will likely not vote to refer one of their nationals or a national of an ally that is not a party to the Rome Treaty to the ICC. As the ICC referral by the UNSC will be a decision made under Chapter VII of the UN Charter (Rome Statute of the ICC, Art. 13(b)), this is subject to the requirement of the affirmative vote of all permanent members of the UNSC (UN Charter, Article 27(3)).[1] Thus, these three permanent members, which refuse to subject themselves to the jurisdiction of the ICC, have taken the opportunity granted them and placed themselves above rule of law (Lomeli, 2014). As can be seen in the vetoes of multiple resolutions coming before the UNSC by China and Russia on behalf of Syria, these permanent members can extend this nullification of ICC jurisdiction to their allies who have likewise not signed the Rome Statute. Thus, the ICC lacks universal jurisdiction over international crimes. Under the protection of a permanent UNSC member's veto, if a despotic government rejects ICC membership, then any crimes committed on its own people within its territory can effectively be beyond the jurisdiction of the ICC. Since Syria is not a party to the Rome Statute, unless in the unlikely event that either Syria refers the situation to the ICC or the UNSC exercises its authority for a referral under the Rome Statute of a case against President al-Assad, there will not be a prosecution by the ICC. Should there be a referral of a situation by the UNSC to the ICC, then the Prosecutor has discretion whether to initiate an investigation. Should the Prosecutor conclude that there is no reasonable basis to proceed, the UNSC can then request the Pre-Trial Chamber to review the negative decision of the prosecutor (Neuner, 2012).

Existing capabilities for implementation of R2P

The jurisdictional framework of the ICC and the related concerns of the principles of R2P are examined in this section. Further, this section explores the procedural limitations of the ICC for the capacity to implement R2P. The discussion concludes with the topic of the discretion of the ICC on whether to choose peace over justice.

Jurisdiction of the ICC and R2P

There are several issues that underscore the jurisdictional framework of the ICC and R2P principles. These include the initial reliance on domestic remedies or complementarity and the nature of the criminal offenses and offenders. The constrained ability of the ICC to determine whether an R2P situation exists is also considered in this section.

Choice of Forum—Complementarity of the ICC and R2P

The ICC is required to determine that a case is inadmissible on the grounds that it is being investigated or prosecuted by a State that has jurisdiction over it, unless the State is unwilling or unable genuinely to carry out the investigation or prosecution (Rome Statute of the ICC, Article 17). The ICC must determine whether a genuine domestic investigation and prosecution is being conducted. Article 17 of the Rome Statute provides that the requisite unwillingness to prosecute can be shown by concluding that there is a purpose of shielding the person concerned from criminal responsibility or the proceedings are being conducted in a manner that is inconsistent with an intent to bring the person concerned to justice. This complementarity principle has led to situations of states engaging in a pretense of investigations. However, where the ICC makes a determination of improper purpose in the domestic prosecution, it has dismissed objections to its investigation where it is has ruled that the State Party had failed to show it was conducting its own investigations (Isanga, 2013).

Syria's UN ambassador has urged that domestic remedies should be exhausted before the situation is referred to the ICC. Bashar Ja'afari claimed that where:

> Syria has established an independent, transparent and credible national commission of inquiry to investigate complaints of human rights violations committed by civilians, [these] domestic remedies have therefore not been exhausted, something that is a primary and fundamental condition before the issue can be referred to international bodies.
>
> (Nichols, 2013)

Critics have found this call for the use of domestic remedies to be an empty proposal (Lomeli, 2014). Yet, since there has not been a UNSC referral of the situation in Syria to the ICC, the genuineness of this domestic alternative has not been formally assessed.

The perspective of R2P that it is the responsibility of both national governments and the international community to prevent atrocity crimes also underlies the establishment of the ICC. The existence of the ICC affirms the obligation that those individuals who commit mass atrocity crimes must be held accountable. Thus, if national courts fail to prosecute genuinely those responsible for such crimes, the ICC may prosecute them. Similar complementarity schemes are seen with the ICC and the principles of R2P. The similarity in their complementarity regimes underscores the common moral commitments manifested by the ICC and R2P:

> R2P obligates governments to protect people from gross human rights abuses, and the International Criminal Court obligates them to prosecute individuals who commit such abuses. Both R2P and the International Criminal Court also affirm that when governments fail to protect people, the responsibility to do so befalls the international community.
>
> (Contarino and Lucent, 2011, pp. 196–197)

The preamble of the Rome Statute observes for the ICC and in turn the World Summit Outcome statement (2005) (Kleffner, 2012, p. 88) notes for R2P the longstanding recognition that a culture of impunity for serious violations of human rights threatens international and human security. The permanency and the breadth of jurisdiction of the ICC at least promise a consistent challenge to this culture of impunity.

The Rome statute, being a consensual document in the form of a treaty, carries with it a continuing condition of a voluntary suspension of state sovereignty. Thus, a case that meets its jurisdictional requirements, where a state is unable or unwilling to handle the matter domestically, comes within the authority of the ICC, by virtue of the agreed upon language of the treaty (Evans, 2008, p. 116). Though, the strength and legitimacy of the tribunal could be stronger if many important states would eventually choose to participate, as a treaty-based institution, the ICC has the advantage of a broad international agreement on its principles from the outset by its States-Parties (International Commission on Intervention and State Sovereignty (2001, ¶3.30, p. 24).[2] This is unlike the ad hoc tribunals, which were created by the authority of UNSC and imposed upon the sovereign authority of the respective countries (Slye and Van Schaack, 2009).

The international criminal law has traditionally placed a responsibility on states to hold to account the perpetrators of mass atrocities. Through the ICC the international criminal law does not implicate state responsibility for the underlying crime, because it is limited to providing a tribunal as an alternative to national courts for holding individuals accountable for crimes rather than nation-states. Thus, the ICC became another possible source of protection for victims by enhancing the reach of international criminal law (Rosenberg, 2010, p. 166).

In addition to a form of deterrence, which seeks to hold perpetrators of mass atrocity crimes accountable, another aspect of deterrence could stem from the ICC's ability to reinforce the societal values protected within the international criminal law. This ability may result from a possible dynamic relationship between the ICC and domestic courts that is a consequence of the complementarity principle. Recognizing that States have the primary responsibility to comply with R2P principles and thus to prevent mass atrocity crimes, the domestic investigation and prosecution will likely rely upon the jurisprudential norms developed and reified by the ICC for these specific international crimes (Contarino and Negrón-Gonzales, 2012). Yet, there is substantial deference to the sovereignty of nation-states given that the jurisdiction shall be complementary to national criminal jurisdictions (see the preamble of the Rome Statute of the ICC). For Syria there are questions about its domestic capacity, let alone its willingness, for bringing to justice those responsible for crimes of atrocity, particularly where the inadequacy of its justice systems have aggravated the conflict, and where the conflict itself is likely to have devastated its judicial institutions (Rapp, 2013).

Jurisdiction Ratione Materia

In the 2005 World Summit statement, the UN General Assembly by consensus vote confirmed the application of R2P in world affairs, specifying the crimes of genocide, war crimes, ethnic cleansing, and crimes against humanity as the predicates for implementing R2P (UN General Assembly, 2005, ¶138). In its multiple references to these crimes (see also UN General Assembly, 2005, ¶139), this collective view of the UN and its Member-state governments makes it clear that the occasion of these mass atrocity crimes precipitates the obligations for R2P (Scheffer, 2007). The Rome Statute of the ICC provides the most sophisticated definitions for such crimes drawn from treaty law and customary international law as both existed in 1998 when it was completed in treaty form (Scheffer, 2007). The advent of the ICC and its international jurisdiction over these international crimes make this institution a key constituent element for facilitating the demands of the R2P principle placed on the international community.

Though not explicitly mentioned in the 2005 World Summit statement, the ICC gets referenced in the 2001 report of the International Commission on Intervention and State Sovereignty (ICISS). The emerging principle identified by the ICISS, that of intervention for human protection purposes, was found by the ICISS to be supported by a wide variety of legal sources, among which was the Rome Statute establishing the ICC (International Commission on Intervention and State Sovereignty, 2001, ¶2.26, p. 16). Such intervention is supportable when major harm to civilians is occurring or imminently threatened, and the State in question is unable or unwilling to end the situation, or is itself the perpetrator.

There is an endorsement of a central role of the ICC by the 2004 Report of the UN Secretary-General's High-level Panel on Threats, Challenges and Change:

> In cases of mounting conflict, early indication by the UNSC that it is carefully monitoring the conflict in question and that it is willing to use its powers under the Rome Statute might deter parties from committing crimes against humanity and violating the laws of war. The UNSC should stand ready to use the authority it has under the Rome Statute to refer cases to the International Criminal Court.
>
> (High-level Panel on Threats, Challenges and Change, 2004, p. 35, ¶90)

The emerging doctrine of R2P identifies, at minimum,[3] the four atrocity crimes (genocide, war crimes, ethnic cleansing and crimes against humanity). For atrocities not defined in the Rome Statute, prosecution by the ICC is problematic. Observers (Blake and Mahmud, 2013) have noted even if there should be a referral of the Syrian situation by the UNSC to the ICC, the ICC will find that it cannot prosecute individuals for the mere use of chemical weapons in a civil conflict since the use of chemical weapons is prohibited by the Rome Statute only in the context of an international armed conflict, unless there can be found a crime against humanity in their use, which is dependent on the finding of widespread and systematic use.

Jurisdiction Ratione Personae

The 2009 report of the Secretary-General, "Implementing the Responsibility to Protect," advises that states should become parties to the ICC (UN Secretary-General (2009, ¶17). However, only individuals may be held legally accountable for crimes under the ICC, in the context of R2P where nations are required to protect their populations these individuals would likely be or involve government officials in positions of authority, such as President al-Assad of Syria. Yet, should these criminal acts become factually attributable to a state, by its failures to abide by its R2P obligations the state will lose legitimacy and its exclusive sovereign rights over its population. For the international community, the identification of these mass atrocity crimes for initiating R2P in Syria rests in the magnitude of collective suffering that is a consequence of the state's failure, attributable from its leadership, to adequately secure the fundamental rights of its citizens. This failure, either by Syria's inability or by its unwillingness to meet its obligations, is a violation of the social contract by the nation and a diminishment of its sovereign legitimacy (Marks and Cooper, 2010).

It is only in this indirect mode that the ICC can indicate that a situation of R2P exists. As presently constituted, the ICC has no authority for determining whether a violation of the R2P principle has occurred. Though it is not of modest consequence, the ICC is limited in its authority to the investigation, prosecution, and punishment of those individuals responsible for commission of certain egregious international crimes. The 2005 World Summit Outcome document specifically observed that the determination of whether there has been a violation of the R2P principles by a nation-state is a dedicated task of the UNSC, not of the ICC (Contarino and Lucent (2011, p. 197). The reliance upon the UNSC for this determination and its ultimate authorization of humanitarian military intervention presents a challenge in the conflicting agendas of the permanent members and the abuses of this authority (Hehir, 2012, p. 205). Thus, as observed by Contarino and Lucent (2011, p. 195), instead of a formal, juridical process by which the ICC could determine when an R2P violation has happened such as in Syria, there is but a political process left with the UNSC.

Yet, though the ICC cannot rule that a government has failed in its R2P obligation, as presently constituted its authority and its investigative processes provide the ICC with the effective expertise and capability to do so. Currently the ICC Pre-Trial Chamber has the authority to decide that a situation has become sufficiently grave to warrant an investigation, by doing so, it could effectively determine that a government, considering that the government official believed to be culpable is sufficiently well placed, has failed in its R2P obligation (Contarino and Lucent (2011, p. 203). Should a juridical process of determining whether there has been an R2P violation be developed, it would allow for the ICC to become an institution that could provide public rules for the practice of R2P, removing the political judgments of states over the questions of discharging the duty of R2P (Roff, 2013). The selectivity of referrals of situations in the Sudan and Libya to the ICC, but not that of Syria, raises questions of legitimacy about a process dependent on the political actors in the UNSC (Bilder and Alvarez, 2013). Until this time the exclusive political nature of this question regarding a violation of the R2P principle will continue, along with the politicized issue of referral by the UNSC for prosecution of individuals of states not parties to the ICC.

Procedural limitations on capacity

In all its responsibilities, the ICC is dependent on the cooperation of states and international organizations to carry out its key functions (Hale and Reddy, 2013). Among the many duties of the ICC, the Rome Statute requires the cooperation of States with respect to the arrest and surrender of suspects (Rome Statute of the ICC, Arts. 89–92), protection and relocation of witnesses (Rome Statute of the ICC, Arts. 87 and 93), and enforcement of sentences (Rome Statute of the ICC, Arts. 103–106). Thus, even if the UNSC refer the situation in Syria to the ICC, the ICC would need the cooperation of the international community to ensure that Syrian leaders are arrested and evidence and witnesses are obtained. Specifically the ICC is dependent on the good will and cooperation of implicated States (Cole, 2014 and Evans, 2008, p. 116).

The Rome Statute, Article 63, requires that the accused be present for the trial to commence, though the accused need not be present for the hearing to confirm charges (Isanga, 2013). Protecting sensitive witness testimony provides a challenge to the desire for public trials (Reed, 2014). The Rome Statute recognizes the need of public hearings, but provides discretion to limit public sessions to protect witnesses, victims, or confidential or sensitive evidence (Rome Statute of the ICC, 64(7), 68(2)). The Rome Statute, Article, 87(7), stipulates that the ICC may make a judicial finding of noncompliance where a state party to the Rome Statute fails to comply with a request for cooperation (Isanga, 2013).

The ICC has stated that States cannot rely on head of state immunity to refuse to arrest a sitting head of state (*Prosecutor v. Bashir*, 2011). Additionally under the Rome Statute, Article 59(4) a State Party is not permitted to question whether an arrest warrant was properly issued (Isanga, 2013). However, as most R2P scenarios will implicate government leaders, State cooperation will likely be forfeited in favor of the government's preference for protecting its alleged perpetrators of mass atrocities. Such was seen in the Darfur situation where the Sudanese government was engaged with the ICC until the first arrest warrants were issued, and Sudan refused to surrender President al-Bashir. Sudan's opposition to the ICC garnered support from many Arab and African leaders, with some States Parties declining to arrest al-Bashir when he was visiting their countries (Haslam and Edmunds, 2014). Clearly, without Syrian government cooperation should the leadership remain unchanged, indictments by the ICC will be extremely challenging to effectuate (Isanga, 2013).

Some International Relations scholarship is suggesting that under certain conditions the ICC could, by inducing the self-surrender of indicted leaders, be self-enforcing (Gilligan, 2006, p. 937). Yet, given the intransigence of the leadership in Syria (Allan, 2013) and the potential for a lack of international cooperation, these conditions may not exist for this situation (Ali, 2014). This option of prosecution by the ICC presents, however, a myriad of procedural difficulties that must be overcome in order for the ICC to be an effective instrument of deterrence (Evans, 2008, p. 116).

With this dependence on both implicated and self-interested countries, indicting a national leader for egregious international crimes can be easier than actually bringing this person to justice at the ICC. An additional justification for a juridical determination of a violation of R2P, as discussed above, is that such a determination has been envisioned by Goldhagen to be the precipitating factor for a reward system of bounties being placed on those responsible for the violations of R2P (Goldhagen, 2012, p. 351). This system could be a significant incentive for private individuals to effect an arrest.

If a purpose for the establishment of the ICC is deterrence of perpetrators of mass atrocity crimes, this is undermined by reliance of the ICC on States to enforce its arrest warrants and to protect witnesses and evidence (Hoover, 2013). This dependence raises challenges for the effectiveness of the ICC as a deterrent to mass atrocity crimes that could in effect precipitate R2P obligations.

Discretion—peace, justice and deterrence

With the requirement in the Preamble to the Rome Statute to "guarantee lasting respect for and the enforcement of international justice" for the "most serious crimes of international concern" (Rome Statute of the ICC, Article 1), questions can be raised regarding whether the demands of justice, that is to end the culture of impunity, should be tempered with concerns of the demands for peace. These demands for peace likely encompass requirements for amnesties and exile.

Article 53 of the Rome Statute gives the ICC Prosecutor the discretion not to pursue an investigation if there are "substantial reasons to believe that an investigation would not serve the interests of justice." Thus, the Prosecutor has discretion to consider the so-called peace versus justice dilemma for situations where there is such a need to advance a peace process that can bring to a close a conflict that has caused much destruction and human suffering, but the prospect of bringing empowered perpetrators to justice threatens this opportunity for peace (Evans, 2008, p. 117). Further, the UNSC could use its authority under Article 16 of the Rome Statute to suspend an investigation or a prosecution on Chapter VII grounds for renewable periods of 12 months, when it is determined that continuing the investigation poses a threat to international peace and security. Presumably this broad authority could be used in this context where the permanent members are convinced of the need to favor the immediate interests of peace over the goals of justice (Evans, 2008, p. 118).

The continuing impunity of the perpetrators may be necessitated where the circumstances are strengthened for ending conflict and saving many lives (Evans, 2008, p. 117). As the co-chair of ICISS, Gareth Evans observed:

> It may shock the conscience to contemplate not pursuing prosecutions when major perpetrators of atrocity crimes are involved, this *can* be helpful in certain circumstances in ending conflict, and in saving as a result a great many more lives.
>
> (Evans, 2008, p. 118)

Evans further cautioned that many several public policy goals are served by the struggle to bring offenders to justice, which should not be discounted. These include retribution, incapacitation, rehabilitation of offenders, truth telling, institutionalization of human rights norms, and, most importantly, deterrence. The threat of criminal prosecutions for a government leader, responsible for mass atrocities, could be a preventative device (Defeis, 2011). Thus, the significance of these goals of justice must be clearly outweighed by the shorter-term costs in prolonging a conflict. Where the trade-off is made to favor immediate peace over justice, there is the risk of developing a perception that the work of the ICC is negotiable, undermining its ability to deter would-be defendants from crimes of mass atrocity (Evans, 2008, p. 118). However, should the UNSC permit the ICC to have jurisdiction over the situation in Syria, this could spur both justice and peace. David Scheffer has noted that if the International Criminal Court obtained jurisdiction over the Syrian situation, following a UNSC referral, al-Assad's departure from Damascus would be accelerated and respect for human rights more likely for the Syrian people (Scheffer, 2013).

Actual abilities to address R2P challenges

Cases that have been referred by the UNSC to the ICC indicate an invocation of the R2P principle by the international community. Where a civil war breaks out in a country such as Syria, which is not a state party to the Rome Statute, the government likely has little interest to refer this situation to the ICC or even to conceal its own involvement in the crimes committed by its troops. Since the Rome Statute does not provide for the possibility of a state referral or *proprio motu* investigation by the prosecutor in civil wars in countries that have not ratified the ICC Statute, the only way to refer civil war situations in the territory of a non-state party to the ICC is usually via a referral by the UNSC. The UNSC on March 31, 2005, referred to the ICC the situation in Darfur and on February 26, 2011, the situation in Libya. Both states continue not to be state parties to the ICC Statute, for the ICC this has meant there was no jurisdiction over the situations until these referrals (Neuner, 2012). This section begins with a discussion of these cases and closes with an examination of the attempts to get the UNSC to engage the ICC in the situation in Syria.

Darfur and Libya

Darfur represents the first case to be referred by the UNSC to the ICC (Charity, 2011). Despite the referral in March 2005, atrocities continued in Darfur for many years. In a trade-off, where justice outweighed peace, as a consequence of making public the arrest warrant, thirteen humanitarian aid agencies (providing 60 percent of all humanitarian assistance in Darfur) were expelled from the Darfur region of Sudan. This loss of humanitarian aid led to a significant risk of further civilian deaths. Sudanese leaders were undeterred (Rosenberg, 2010, p. 178); among other things, the government of Sudan continued to arm militias responsible for mass death, destruction, and displacement, reneged on its numerous promises to disarm them, and expelled the Special Representative of the UN Secretary-General from the country in October 2006 (Anonymous, 2007).

President Al-Bashir became the first sitting head of state indicted by the ICC. The African Union refused to arrest and extradite al-Bashir to the ICC. Some of these government leaders said that this refusal was a signal to the West not to impose its ways on Africa (Thakur, 2011).[4] Though the UNSC did not reinforce its referral with effective efforts to bring perpetrators, such as al-Bashir, before the ICC, the ICC process in the Darfur crisis has at best been seen as representing a positive first step in legitimizing the role of the ICC to address an R2P situation (Contarino and Negrón-Gonzales, 2012). The resolution of this R2P crisis still depends on the international community to utilize R2P strategies other than what can be presently offered by the ICC (Anonymous, 2007).

In a unanimous vote on February 26, 2011, the UNSC, in addition to taking binding measures under Article 41 of the Charter that included imposing an arms embargo, a travel ban, and an asset freeze, referred the situation in Libya to the ICC, UNSC action was required as Libya is not a state party to the ICC. In the Preamble to Resolution 1970, the UNSC observed that the widespread and systematic attacks currently taking place in the country against the civilian population could amount to crimes against humanity. Resolution 1970 represents the first time the UNSC took coercive action against a government explicitly on R2P grounds. This Resolution also is the first time for the US to vote in favor of a referral to the ICC, having abstained from the earlier referral of Darfur. In its provisions, Resolution 1970 indicates how the international community is to facilitate the efforts of the ICC. In ¶5, the Libyan authorities are to cooperate fully with the ICC and all States, including those not party to the Rome Statute, and regional and other international organizations are urged to cooperate fully with the ICC (Crook, 2011).

On March 3, 2011, the ICC Prosecutor announced his investigation into alleged crimes against humanity committed in Libya, identifying certain individuals in formal or de facto authority, thus placing them on notice of their exposure to criminal responsibility. Members of opposition groups were informed in this announcement that they also could be included in the investigation (Cerone, 2012). The Libyan government's attacks on its population were not halted by the sanctions coupled in Resolution 1970 against the Libyan government with the threat of criminal prosecution by the ICC. This led the UNSC to adopt Resolution 1973 on March 17, 2011, which authorized the use of armed force against the Libyan government. The more limited effects of the referral to the ICC under Resolution 1970 raises questions regarding the operational viability of this response by the ICC under R2P principles (Murphy, 2011).

Later in May, 2011, the ICC prosecutor submitted a request, within weeks of the referral in Resolution 1970, to the Pre-trial Chamber for arrest warrants against Muammar Gaddafi and his son, Saif, and the head of Libyan intelligence (Wald, 2012). Though the warrants were widely supported by Western nations and some African countries, the African Union (AU) condemned the ICC action as being biased, and instructed its members to ignore the warrants (Wald, 2012). Colonel Gaddafi has been confirmed dead (*Prosecutor v. Gaddafi* (2011), his case is now closed and the Libyan authorities have custody of the other two ICC defendants and have refused to surrender them (Sadat, 2013). Yet, it was a regime change in Libya, which has not occurred in Syria that led to domestic actions that facilitated the arrests of the ICC-defendants, in contrast to the situation in Darfur, where the leadership in Sudan remains.

The Libya situation has demonstrated an effort at coordination between the UNSC and the ICC that is an improvement over the Darfur experience. Libya is obligated under Resolution 1970 to cooperate with the ICC. Though there is a prospect of prosecution by domestic authorities, the risk for the ICC, should Libya not fulfill its obligations under the complementarity principle, is that the UNSC will fail to assist the ICC in enforcing its outstanding arrest warrants. Such a result would be another demonstration of the dependence of the ICC upon the UNSC (Contarino and Negrón-Gonzales, 2012).

Syria

Quite distinct from the active efforts of the UNSC to utilize the ICC for the effort to confront the crises in Darfur and Libya, there has been no such exertion with the conflict in Syria. National interests are preventing the crisis situation in Syria from being referred to the ICC. There is disagreement among member-states of the UNSC as to the propriety of deploying the ICC, let alone other measures, for this situation. However, with Syria not being a State Party to the Rome Statute, the ICC remains without jurisdiction, and thus without influence, until the stalemate is resolved on the political issues within the UNSC (Triponel and Williams, 2013). Even though there has been success in the recent resolution requiring Syria to cooperate fully in the UN effort to secure and destroy its stockpile of chemical weapons, there was no inclusion of a referral of the matter to the ICC (Lomeli, 2014).

The stalemate cannot be due to a comparative level of seriousness not seen in Syria (Cole, 2014). The Libyan death toll was estimated at over 1,000 on February 23, 2011, only weeks before the UN authorized the intervention in Libya and NATO began airstrikes over the country (Guiora, 2013). It is reported that well over 100,000 persons have been killed since the start of the conflict in Syria due to the regime's use against civilians of air bombardment and other heavy weaponry and chemical weapons (Cole, 2014). This number of casualties has continued to rise since this estimate.

Political motivations likely play a key role in the opposition by Russia and China to intervention by the ICC. Russian protection of the Assad regime can be linked to Russia's only Mediterranean naval base being situated in Syria (Triponel and Williams, 2013). Further, the opposition by both Russia and China to referral to the ICC may also be in reaction to the UNSC's action in Libya, where both countries had attempted to negotiate a restriction on the scope of the authorization to use force. However, the resulting regime change in Libya that resulted from NATO's intervention served only to reinforce the original hesitation by Russia and China to the actions of the UNSC (Triponel and Williams, 2013).

In August of 2011, the UNSC gave approval to a statement by its President, wherein the UNSC condemned the widespread violations of human rights and called for an end to the violence in Syria. However, a proffered resolution that would have referred the situation to the ICC was threatened by a Russian veto and opposed by China, Brazil, India and South Africa (Murphy, 2011). Since 2011, high-level UN human rights officials have released reports that have found human rights violations committed by the Syrian government on a systematic basis (UN Human Rights Council, 2011). In early 2013, invoking the work of the UN Commission of Inquiry on Syria, which reported widespread, systematic, and gross human rights violations by Syrian forces (Petty, 2013), the UN High Commissioner for Human Rights Navi Pillay, renewed her call for a UNSC referral of the situation in Syria to the ICC, and the UN Human Rights Council's independent commission of inquiry on Syria released a report in 2013 to Pillay that included a confidential list of individuals who could be charged with crimes against humanity (Schank, 2014). In December 2013 Navi Pillay reported on the evidence collected by a panel of investigators that linked President Bashar al-Assad of Syria to war crimes and crimes against humanity for the first time (Cumming-Bruce, 2013). During a briefing with the UNSC on April 8, 2014 Pillay renewed the call that the UNSC refer the situation to the ICC (Human Rights Watch, 2014).

The UN Human Rights Council has continued the mandate of the Commission of Inquiry on Syria. This approach, to press for commissions of inquiry by the UN Human Rights Council, does allow for at least the gathering of facts and the beginning the process of investigation in Syria. This will likely prove useful for documenting atrocity crimes and for building a case for a future prosecution of war criminals before the ICC or domestic Syrian courts (Petty, 2013). On March 5, 2014, the UN Syria Commission of Inquiry issued its latest report finding that all sides to the Syria conflict have continued to commit serious crimes under international law and observed that the UNSC was failing to take action to end the state of impunity. The Commission recommended that the UNSC give the ICC a mandate to investigate abuses in Syria (Human Rights Watch, 2014).

In its most recent failed effort the UNSC saw Russia and China on May 22, 2014 vetoing a resolution to refer the situation in Syria to the ICC (UN Security Council Meetings Coverage, 2014). This resolution had been presented by France and 65 sponsors (Journalists for Justice, 2014). Additionally, on May 15, 2014 over 100 civil society groups from around the world had issued a statement urging the UNSC to approve a resolution to refer the situation in Syria to the ICC (Civil Society Organizations on Need for Justice (2014). Many national foreign ministers have called on the ICC to take action in Syria (Lomeli, 2014). The world community has noted the toll on the rule of law from the inability to refer the situation in Syria to the ICC. During recent meetings of the General

Assembly state delegates have heard a call for the five permanent members of the UNSC to give up their veto authority on issues involving mass atrocities (Lomeli, 2014). Despite a global outcry against the Syrian conflict and calls for a referral by the UNSC to the ICC, the issue of UNSC intervention remains intensely contested among permanent Council members, with Russia and China vetoing UNSC resolutions (Coalition for the International Criminal Court (n.d.).

With the continuing impasse in getting the referral of the situation in Syria from the UNSC to the ICC, there is the possibility of establishing an ad hoc tribunal uniquely devoted to this crisis. Such has been established for Sierra Leone, Lebanon, Cambodia and East Timor. These specialized tribunals were created for situations that arose prior to the temporal jurisdiction of the ICC for these situations. However, the consequences for the ICC should such an alternate tribunal be established could be the denigration of the legitimacy of the ICC raising profound questions as to the purpose for having established this international court where it cannot take on a devastating humanitarian crisis such as that in Syria (Lomeli, 2014).

Conclusion

Given their common objectives, the ICC and the R2P principles have the potential to strengthen one another. The developments in jurisprudence from the ICC on the legal norms for mass atrocity crimes will strengthen the R2P principle by clarifying these international legal standards that serve as the prerequisite for R2P principles. Thus, while there is yet no clear agreement on the precise threshold for which an unwillingness of a state to protect its people reaches a point that R2P principles are triggered (Breakey, 2013, p. 52) and there is no forum for a juridical determination of such a failure, the contribution of the ICC to this conceptual development in its jurisprudence will be instrumental to the success of R2P.

It is the political impasse in the UNSC and the ICC's dependence on the UNSC to exercise its authority over non-states parties that impede any successful role for the ICC with the situation in Syria. David Scheffer, the first US Ambassador-at-Large for War Crimes Issues, recognized the "tremendous amount of angst" held by countries in their view that the UNSC is failing to refer Syria to the ICC. He finds it a fascinating irony that a decade and a half after the finalization of the Rome Statute was finalized, there are countries seeking the help of the UNSC, because the UNSC actually has the ability to require some compliance with the ICC (Scheffer, 2013). The effectiveness of the ICC in facilitating the principles of R2P for Syria is dependent on the political agendas of the permanent members of the UNSC. How the crisis in Syria will be resolved will determine not just the future of this country, but likely that of the ICC and R2P as well (Murphy, 2011).

Notes

1 By contrast, there is a requirement for members of the UNSC to abstain from voting for those matters coming under Chapter VI or under Article 52(3) of the Charter, if they are a "party to the dispute." UN Charter, Article 27(3).
2 The ICISS found that the establishment of the ICC was a welcome measure to avoid the accusations of double standards and "victor's justice," which are periodically aimed at these specialist tribunals. (International Commission on Intervention and State Sovereignty, 2001, ¶3.30, p. 24).
3 The ICISS principles on the predicate for implementing R2P extend beyond atrocity crimes, having a broader range than what was adopted in the *2005 World Summit Outcome*. Thus, the measure of "large scale loss of life" under the ICISS, need not necessarily be precipitated by the crimes of genocide, war crimes, ethnic cleansing and crimes against humanity, but could be precipitated by natural disasters and an ineffective government response (Scheffer, 2007).
4 There has been considerable attention paid by the ICC to situations in Africa. African countries have been at the forefront of protesting at the Africans-only prosecution of alleged war criminals by the ICC. It has been observed that there is selectivity in its African targets, where attention is given governments, which are adversaries of the US and US allies are ignored. (Mamdani, 2011, p. 131). This has resulted in African leaders complaining about a possible bias toward prosecution only of Africans by the ICC. At the thirteenth African Union summit of heads of government/state in July 2009, Africa's leaders agreed to denounce the ICC for its March 2009 issuance of an arrest warrant for Sudan's President, Omar al-Bashir following the indictment by the ICC for war crimes and crimes against humanity. (Thakur, 2011, p. 121). Countering this protest of the African centered approach to ICC prosecutions, is the recognition that African states continue to refer situations the Court, is indicated by the referrals of Mali and Côte d'Ivoire (Cole, 2014).

References

Ali, N. (2014). Bringing the guilty to justice: Can the ICC be self-enforcing? *Chicago Journal of International Law*, 14, 408–451.

Allan, J. (2013). Ineffective, opaque, and undemocratic: The IOUs of – too much – International law and why a bit of skepticism is warranted. *San Diego Law Review*, 50, 833–866.

Anonymous (2007). Ensuring a responsibility to protect: Lessons from Darfur. *Human Rights Brief 14*, 26–29.

Bilder, R. B. and Alvarez, J. E. (2013). Book review: Globalization and sovereignty: Rethinking legality, legitimacy, and constitutionalism. *American Journal of International Law*, 107, 697–703.

Blake, J. and Mahmud, A. (2013). A legal 'red line'?: Syria and the use of chemical weapons in civil conflict. *UCLA Law Review Discourse*, 61, 244–260.

Breakey, H. (2013). R2P + POC (+IHRL) = R2PC: The United Nations UNSC and the hybridisation of international protection principles. In Sampford and Thakur (eds.). *Responsibility to protect and sovereignty* (pp. 41–61). Ashgate Publishing: Surrey, UK.

Coalition for the International Criminal Court (n.d.) UNSC. Retrieved from: www.coalitionfortheicc.org/?mod=sc&idudctp=14&show=all (accessed August 30, 2014).

Cerone, J. (2012). Civilian casualties in modern warfare: The death of the collateral damage rule: expanding the R2P tool-kit: New political possibilities and attendant legal uncertainties. *ILSA Journal of International & Comparative Law*, 18, 531–563.

Charity, M. H. (2011). The International Criminal Court, the responsibility to protect, and Darfur, Republic of Sudan. *Ohio Northern University Law Review*, 37, 67–110.

Civil society organizations on need for justice (2014, May 15). *Syria: Groups call for ICC referral*. FIDH. Retrieved from: www.fidh.org/en/north-africa-middle-east/syria/15321-syria-groups-call-for-icc-referral (accessed August 30, 2014).

Cole, R. J. V. (2014). Africa's relationship with the International Criminal Court: More political than legal. *Melbourne Journal of International Law*, 14, 670–698.

Contarino, M. and Lucent, S. (2011). Stopping the killing: The International Criminal Court and juridical determination of the responsibility to protect. In Alex J. Bellamy, Sara E. Davies and Luke Glanville (eds.). *The Responsibility to Protect and International Law* (pp. 193–216). Leiden, Netherlands: Koninklijke Brill.

Contarino, M. and Negrón-Gonzales, M. (2012). The International Criminal Court. In Gentian Zyberi and Kevin Mason (eds.). *An institutional approach to the responsibility to protect* (pp. 411–435). Cambridge, UK: Cambridge University Press.

Crook, J. R. (2011). United States joins in strong measures against Libya, including UN-sanctioned use of force. *American Journal of International Law*, 105, 568–574.

Cumming-Bruce, N. (December 4, 2013). U.N. official links Assad to crimes in Syria. *International New York Times*, p. 8. Retrieved from: www.nytimes.com/2013/12/03/world/middleeast/top-un-rights-official-links-assad-to-crimes-in-syria.html?_r=0 (accessed August 30, 2014).

Defeis, E. F. (2011). The responsibility to protect and international justice. *Journal of International Business & Law*, 10, 91–98.

Evans, G. (2008). *The Responsibility to protect: Ending mass atrocity crimes once and for all*. Washington DC: Brookings Institution Press.

Gilligan, M. J. (2006). Is enforcement necessary for effectiveness? A model of the international criminal regime. *International Organizations*, 60, 935–967.

Goldhagen, D. J. (2012). Ending our age of suffering: A plan to end of genocide. In Julia Hoffmann and André Nollkaemper (eds.). *Responsibility to protect from principle to practice* (pp. 347–354). Amsterdam: Pallas Publications.

Guiora, A. N. (2013). Humanitarian intervention and sovereignty under the umbrella of geo-politics. *University of Pennsylvania Journal of International Law*, 34, 411–430.

Hale, C. and Reddy, M. K. (2013). A meeting of the minds in Rome: Ending the circular conundrum of the US–ICC relationship. *Washington University Global Studies Law Review*, 12, 581–620.

Haslam, E. and Edmunds, R. (2014). Victim participation, politics and the construction of victims at the International Criminal Court: Reflections on proceedings in Banda and Jerbo. *Melbourne Journal of International Law*, 14, 727–747.

Hehir, A. (2012). *The responsibility to protect: rhetoric, reality and the future of humanitarian intervention*. London: Palgrave Macmillan.

High-level Panel on Threats, Challenges and Change (2004). A more secure world: Our shared responsibility. (Report of the Secretary-General's high-level panel on threats, challenges and change). Retrieved from: www.un.org/en/peacebuilding/pdf/historical/hlp_more_secure_world.pdf (accessed August 30, 2014).

Hoover, J. (2013). Moral practices: Assigning responsibility in the International Criminal Court. *Law and Contemporary Problems*, 76, 263–286.

Human Rights Watch (2014). *UN Security Council: Give ICC mandate in Syria: Russia, China should not veto referral*. Retrieved from: www.hrw.org/news/2014/05/13/un-security-council-give-icc-mandate-syria (accessed August 30, 2014).

International Commission on Intervention and State Sovereignty (2001). *Report on the responsibility to protect*. Retrieved from: http://responsibilitytoprotect.org/ICISS%20 Report.pdf (accessed August 30, 2014).

International Criminal Court (2014). *Situations and cases*. Retrieved from: www.icc-cpi.int/en_menus/icc/situations%20and%20cases/Pages/situations%20and%20cases.aspx (accessed August 30, 2014).

Isanga, J. M. (2013). The International Criminal Court ten years later: Appraisal and prospects. *Cardozo Journal of International and Comparative Law*, 21, 235–323.

Journalists for Justice (2014, May 23). *Russia and China veto resolution to refer Syria to the ICC*. Retrieved from: www.jfjustice.net/russia-and-china-veto-resolution-to-refer-syria-to-the-icc/ (accessed August 30, 2014).

Kleffner, J. (2012). The scope of the crimes triggering the responsibility to protect. In J. Hoffman and P. A. Nollkaemper (eds.). *Responsibility to protect. From principle to practice* (pp. 85–92). Amsterdam: Pallas Publications-Amsterdam University Press.

Lomeli, M. C. (2014). "Never again" again and again: The international criminal court's inability to deter mass atrocities and the security council's failure to act. *Arizona Journal of International and Comparative Law*, 31, 81–123.

Mamdani, M. (2011). Responsibility to protect or right to punish? In Phillip Cunliffe (ed.). *Critical perspectives on the responsibility to protect* (pp. 125–138). London: Routledge.

Marks, S. P. and Cooper, N. (2010). The responsibility to protect: Watershed or old wine in a new bottle? *Jindal Global Law Review*, 2, 86–130.

Murphy, J. F. (2011). International law in crisis: Challenges posed by the new terrorism and the changing nature of war. *Case Western Reserve Journal of International Law*, 44, 59–92.

Neuner, M. (2012). The UNSC and the ICC: Assessing the first ten years of coexistence. *New England Journal of International and Comparative Law*, 18, 283–310.

Nichols, M. (2013, January 25). Syria says ICC call hinders search for end to conflict, Reuters. Retrieved from: www.reuters.com/article/2013/01/25/us-syria-crisis-un-idUS BRE90O12C20130125. (accessed August 30, 2014).

Petty, K. A. (2013). Humanity and national security: the law of mass atrocity response operations. *Michigan Journal of International Law*, 34, 745–827.

Prosecutor v. Bashir (2011, December 12). *Case No. ICC-02/05–01/09–139*. Decision on the Failure by the Republic of Malawi to Comply with the Cooperation Requests Issued by the Court.

Prosecutor v. Gaddafi (2011, November 22). *Case No. ICC-01/11–01/ 11*. Decision to Terminate the Case Against Muammar Mohammed Abu Minyar Gaddafi.

Rapp, S. J. (2013). The reach and the grasp of international criminal justice: How do we lengthen the arm of the law? *Case Western Reserve Journal of International Law*, 45, 651–670.

Reed, K. (2014). Compensation for extraordinary rendition: A comparative study and the need for a domestic cause of action in the United States. *Pacific McGeorge Global Business & Development Law Journal*, 27, 131–152.

Roff, H. (2013). *Global justice, Kant and the responsibility to protect: A provisional duty*. London: Routledge.

Rosenberg, S. P. (2010). Responsibility to protect: A framework for prevention. In A. Bellamy, S. Davies and L. Glanville (eds.). *The responsibility to protect and international law* (pp. 157–192), Leiden: Martinus Nijhoff.

Sadat, L. N. (2013). Crimes against humanity in the modern age. *American Journal of International Law*, 107, 334–377.

Schank, A. (2014). Sectarianism and transitional justice in Syria: Resisting international trials. *Georgetown Journal of International Law*, 45, 557–587.

Scheffer, D. (2007). Prevention: Atrocity crimes framing the responsibility to protect. *Case Western Reserve Journal of International Law*, 40, 111–135.

Scheffer, D. (2013). Chasing leadership impunity: The rapid evolution of international criminal law. *Chapman Law Review*, 16, 395–405.

Slye, R. C. and Van Schaack, B. (2009). International Criminal Law. New York: Aspen Publishers.

Thakur, R. (2011). *The responsibility to protect: Norms, laws and the use of force in international politics*. New York: Routledge.

Triponel, A. F. and Williams, P. R. (2013). The clash of the titans: Justice and realpolitik in Libya. *American University International Law Review*, 28, 775–834.

UN General Assembly (2005). *UN world summit outcome document*. (U.N. Doc. A/RES/60/L.1). Retrieved from: www.un.org/womenwatch/ods/A-RES-60-1-E.pdf (accessed August 27, 2014).

UN Human Rights Council (2011, September 15). *The current human rights situation in the Syrian Arab Republic in the context of recent events*. (U.N. Doc. A/HRC/18/53). Retrieved from: www.refworld.org/docid/4e89a9010.html (accessed August 27, 2014).

UN Secretary-General (2009, January 12). *Implementing the responsibility to protect*. U.N. Doc. A/63/677.

UN Security Council Meetings Coverage (2014, May 22). *Referral of Syria to International Criminal Court fails as negative votes prevent Security Council from adopting draft resolution*. Meetings Coverage and Press Releases. Retrieved from: www.un.org/News/Press/docs/2014/sc11407.doc.htm (accessed August 27, 2014).

Wald, P. M. (2012). Apprehending war criminals: Does international cooperation work? *American University International Law Review*, 27, 229–262.

5 Organisation for the Prohibition of Chemical Weapons (OPCW)

John Janzekovic

The Organisation for the Prohibition of Chemical Weapons (OPCW) became directly involved in the Syrian civil war in 2013 after allegations surfaced of chemical weapons, including highly lethal nerve agents, being used in Syria. The OPCW is the monitoring, investigating, and implementing body of the 1997 Chemical Weapons Convention (CWC). The Convention's primary provisions are to destroy chemical weapons under international verification by the OPCW and to prevent the proliferation of chemical weapons. Today, 190 member-states including Syria are a party to the CWC. Israel and Myanmar have signed but not ratified the CWC, while Angola, Egypt, North Korea and South Sudan have neither signed nor acceded to the convention (OPCW, 2014).

A joint OPCW-UN mission authorized by the United Nations (UN) Secretary-General, Ban Ki-moon, on March 21, 2013 was mandated under the requirements of the CWC, Annex to Part XI, to investigate the rapidly increasing number of claims and counterclaims (OPCW, 2013a). President Bashar Assad's government and the opposition rebels accused each other of using chemical weapons and both have denied it. Syria became the 190th member and therefore a party to the CWC after President Assad signed a legislative decree of assent on September 12, 2013. Syria was not a party to the convention prior to 2013 therefore it was not legally committed to CWC prohibitions against the development, production, or use of chemical weapons. However, Syria had ratified the 1925 Geneva Protocol in 1968, which bans the use of bacteriological and chemical methods of international warfare (Spence, 2012).

The closest some of the major powers came to direct intervention in Syria was in mid-2013 (CBCNews, 2014). US officials stated in June 2013 that a "red line" had been crossed by the use of chemical weapons. In August 2013, Britain's Prime Minister David Cameron argued for a military response but the House of Commons rejected this. France's foreign minister, Laurent Fabius supported calls for a military strike in Syria, but not without such a strike being led by the Americans. The direct inference by the US, Britain and France was that the Assad regime used prohibited weapons against regime opponents and civilians. Russia's President Vladimir Putin stated in June 2013 that he shared an interest with the US in stopping the violence, but he firmly opposed any forcible military intervention by outside powers. Russia is one of Syria's most important international allies and top supplier of its weapons. The American President Barack Obama agreed to pursue a diplomatic solution with Russia before launching any military strikes while China and Russia in the UN Security Council continued to reject any calls for direct intervention and limited their responses to statements of concern.

On August 21, 2013 the OPCW-UN investigators confirmed that a large-scale sarin attack was delivered by rockets hitting the Ghouta area in Damascus. This resulted in the deaths of an estimated 1,400 people and it was a clear violation of the CWC. The attack also violated the Responsibility to Protect (R2P) principles and the UN General Assembly (UNGA) Resolution (2009) that formalized R2P's protective and preventative implementation as an international norm (UN General Assembly, 2009a; UN General Assembly, 2009b). According to the R2P principles of and the UN resolutions, the State carries the primary responsibility for protecting populations from genocide, war crimes, crimes against humanity and ethnic cleansing. Under R2P, the international community also has a specific responsibility to use diplomatic, humanitarian and "other means" to protect populations from these crimes (UN General Assembly, 2005). This responsibility is not solely dependent on identifying those who use these prohibited weapons rather it is use of these weapons itself that obliges an international response. On September 14, 2013, the US and Russia agreed to a framework in conjunction with the OPCW to remove then destroy Syria's chemical arsenal. The agreement stopped the prospect of US-led military strikes on Syria as a result of the August 21, 2013 OPCW report regarding the chemical weapons attack in Damascus (OPCW, 2013a).

OPCW mandate and R2P in Syria

The International Coalition for the Responsibility to Protect (ICRtoP) outlines the many efforts by the UN and various state sponsored special envoys to halt the widespread violence in Syria. The majority of these efforts, and personal pleas by world leaders to stop the fighting, have been rebuffed outright or simply ignored by all parties. The R2P convention and CWC protocols include the possibility for forcible humanitarian intervention in Syria but the ICRtoP also warned that,

> The Responsibility to Protect norm, as agreed to in the 2005 World Summit Outcome Document, does not sanction a unilateral military response or a response by a 'coalition of the willing.' Any military response under R2P must be authorized by the Security Council.
>
> (ICRtoP, 2014)

Any possible UN sponsored direct action in Syria is further complicated by reports that all sides in the Syria conflict are engaging in serious human rights abuses either against each other or against civilians.

The lack of any consensus by the major powers in the UN appears to be an insurmountable hurdle for the international community as it tries to deal with the ever-increasing levels of violence throughout Syria. The exception is the OPCW-UN mission to Syria. However, the mission was mandated to investigating whether chemical weapons had been used, not to determine who used them (Brühl, 2013; UN News Centre, 2013). Russia, for example, made it very clear how it viewed the role of the OPCW and its mandate in Syria, "... there should be no attempts of reorienting the OPCW to deal with irrelevant issues that are in the competence of other international organizations. Otherwise such attempts will result in weakening of the OPCW mandate, which is obviously unacceptable" (Kalamanov, 2013).

R2P is essentially a political concept. It is not a new norm of international law despite basing many of its arguments on the existing body of such laws (Pommier, 2011). R2P is also not primarily intended as a new validation aimed at authorizing military intervention rather it claims to be focused on preventive efforts to address potential humanitarian crises. In reality much of the rhetoric and practicality about R2P is underpinned by well-established principles of existing international law. That is, states already have legal obligations to address genocide, war crimes and crimes against humanity, to assist each other to fulfill obligations under international humanitarian law, and to promote compliance with the law.

The many reports, commissions and declarations by key stakeholders in the formal development of R2P make it clear that the fundamentals of the international obligation to protect at risk populations, and to prevent such populations from becoming at risk in the first place, are to be realized through the legal formalities inherent in the UN Charter. The concern is that unless the UN is directly involved in the instigation and implementation of R2P then other agencies with their own agendas might undertake intervention under the guise of responsibility to protect or prevent (International Commission on Intervention and State Sovereignty, 2001, ¶71).

R2P's three-pillar approach to the ongoing humanitarian disaster in Syria firmly underscores the realpolitik divide between the major powers and the international community generally. The one, perhaps the only one, indication that at least R2P's prevention strategy is having some success is in the UN-led mission to investigate allegations of the use of chemical weapons. The overall deteriorating situation in Syria threatens the foundations of R2P because the majority of the basic protective essentials are not being addressed and, equally concerning, there is no indication that the application of a R2P framework is edging towards any sort of coherent plan or strategy.

An important pillar of the R2P thesis is the responsibility to prevent the need for direct and immediate protection in the first place. If the desperate need for protection ends up as a response to some human instigated disaster then prevention has either largely failed or it has not been effective in the first place (Janzekovic and Silander, 2013, p. 65). In the case of Syria, the preventative approach regarding the further use of chemical weapons was successful with the Director-General OPCW, Ahmet Üzümcü, reporting that identification and removal of chemical and nerve agents in Syria was completed on June 23, 2014. This is a significant achievement underpinned by the R2P preventative pillar. The Carnegie Commission on Preventing Deadly Conflict, in its final 1999 report, identified three broad aims of preventative action: prevent the emergence of violent conflict, prevent ongoing conflicts from spreading, and prevent the re-emergence of violence (Carnegie Commission, 1997, pp. xviii–xxviii). Here the broader stated aims of prevention have been far less successful in halting the ongoing, wide ranging violence in Syria. This Commission proposed in its report that prevention required the alleviation of risk factors that triggered violent conflict and that it required resolution to the underlying root causes of violence. However, the Commission did not explain how this was to be done except to propose that prevention may be operational or structural in nature. Operational prevention is claimed to focus on responding to the immediacy of conflict, while structural prevention is aimed at identifying and responding to the underlying causes of conflict. The practical, real-world application of the prevention thesis is rarely realized with such fine-sounding but ultimately obscure principles and ideals. The most that can be hoped for is that there are at least some protection and prevention initiatives that are effective. The OPCW-UN mission in Syria is an example of how the international community is able to respond effectively to a very serious situation that potentially saved many lives.

The complexity of diplomatic maneuverings between the major powers and with Syria itself, and then the successful implementation of the OPCW-UN mandate, shows that it is possible for the international community to act swiftly and directly. However, the international response to these events in Syria shows that it takes an extreme and very specific danger before a practical and effective response is forthcoming. There remain many serious challenges confronting the people in Syria and the international community needs to do much more if the obligation to prevent and protect thesis is to have any real meaning. Sigrid Kaag, the Special Coordinator of the OPCW judged that the removal of chemical weapons from Syria was, "A modest but meaningful contribution to peace and security in Syria." (Kaag, 2014). So, while the critical work of this mission cannot be understated, there remain significant challenges for the international community to more effectively respond to the many serious human rights abuses in Syria.

Civil discontent in Syria

Syria has a decades-long history of regime intolerance to civil discontent. In 1982, thousands of Syrians were killed after a clampdown by President Hafez Assad against a Muslim Brotherhood uprising in Hama. Sectarian and ethnic unrest flared in the region resulting in the torture and killings by the regime during the Druz uprising in 2000 and the Kurdish rebellion in 2004. Three former war crimes prosecutors presented the "Caesar Report" to the UN Security Council in April 15, 2014 and stated that 11,000 detainees were tortured and killed between 2011 and 2013 in Syrian government detention centers (Cinq-Mars *et al.*, 2014).

Civil discontent in Syria has for a long time been directed against the many failures of promised political and economic reforms, and against the cycle of regime hard-line responses to civil protests and disturbances. The genesis for the current civil war in Syria is unclear. Some argue that the catalyst was the jailing and killing of children in March 2011 after they painted anti-regime slogans and graffiti on walls in the southern, predominately Sunni city of Daraa (Stirling, 2012). Public protests erupted after news spread of the failure of authorities to punish those responsible for the jailing, beatings, torture and killings. Protests increased after evidence surfaced that the authorities were also involved in abuses against children and others. What started as a rural and provincial-driven uprising quickly spread throughout Syria. Others claim that the civil war in Syria emulated the violent uprisings elsewhere in the Arab world. These uprisings saw the collapse of civil order in Tunisia, Egypt and in other neighboring countries where long-held animosities and dissatisfaction with governments resulted in civil protests and the subsequent brutal crackdown by authorities (BBC News, 2011).

In April 2011, protests in Syria became a full-scale armed rebellion after the Syrian Army fired on demonstrators, killing at least 260 people in the village of Ezra, the Damascus district of Barzeh and the city of Homs. The Syrian Observatory for Human Rights based in Britain claimed that by mid-2014 it had documented 162,402 deaths in the conflict but this organization argues that the real toll is likely to be significantly higher at around 220,000 deaths of civilians, rebels and members of the Syrian military (Surk, 2014). Up to three million people have fled Syria, there are over 6.5 million internally displaced persons (IDPs) and there are at least 10.8 million Syrians in need of humanitarian assistance (Cinq-Mars *et al.*, 2014).

Today, the violence in Syria is exacerbated by conflict between Assad regime opponents and by regime loyalists and their supporters. One of the many opponents to the regime is the Free Syrian Army (FSA) that was formed in July 2011. The FSA is comprised of different jihadists with diverse and often extreme religious agendas, various tribal groups, disaffected locals, foreign opportunists, and genuine Syrian freedom fighters. In November 2012 parts of the FSA morphed into the National Coalition for Syrian Revolutionary and Opposition Force. The result is a confusing mix of poorly organized, ad hoc arrangements of convenience between militias with a range of agendas claiming to be directed against the Assad regime but also against anyone not belonging to a particular rebel faction. Caught up in the middle of all these warring factions and the Assad regime are the civilians of Syria, and reports of the use of chemical weapons in Syria raised international concerns to a new, much higher level (Elleman *et al.*, 2012; Nikitin *et al.*, 2013, pp. 3–4).

Syria's chemical weapons development

Syria's chemical weapon's program has long been shrouded in secrecy with analysts estimating that Syria acquired delivery systems and chemical weapons from

Egypt, Iran and possibly Russia before the 1973 Yom Kippur or Ramadan War between Israel and Egypt/Syria (Nikitin *et al.*, 2013). In 1989, the US Central Intelligence Agency (CIA) stated that, "Western European firms were instrumental in supplying the required chemicals and equipment. Without the provision of these key elements, Damascus would not have been able to produce chemical weapons" (US House, 2003, p. 7). The CIS identified several German firms involved in selling dual-use items. Dual-use items are chemicals that can be used for both civil and military purposes. Germany exported 111 tonnes of hydrogen fluoride, ammonium hydrogen fluoride, sodium fluoride, potassium cyanide and sodium cyanide between 2002 and 2006. The German government confirmed reports that successive German governments had approved deliveries of chemicals between 2002 and 2006 to Syria that can be used to make sarin gas (DW News, 2013). These chemicals are not listed in CWC schedules but they are subject to export control because they are classified as dual-use and chemical weapons precursors (Australia Group, 2009).

The CWC identifies three lists of schedules according to their sensitivity. The most sensitive of these schedules are chemicals in Schedule 1, which the CWC stipulates should not be transferred to any other country except under very tightly controlled conditions. The transfer of both Schedule 1 and Schedule 2 chemicals to non-state parties is prohibited. Jan van Aken, foreign affairs spokesman for Germany's Left Party and a former UN Weapons Inspector condemned the sale of the chemicals to Syria—a country which, "the whole world knew had a huge chemical weapons program" (Hudson, 2013). The CWC schedules listing and associated export control system is an important part of an overall attempt to manage the transfer of potentially dangerous chemicals that may be used in the manufacture of chemical weapons. The CWC requires parties to promise not to assist, encourage, or induce anyone to engage in activities prohibited by the convention. It requires all states parties to adopt national measures to implement the CWC but it does not provide details on how states are to do this.

There are inherent difficulties in managing the international transfer of chemicals. Ian Anthony, Director of the SIPRI Arms Control and Nonproliferation Programme argues that after dual-use goods have left the EU it is very difficult, if not impossible, to supervise their use, despite laws that require prior authorization from responsible national authorities before controlled items are exported (Anthony, 2014). He claims that the majority of dual-use exports pose either a very small or no proliferation risk and that an export that is subject to licensing will rarely be blocked. However, where dual-use chemicals are combined with a capability to be used as a chemical weapons precursor then the level of concern should rise exponentially particularly with the lack of an effective monitoring system.

Germany's exports of 111 tons of dual-use chemicals that may be used as chemical weapons precursors cannot be considered to be a very small or an absence of a proliferation risk. Syria was not party to the CWC until 2013. Five chemicals not on the common control list of chemical weapon precursors—

ethylene oxide, hydrogen sulfide, sulfur trioxide, white and yellow phosphorus, and thiophosphoryl—were determined by the 41 states of the Australia Group Forum to be of particular concern regarding Syria and that all dual-use chemical transfers to Syria required "special vigilance."

The Center for Strategic and International Studies (CSIS) reported in 2008 that Syria's chemical warfare program began in the mid-1970s under President Hafez al-Assad with facilities that successfully produced VX nerve gas, sarin nerve agents and mustard blister agents. Hundreds of tons of hydrochloric acid and ethylene glycol imported from Iran were precursors for the production of chemicals that could be mounted on Scud warheads or onto conventional aerial bombing delivery systems (Cordesman and Burke, 2008, p. 2). Iran's involvement with Syria's chemical weapons program included plans to supply Syria with chemical manufacturing equipment and chemical detection sensors for airborne agents. Iran further intended to provide technical assistance to Syria's Scientific Studies and Research Centers (CERS) to produce and pilot a number of CW facilities throughout Syria. CERS is the Syrian government agency that together with the Ministry of Defence reports directly to the President. CERS is responsible for the facilities that produced chemical agents in Dumayr, Khan Abu Shamat, and Furqlus, located north of Damascus in Hamah, and in Al-Safirah, southeast of Aleppo.

The capability to independently manufacture and the means to deliver chemical weapons have long been goals by Syria. There is much conjecture as to why Syria wants such a capability in the first place. Russian President Vladimir Putin claimed that Damascus' chemical weapons arsenal was a response to a significant imbalance of power with Israel (Dermy, 2013; RT News, 2013). Syria's humiliating defeat against Israel during the Yom Kippur War and the subsequent occupation of the Golan Heights, Israel's rapid development of its own nuclear arsenal, a series of setbacks against Israel in Lebanon in the 1980s, and Israel's destruction of Syria's nuclear program in 2007, all contributed to shaping Syria's mindset and strategic outlook.

OPCW in Syria

The United Nation's Mission to Investigate Allegations of the Use of Chemical Weapons in the Syrian Arab Republic Report, submitted to the United Nations (UN) Secretary-General Ban Ki-moon in September 15, 2013, concluded that in the Ghouta Area of Damascus on August 21, 2013, "chemical weapons have been used in the ongoing conflict between the parties in the Syrian Arab Republic, also against civilians, including children, on a relatively large scale" (UN Mission, 2013). The subsequent final report released in December 12, 2013 presented a timeline of events in Syria, the actions of the UN, and evidence that led to the conclusion that chemical weapons were used. The Secretary-General stated that the use of these weapons was a war crime and a grave violation of the 1925 Protocol for the Prohibition of the Use in War of Asphyxiating, Poisonous or Other Gases, and of Bacteriological Methods of Warfare (UN Mission, 2013).

The UN investigation was prompted by 16 allegations of separate incidents involving the use of chemical weapons reported to the Secretary-General by France, Qatar, the Syrian Arab Republic, Britain, Northern Ireland and the US. The UN Mission agreed to investigate seven of the 16 allegations based on the credibility and sufficiency of information received—Khan Al Asal (March 19, 2013), Sheik Maqsood (April 13, 2013), Saraqueb (April 29, 2013), Ghouta (August 21, 2013), Bahhariyeh (August 22, 2013), Jobar (August 24, 2013) and Ashrafiah Sahnaya (August 25, 2013). The UN Mission's final report concluded that chemical weapons had been used in the ongoing conflict between the parties in the Syrian Arab Republic, primarily in the Ghouta area of Damascus, but also in Jobar, Saraquebon, Ashrafiah Sahnaya and Khan Al Asal (UN Mission, 2013).

Syria's Foreign Minister Walid al-Moualem agreed on September 10, 2013 to accept a Russian proposal supported by China and Iran for Syria to place its estimated 1,000 tons of chemical weapons stockpile under international control for dismantling, "We are ready to inform about the location of chemical weapons, halt the production of chemical weapons and also show these objects to representatives of Russia, other states and the United Nations." (Jamieson *et al.*, 2013). The change of heart by Syria to allow UN and OPCW inspectors to oversee the destruction of its chemical weapons was significant because up until the September 2013 declaration by Syria's Foreign Minister, Syria had refused to admit that it even had any chemical weapons. Syria and the international community had reached this point only after 12 months of intense, international diplomatic pressure on Russia, China and Iran and talk by the US of a red line regarding a direct and forcible response to the use of chemical weapons. Should Syria not comply with the UN and OPCW demands then a US led strike against Syria was increasingly likely (Daalder, 2013).

Syria provided a disclosure statement to the OPCW-UN on September 21, 2013 regarding the location and status of its chemical weapons stockpiles. OPCW-UN Inspections of Syria's chemical weapons stockpiles began on October 1, 2013 (OPCW, 2013a). In October 24, 2013, Syria submitted to the OPCW a formal declaration covering its chemical weapons program with a further submission on November 21, 2013 increasing the total amount of previously declared munitions to 1,260 items. Syria also provided information regarding its chemical weapons program between 1982 and 2010 (OPCWb, 2013). After two years of war and over 100,000 deaths, the news of these events was met with significant skepticism by Syrian rebels and activists who considered the handing over of these weapons to be a ploy to detract attention away from the increasing death and destruction in Syria. The OPCW-UN stated on December 28, 2013 that it was now ready to assist with the removal of chemicals from the Syrian Arab Republic for disposal outside its territory (OPCW, 2013c).

According to OPCW-UN directives, Syria was to prepare, package, then transport the chemicals from its 12 chemical weapons storage facilities to the shipping port of Latakia. The US, Britain, Northern Ireland, China, Denmark, Norway, Russia and Finland were all involved in the complex management of transportation, security, emergency response capabilities, and provision of chemical weapons destruction facilities. Thirty different countries have contributed €47.5 million to the Syria Trust Fund for the Destruction of Chemical Weapons but the whole destruction costs are likely to be at least €190 million (Notman, 2014). The OPCW's plan for all the chemical weapons to be destroyed by June 20, 2014 was realized and on June 23, 2014 the OPCW-UN announced that the removal or destruction of Syria's chemical weapons material was now complete (UN News Centre, 2014).

Despite widespread suspicion and many allegations in the international media, the Assad regime has not been clearly identified as the perpetrator of the chemical attack on August 21, 2013. Photos, videos and eyewitness accounts appeared on the internet with a variety of experts claiming that the nerve agent sarin was used. 1,429 people, including children, were killed as a result of the chemical attack according to the White House media press release in August 30, 2013. The final report of the UN inquiry into chemical weapons use in Syria stated that the nerve agent sarin was likely used in four locations in addition to the confirmed attack near Damascus in August. The US government proclaimed that the Syrian Government carried out the chemical weapons attack in the Damascus suburbs:

> We assess with high confidence that the Syrian government carried out the chemical weapons attack against opposition elements in the Damascus suburbs on August 21. We assess that the scenario in which the opposition executed the attack on August 21 is highly unlikely.
>
> (White House, 2013a)

A lengthy investigation and a detailed technical report in January 14, 2014 presented by Richard Lloyd, a former UN Weapons Inspector and Theodore Postol, Professor of Science, Technology and National Security Policy at the Massachusetts Institute of Technology (MIT) strongly challenged the US analysis and subsequent findings regarding the Damascus attack. In particular, they disputed the firm assertion by the White House that the chemical munitions rockets were fired from the heart of the Syrian government controlled area (White House, 2013a).

The central issue of contention is the maximum possible range of the chemical launch and delivery vehicles. Two different types of munitions were linked to the sarin attack. A Soviet made M14 140 mm artillery rocket fitted with a sarin warhead used with a BM-14 launching system and a modified 330 mm surface-to-surface artillery rocket. The modified 330 mm rockets are compatible with the Iranian made 333 mm Falaq-2 launcher possessed by the Syrian government. The White House maps published on August 30, 2013 outlined the Syrian Government controlled area and the ring of maximum ranges from where chemical munitions could have been launched (White House, 2013b).

Figure 5.1 indicates the Syrian Government and opposition forces areas and locates the reported regions affected by August 21, 2013 chemical weapons attack. If the weapons were launched from the centre of the Syrian government

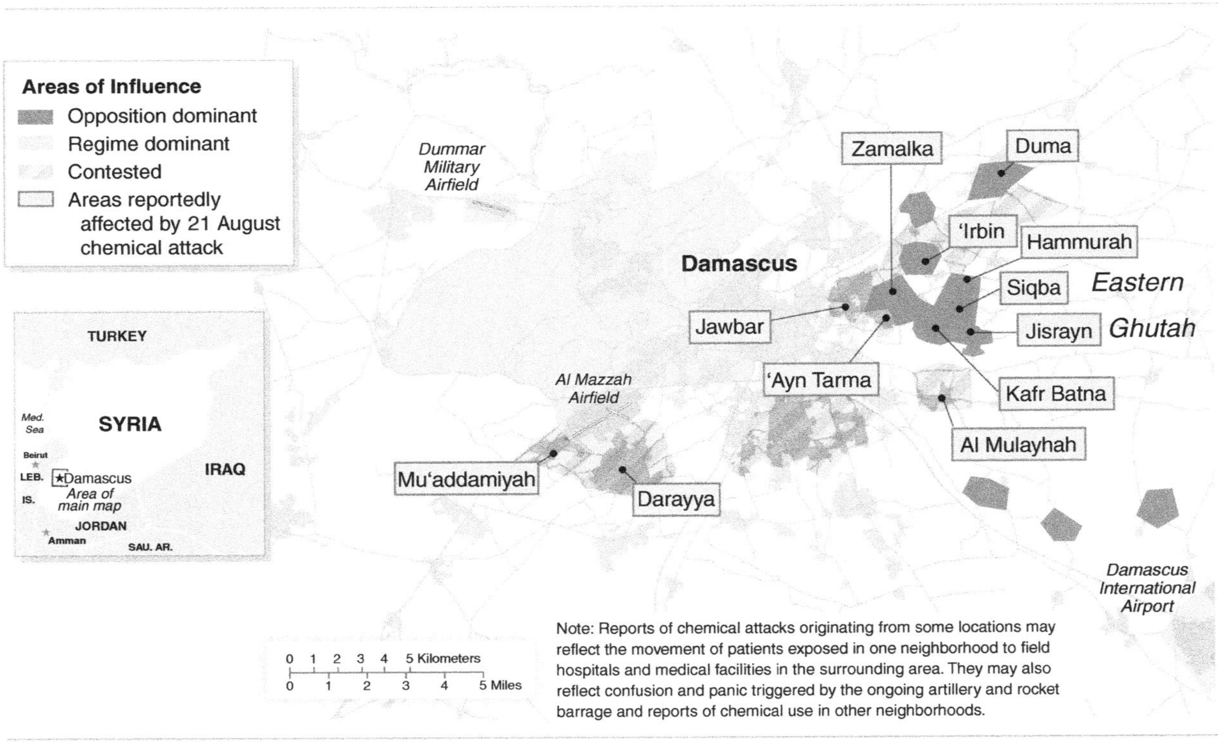

Figure 5.1 Syria: Damascus areas of influence and areas reportedly affected by August 21 chemical attack (source: White House Press Release August 30, 2013: *Government Assessment of the Syrian Government's Use of Chemical Weapons on August 21, 2013*).

controlled area as stated by the US government then the rockets would have to travel up to ten kilometers (6.2 miles) to reach their destination in the opposition dominated areas in Damascus. Even if the rockets were launched from the edge of the Syrian controlled areas they would still need to travel a distance of six kilometers (3.7 miles) to impact on the reported targets, which included Kafr Batna, Jawbar, Ayn Tarma, Darayya and Mu'addamiya. Lloyd and Postol claimed that the Syrian improvised chemical munitions that were used in the August 21 nerve agent attack could not have had the range to reach their targets. They concluded that:

> Due to volume and fuel density constraints, our assumption of rocket propellant carried by the munition is at the top end of what is possible … this means that our estimated maximum range of 2 km for the improvised munition is close to its upper possible range! In turn, it means that the US government's interpretation of the technical intelligence it gathered prior to and after the August 21 attack cannot possibly be correct.
>
> (Lloyd and Postol, 2014)

There are other areas of contention. Seymour Hersh argues that the White House did not acknowledge that the Syrian army is not the only party capable of producing the chemical sarin. The al-Nusra Front, an al-Qaida associated jihadi organization, had mastered the procedure of creating the chemical and was capable of manufacturing sarin in significant quantities. He cited his discussions with Theodore Postol stating that the improvised munition container and launch system was very likely manufactured locally and that it was, "something you could produce in a modestly capable machine shop" (Hersh, 2013).

Chemical weapons in Syria and international law

Some have argued that the use of chemical weapons in Syria is a serious violation of international law based on a range of treaties from the 1925 Geneva Gas Protocol prohibiting the use of chemical and biological weapons in war through to the 1933 Chemical Weapons Convention, and the Rome Statute of the International Criminal Court (ICC). However, most treaty law applies to the use of such weapons in international conflicts not in non-international armed conflict. Under the Rome Statute there is no individual criminal liability for the use of chemical or biological weapons. The 1925 Geneva Gas Protocol legally applies to Syria should it use these weapons against its neighbors or other states but it does not apply if Syria was to use chemical weapons in a civil war nor does it apply to the stockpiling or manufacture of chemical weapons. Syria is also a party to the 1949 Geneva Conventions and Protocols. Common Article 3 binds together the four Geneva Conventions and it applies to both international and non-international conflicts but chemical weapons and their use are excluded (Asser Institute: Centre for International Law, 2014; Sandesh, 2012, p. 394). The lack of a historical, firm legal framework dealing with the use of chemical weapons prompted the development of the CWC, which became part of international treaty law entering into force in 1997.

It could be argued that international law treats the prohibition on the use of chemical weapons in war against civilians or soldiers as a "*jus cogens norm*" (International Law Commission (ILC, 1980, para. 17). Crimes against humanity, war crimes, and genocide are examples of *jus cogens* norms. *Jus cogens* is a particular category of international law that permits no derogation under any circumstances. However, classifying a violation of the CWC in this way is problematic because chemical weapons have been repeatedly used in the past with impunity. For example, by Saddam Hussein against Iran in the 1980–88 war and against Iraqi Kurds in 1988.

There are two elements required to be present for a crime to be *jus cogens*, (1) it must threaten the peace and security of humankind; and (2) it must shock the conscience of humanity (Bassiouni, 1999, p. 42). While the chemical attacks in Syria have indeed shocked the conscience of humanity there is little if any indication that these limited, isolated attacks in any way threaten the peace and security of humankind. Under a *jus cogens* norm there is the clear duty to prosecute or extradite (*aut dedere aut judicare*), any statutes of limitations become inapplicable, the theory of universal jurisdiction applies, and states have the specific obligation (*erga omnes*) not to grant impunity to the violators (Bassiouni, 1999, p. 39). A complication regarding the use of chemical weapons in Syria is that, until the perpetrators are identified, these legal options cannot apply.

The CWC prohibits the development, production, stockpiling or use of these weapons however as Syria was not a Party to the CWC in 2012 it was not legally committed to the convention's prohibitions. Under this regime, the UN had no legal mandate to conduct inspections in Syria to verify the possible existence of chemical weapons or related activities. Syria was a party to the 1925 and the 1968 Geneva Protocols that ban the use of chemical and bacteriological methods of warfare (OPCW, 2013a). Syria formally renounced both first and retaliatory use of chemical or biological weapons against a State as a result of being party to the Protocol. The chemical attack also does not fit neatly under the definition of a crime against humanity. Under Article 7 of the Statute of the International Criminal Court (SICC) certain enumerated acts, including murder and extermination, constitute crimes against humanity when "committed as part of a widespread or systematic attack directed against any civilian population, with knowledge of the attack" (Art. 7 SICC, 2002).

The isolated and sporadic chemical attacks in Syria could not be classified as widespread or systemic and no individual or group has been clearly defined as the instigators of the attacks. Ms. Del Ponte, a member on the Independent International Commission of Inquiry on Syria, said that, "testimony from victims and doctors had given rise to strong, concrete suspicions but not yet incontrovertible proof" (BBC Middle East News, 2013). The lack of evidence identifying who carried out the attack is problematic even if the use of such weapons could be classified as a war crime under the SICC because, (a) The crime must have been committed in the territory of an ICC member-state—Syria has not ratified the

SICC, and (b) The State in question must agree to the jurisdiction of the ICC (Art. 7 SICC, 2002).

It is highly unlikely that Syria would agree to the jurisdiction of the ICC given the extent of potential war crimes for which Assad's regime may be accused. Should the concept of universal criminal jurisdiction apply then Syria's agreement is not required but the practical application of this approach is fraught with challenges. Up to ten countries have endeavored to prosecute crimes under laws on universal jurisdiction, however such attempts have been largely ignored by alleged perpetrators particularly those who are or have been heads of state.

Kenneth Anderson provides an alternative approach to the *formalist approach* in the application of international law and in particular regarding the use of chemical weapons in Syria (Anderson, 2013). He argues that the use of chemical weapons in an internal armed conflict against civilians might incur few or no real world consequences. This is due in large part because of legal arguments that those who might respond to preserve an important humanitarian norm could not lawfully do so under formal law mechanisms. He posits what some term the *pragmatic approach* to international law, which asserts that law among nations is of necessity enmeshed with policy, politics, diplomacy and real world consequences of actions. This approach attempts to address the dilemma of what states should do when there is a great divide between what formal international law requires and what morality dictates.

Had the UN and the international community not been able to come to a consensus regarding the destruction of Syria's chemical weapons then a pragmatic approach based on the crossing of the red line would shift focus away from questions of legality of forcible intervention towards questions of legitimacy of intervention. That is, any international response may be "illegal but legitimate" (Roberts, 2008). The result is that politics, policy and diplomacy are not separate to law (the formalist approach); rather they are an important and integral part of law (the pragmatic approach). The problem with legal pragmatism is that it would be very easy to overly weight certain actions and counter actions towards policy or other means of political necessity with some selective elements of formal international law thrown in to satisfy the pragmatic law and necessity approach.

The pragmatic approach to international law trumpets necessity, and so called real-world requirements, responses and outcomes as a way of looking at international law but the danger here is that political or ideological pragmatism may simply override all other formal, legal requirements. Steven Blockmans supports the pragmatic approach where, in the case of Syria, "formal interpretations of international law should give way to a more pragmatic approach" (Blockmans, 2013). He argues this approach should be applied when thinking about some sort of direct intervention. This is presumably because a red line has been crossed and because those who might respond to preserve a pre-emptory humanitarian norm could not lawfully do so under the formal, but partially outdated, law of the UN Charter. One could only surmise that many states would readily embrace the need for a certain level of rough order based on national security and self-defense in the application of formalized international law.

Despite the frustration by many that the perpetrators of the chemical attacks in Syria have not been clearly identified, to take the pragmatic path is the slippery slope to the sidelining even making irrelevant international law. This would lead to a very selective application and interpretation of what law actually means leading to convenience rather than adherence to law that has undergone a lengthy and tortuous path to relevance. There are many challenges to the formalized approach to the application and to the relevance of international law, the SICC, the UN Charter, and the many other legal instruments and institutions but the rubbery approach is not the way to deal with deficiencies in international law. Concerted efforts must be made to rectify them but not to pick and choose or even disregard altogether established legal custom and procedures.

Conclusion

There is little indication that the major powers or the UN collectively are progressing in the formulation of a coherent, practical response of what to do overall about the ever-increasing violence in Syria. One could argue that the R2P thesis is stymied by the "no good options" dilemma because the conflict in Syria is a battle between two malevolent forces. The Assad regime and its supporters continue to deliberately engage in extreme acts of brutality against the people of Syria and the various rebel factions are equally complicit in a lack of restraint against any opposition to their various causes and agendas. However, this approach misses the point of what R2P aims to achieve. That is, there is a clear and immediate obligation for the international community to protect civilians and other non-combatants in Syria regardless of no good options, and especially where there are no good domestic options. This requires a more mature understanding and acceptance of what the R2P norm is supposed to mean. The international community is a long way from such an understanding or acceptance.

The UN investigation into allegations that chemical weapons had been used in Syria in 2013 raised a number of important questions for the international community. Most importantly, how should the international community respond and was R2P a cornerstone or even relevant in the response? The OPCW-UN reaction to events in Syria was a critical test for the UN and the international community generally. The test was whether the prevention and protection pillars of R2P were timely and effective in removing Syria's capacity for engaging in chemical warfare. By this measure, the international response was effective with many countries acting in unison to dismantle and then remove Syria's chemical weapons capability but the effectiveness is tempered with at least two qualifications. One relates to the strictly mandated limits of the investigation that did not permit any investigation for culpability into who carried out the attacks. The other relates to the overall increasing levels of violence, death, and destruction in Syria, which continues unabated despite the critical work of the OPCW-EN mission to reduce the threat of the use of chemical weapons.

The OPCW's primary roles are demilitarization and non-proliferation of chemical weapons and it is not structured to pursue responsibility. However, without an investigation into who is to blame this leaves any possible further response to the use of chemical weapons in limbo. This was the cost of the consensus between all parties so that the weapons inspectors were permitted to do their work in the first place but the central issue of blame must not be simply forgotten and it must be addressed in the future. The lack of effective international engagement to reduce the overall death and destruction in Syria challenges many of the core ideals inherent in the notion of R2P.

References

Anderson, K. (2013). Legality of intervention in Syria in response to chemical weapon attacks. *ASIL Insights*, 17(21), 5–6. Retrieved from: www.asil.org/insights/volume/17/issue/21/legality-intervention-syria-response-chemical-weapon-attacks (accessed July 16, 2014).

Anthony, I. (2014). Exports of dual-use chemicals to Syria: An assessment of European Union export controls. *EU Non-Proliferation Consortium: Non-Proliferation Papers*, 35,1–3. Retrieved from: www.sipri.org/research/disarmament/eu-consortium/publications/non-proliferation-paper-35 (accessed July 16, 2014).

Asser Institute: Centre for International Law (2014, July). *International humanitarian law applicable in non-international armed conflicts*. Asser Institute. Retrieved from www.asser.nl/default.aspx?site_id=9&level1=13336&level2=13374&level3=13463. (accessed July 16, 2014).

Bassiouni, M. C. (1999). *The sources and theory of international criminal law: A theoretical framework*. New York: Transatlantic Publishers Inc.

BBC Middle East News (2013, May 6). *UN commission downplays claim Syria rebels used sarin*. Retrieved from: www.bbc.co.uk/news/world-middle-east-22428496 (accessed December 30, 2014).

BBC News (2011, April 22). Syria unrest: 'Bloodiest day' as troops fire on rallies. Retrieved from: www.bbc.co.uk/news/world-middle-east-13167433 (accessed July 4, 2014).

Blockmans, S. (2013, September 4). *CEPS Commentary: Syria and the red lines of international law, Centre for European Policy Studies*. Retrieved from: www.ceps.be/book/syria-and-red-lines-international-law (accessed July 12, 2014).

Brühl, J. (2013, September 25). *Where did Syria's chemical weapons come from? Propublica*. Retrieved from: www.propublica.org/article/where-did-syrias-chemical-weapons-come-from (accessed July 11, 2014).

Carnegie Commission. (1997). *Preventing deadly conflict: final report with executive summary*. Washington, DC: The Commission. pp. xviii–xxviii. Retrieved from: www.janeliunas.lt/files/Preventing%20Deadly%20Conflict.doc (accessed July 11, 2014).

CBC News. (2014, April 3). *Syria's civil war: key facts, important players. What's at stake in an increasingly bloody and dangerous conflict*. Retrieved from www.cbc.ca/news2/interactives/syria-dashboard/ (accessed April 3, 2014).

Cinq-Mars, E., D'Souza, R., Karr, C., Khudayberdieva, N. and Naomi, K. (2014, July 15). Current crisis: Mass atrocity crimes are occurring and urgent action needed. *R2P Monitor*, (16), 2–3. Retrieved from: www.globalr2p.org/media/files/r2p_monitor_july2014_final.pdf (accessed July 15, 2014).

Cordesman, A. H. and Burke, A. A. (2008, June 2). Syrian weapons of mass destruction: An overview. *Center for Strategic & International Studies*, 2. Retrieved from: http://csis.org/files/media/csis/pubs/080602_syrianwmd.pdf (accessed June 24, 2014).

Daalder, I. (2013, September 10). Russia's Syria chemical weapons proposal is welcome, in principle. *Financial Times*. Retrieved from: www.ft.com/cms/s/0/74e 99164-1a07-11e3-93e8-00144feab7de.html#axzz2p09WPPP5 (accessed August 17, 2014).

Dermy, E. (2013, September, 19). Putin says Syria chemical arms moves 'inspire confidence'. *DefenseNews, Gannett Government Media*. Retrieved from: www.defensenews.com/article/20130919/DEFREG04/309190011/Putin-Says-Syria-Chemical-Arms-Moves-Inspire-Confidence- (accessed August 17, 2014).

DW News (2013, September 18). Germany confirms past chemical deliveries to Syria. *Deutsche Welle*. Retrieved from: www.dw.de/germany-confirms-past-chemical-deliveries-to-syria/a-17098815.

Elleman, M., Esfandiary, D. and Hokayem, E. (2012, July). Syria's proliferation challenge and the European Union's response. *EU Non-Proliferation Consortium: Non-Proliferation Papers, July 2012*. Retrieved from: www.sipri.org/research/disarmament/eu-consortium/publications/nonproliferation-paper-20 (accessed July 12, 2014).

Hersh, S. (2013). Whose sarin? *London Review of Books*, 35(24), 9–12.

Hudson, A. (2013, September 18). Germany sold Syria chemicals with military potential: government. *Reuters*. Retrieved from: www.reuters.com/article/2013/09/18/us-syria-crisis-germany-sarin-idUSBRE98H0QB20130918 (accessed June 25, 2014).

ICRtoP (2014). *The crisis in Syria. International coalition for the responsibility to protect*. Retrieved from: www.responsibilitytoprotect.org/index.php/crises/crisis-in-syria (accessed December 12, 2014).

International Commission on Intervention and State Sovereignty (2001). The Responsibility to Protect. *International Development Research Centre*, 71. Retrieved from: www.iciss.ca/pdf/Commission-Report.pdf (accessed December 1, 2014).

International Law Commission (1980). Vienna convention on the law of treaties. United Nations. Retrieved from: www.worldtradelaw.net/misc/viennaconvention.pdf (accessed December 12, 2014).

Jamieson, A., Kovalyova, A. and Simmons, K. (2013, September 10). Syria's foreign minister: We'll declare chemical weapons, sign arms ban. *NBC News*. Retrieved from: http://worldnews.nbcnews.com/_news/2013/09/10/20416189-syrias-foreign-minister-well-declare-chemical-weapons-sign-arms-ban?lite (accessed December 30, 2014).

Janzekovic, J. and Silander, D. (2013). *Responsibility to protect and prevent: Principles, promises and practicalities*. London: Anthem Press.

Kaag, S. (2014, June 23). "Modest but meaningful contribution" to peace in Syria after removal of chemical weapons. *News & Media: United Nations Radio*. Retrieved from: www.unmultimedia.org/radio/english/2014/06/modest-but-meaningful-contribution-to-peace-in-syria-after-removal-of-chemical-weapons/#.U8XYnHnlqpo (accessed July 20, 2014).

Kalamanov, G. (2013, April 10). *Statement by the Deputy Minister of Industry and Commerce of the Russian Federation Mr. Georgiy Kalamanov at the Third Session of the Conference to Review the Operation of the Chemical Weapons Convention, Russian Embassy*. Retrieved from: www.rusembassy.nl/index.php/en/mission-opcw/246-kalamanov-april-2013 (accessed July 16, 2014).

Lloyd, R. and Postol, T. (2014, January 14). Possible implications of faulty US technical intelligence in the Damascus nerve agent attack of August 21, 2013, Massachusetts Institute of Technology (MIT). *Science, Technology, and Global Security Working Group*. Retrieved from: www.documentcloud.org/documents/1006045-possible-implications-of-bad-intelligence.html#storylink=relast. (accessed April 23, 2014).

Nikitin, M., Kerr, P. and Feickert, A. (2013, September 30) Syria's chemical weapons: Issues for Congress. Congressional Research Service. *Report for Congress*. Retrieved from: http://fas.org/sgp/crs/nuke/R42848.pdf (accessed June 24, 2014).

Notman, N. (2014, May 21). Eliminating Syria's chemical weapons. *Chemistryworld*. Retrieved from: www.rsc.org/chemistryworld/2014/05/syrian-chemical-weapons-feature (accessed July 23, 2014).

OPCW (2012, July 18). Organisation for the Prohibition of Chemical Weapons. *News, Syria and the OPCW*. Retrieved from: www.opcw.org/news/article/syria-and-the-opcw/ (accessed March 15, 2014).

OPCW (2013a, March 21). Organisation for the Prohibition of Chemical Weapons. *News, Syria and the OPCW*. Retrieved from: www.opcw.org/news/article/statement-on-syria-investigation/ (accessed March 15, 2014).

OPCW (2013b, December 28). *Organisation for the Prohibition of Chemical Weapons. Statement by the Director-General*. Retrieved from: www.opcw.org/news/article/statement-by-the-director-general-6/ (accessed March 15, 2014).

OPCW (2014, August 17). *Signatory states which have not yet ratified the Chemical Weapons Convention*. Retrieved from: www.opcw.org/news/article/syria-and-the-opcw/ (accessed March 15, 2014).

OPCW Executive Council (2013, September 27). *Decision: Destruction of Syrian chemical weapons*. [EC-M-33/DEC.1]. Retrieved from: www.opcw.org/fileadmin/OPCW/EC/M-33/ecm33dec01_e_.pdf (accessed August 17, 2014).

OPCW Executive Council (2013b, November 25). *Progress in the Elimination of the Syrian Chemical Weapons Programme*. [EC-M-35/DG.1]. Retrieved from: www.opcw.org/index.php?eID=dam_frontend_push&docID=16886 (accessed March 3, 2014).

Pommier, B. (2011). The use of force to protect civilians and humanitarian action: the case of Libya and beyond. *International Review of the Red Cross*, 93(884), 1063–1083.

Roberts, A. (2008). Legality vs. Legitimacy: Can Uses of Force be Illegal but Justified? In P. Alston and E. MacDonald (eds). *Human rights, intervention and the use of force* (pp. 179–181). Oxford, New York: Oxford University Press.

RT News (2013, September 20). *UN nuclear meeting rejects Arab push for Israel to join weapons pact*. Retrieved from http://rt.com/news/israel-nuclear-arabs-iaea-129/ (accessed August 17, 2014).

Sandesh, S. (2012). *The law of non-international armed conflict*. Oxford, UK: Oxford University Press.

Spence, S. (2012, October 5). *Syria revisited – International law and the use of biological weapons. The Verification Research, Training and Information Centre (VERTIC), Strategic Vision and Technical Delivery of the National Implementation Measures Programme*. Retrieved from: www.vertic.org/pages/posts/syria-revisited--international-law-and-the-use-of-biological-weapons-381.php (accessed August 17, 2014).

Stirling, J. (2012, March 1). Daraa: The spark that lit the Syrian flame. *CNN International*. Retrieved from: http://edition.cnn.com/2012/03/01/world/meast/syria-crisis-beginnings/ (accessed May 3, 2014).

Surk, B. (2014, June 19). Death toll in Syria's war tops 160,000: Activists. *The World Post: Huffington Post and Berggruen Institute on Governance*. Retrieved from: www.huffingtonpost.com/2014/05/19/syria-war-death-toll_n_5353021.html (accessed May 3, 2014).

UN General Assembly (2005, October, 24). *2005 World Summit Outcome*. (U.N. Doc A/RES/60/1). Retrieved from: www.un.org/en/preventgenocide/adviser/pdf/World%20Summit%20Outcome%20Document.pdf#page=30 (accessed June 23, 2014).

UN General Assembly (2009a, January 12). *Follow-up to the outcome of the Millennium Summit – Implementing the responsibility to protect, Report of the Secretary-General.* (UN Doc A/63/677). Retrieved from: www.un.org/en/ga/search/view_doc.asp?symbol =A/63/677 (accessed June 23, 2014).

UN General Assembly (2009b, September 14). *The responsibility to protect.* (U.N. Doc A/RES/63/308). Retrieved from: www.un.org/en/ga/search/view_doc.asp?symbol=A/ RES/63/308&Lang=E (accessed June 24, 2014).

UN General Assembly (2013, September 16). *Report of the United Nations mission to investigate allegations of the use of chemical weapons in the Syrian Arab Republic on the alleged use of chemical weapons in the Ghouta area of Damascus on 21 August 2013.* (U.N. Doc A/67/997-S/2013/553). Retrieved from: www.securitycouncilreport. org/atf/cf/%7B65BFCF9B-6D27-4E9C-8CD3-CF6E4FF96FF9%7D/s_2013_553.pdf (accessed July 4, 2014).

UN Mission (2013). *United Nations mission to investigate allegations of the use of chemical weapons in the Syrian Arab Republic.* Retrieved from: https://unoda-web.s3.amazonaws.com/wp-content/uploads/2013/12/report.pdf. (accessed July 4, 2014).

UN News Centre (2013, September 16). *Clear and convincing evidence of chemical weapons use in Syria, UN team reports.* Retrieved from: www.un.org/apps/news/story. asp?NewsID=45856#.U79KKXnlqos (accessed July 9, 2014).

UN News Centre (2014, June 23). *Removal of Syria's chemical weapons material complete, announces OPCW-UN mission.* Retrieved from: www.un.org/apps/news/story. asp?NewsID=48103#.U6iuRXnlqos (accessed July 4, 2014).

United States House (2003, September 16). *Syria: Implications for U.S. security and regional stability hearing* (Serial No. 108–66 7). United States House of Representative Subcommittee On The Middle East and Central Asia of the Committee on International Relations. Retrieved from: http://commdocs.house.gov/committees/intlrel/ hfa89406.000/hfa89406_0f.htm (accessed July 4, 2014).

White House (2013a, August 30). *Government assessment of the Syrian government's use of chemical weapons on August 21, 2013,* Office of the Press Secretary. Retrieved from: www.whitehouse.gov/the-press-office/2013/08/30/government-assessment-syrian-government-s-use-chemical-weapons-august-21 (accessed June 23, 2014).

White House (2013b, August 30). *Syria: Damascus Areas of Influence and Areas Reportedly Affected by 21 August Chemical Attack.* Retrieved from: www.whitehouse.gov/ the-press-office/2013/08/30/government-assessment-syrian-government-s-use-chemical-weapons-august-21 (accessed August 17, 2014).

6 Organization of Islamic Cooperation (OIC)

Melinda Negrón-Gonzales

The Organization of Islamic Cooperation (OIC) (formerly Organization of the Islamic Conference) is the world's second largest intergovernmental organization, after the United Nations (UN), with 57 state members spread over four continents. Established in 1969, its 25 founding states aimed to engender solidarity among Muslims in disparate locations and promote the interests of the global Muslim community, or *ummah*. Its members' fluctuating interests and an ever-changing international environment have shaped its institutional form and objectives. Created by weak states led by autocrats with a tenuous hold on power, the OIC was deliberately loosely structured to avoid encroachments of national sovereignty, and primarily functioned as a platform for dialogue. However, the OIC has undergone a significant transformation in the past decade. Beginning in 2005, a reformist Secretary-General set the foundation for a more robust organization with an expanded mandate that includes the promotion of good governance and human rights and a more active role in conflict resolution (OIC, 2005; see also Ihsanoglu, 2010).

Insofar as the expanded mandate and institution-building generate an organization better equipped to promote, monitor and enforce principles related to the Responsibility to Protect (R2P), the OIC can serve as a major global player in the advancement of R2P. According to the Global Centre for the Responsibility to Protect:

> [R]egional organizations should enhance the capacity of their member states to prevent and address mass atrocities ... have a special position from which to design and implement regional strategies to prevent mass atrocities, including through the establishment and operationalization of effective early warning systems ... and furthermore, "[g]iven the limited capacity of many countries, regional organizations could play a robust role in leading on the foreign policy aspects of R2P implementation, especially in connection with country-specific crises".
>
> (Global Centre for the Responsibility to Protect, 2013)

The OIC is certainly well positioned to fulfill this role, due to its size and geographic scope. However, this does not mean it is well equipped to do so. In addition to its size, the OIC is important to the future of R2P because of the instability in its member countries. Almost half of the organization's 57 member-states have experienced armed conflict in the past two decades, and some of those conflicts have been marked by the type of violence that escalated or has the potential to escalate into atrocity crimes (e.g., Sudan, Libya, Iraq).

There are two obstacles that preclude the OIC from significantly advancing R2P. The first obstacle is ideational. Despite a new charter with an expanded mandate, the OIC remains firmly committed to state sovereignty and non-interference in the internal affairs of its members. The second obstacle is structural and is a product of the first. Despite recent institution-building, the OIC remains institutionally weak vis-à-vis member-states, given that it lacks instruments to monitor and enforce compliance with the R2P-type principles enshrined in its new charter. This chapter will first examine the OIC's institutional structure and objectives to determine its commitment and capacity to promote and implement R2P. This is followed by an in-depth analysis of the organization's response to the humanitarian crisis in Syria. Lastly, this chapter explores the potential and likelihood of the OIC's promotion and operationalization of R2P in the near future.

OIC institutional structure and objectives and the responsibility to protect

The first meeting of the Islamic Conference of Foreign Ministers, the highest body of the Organization of the Islamic Conference, was held in Jeddah, Saudi Arabia in 1970, after which leaders decided to create a permanent secretariat in Jeddah. The Secretariat, and the organization as a whole, served as little more than a platform for discussion. This has changed in recent years. The Secretariat is now headed by a Secretary-General who is elected by the Council of Foreign Ministers (CFM) (until 2004, the Secretary-General was appointed rather than elected).[1] The first Secretary-General to be elected was Ekmeleddin Ihsanoglu of Turkey, in 2004. This operational modification was but one in a wave of changes made in the 2000s, including a name change in 2011 from the Organization of the Islamic Conference to the Organization of Islamic Cooperation (OIC). The new name signals a transformation from a loosely configured body to a more complex and institutionally robust organization. During his tenure as Secretary-General (December 31, 2004—January 21, 2014), the reformist Ihsanoglu set the OIC on a path to promote "modernization and moderation" (Ihsanoglu, 2010) among its member-states and oversaw the restructuring of the organization. These extensive reforms greatly shape the OIC's present capacity to impact the diffusion of the R2P international norm and also assist states in meeting their R2P obligations.

In the past several years, proponents of R2P have highlighted the ways regional organizations, such as the OIC, can play a greater role in the promotion and implementation of this possible norm-in-formation. For instance, UN Secretary-General Ban Ki-Moon's report on "The Role of Regional and Sub-regional Arrangements in Implementing the Responsibility to Protect" (UN General Assembly and Security Council, 2011) underscored the critical prevention and protection roles that could be played by neighbors and regional and sub-regional organizations. Specifically, regional organizations have a direct role to play in the implementation of R2P's first pillar by encouraging states to recognize their obligations to protect citizens from atrocity crimes, and its second pillar, by providing international assistance and capacity-building, and third pillar, by ensuring timely and decisive response to episodes of violence.[2] Regional organizations should also be heavily involved in the United Nations Security Council's decision-making process concerning timely and decisive response, and the report states that "collective action under Chapter VII is to be considered 'on a case-by-case basis and in cooperation with relevant regional organizations as appropriate'." (UN Secretary-General (2011, ¶3; see also International Coalition for the Responsibility to Protect, 2011).

OIC Secretary-General Ihsanoglu's reforms clearly set the groundwork for the OIC to meet the aforementioned expectations underscored by UN Secretary-General Ban Ki-Moon. For instance, the OIC's "Ten Year Program of Action to Face the Challenges of the Twenty-First Century," adopted in the third extraordinary session of the Islamic Summit in 2005, set forth an ambitious agenda which emphasized the need to promote good governance and human rights in the Muslim world, especially with regard to the rights of children, women and the elderly. The action plan also committed the OIC to pursue activities related to conflict prevention and resolution, as well as post-conflict peace-building (OIC, 2005). Additionally, in 2008, a new OIC Charter was adopted which reiterated and further elucidated the vision laid out in the action plan. From an R2P perspective, it is promising. The new Charter, like the Ten Year Program, seeks "to promote human rights and fundamental freedoms, good governance, rule of law, democracy and accountability in Member States" (OIC, 2008).

To this end, the OIC is enhancing its capacity to provide institution-building assistance to its member-states (which meets R2P's pillar two expectations), creating, for example, an election-monitoring outfit to help ensure free and fair elections (OIC, 2014). This is integral to preventing post-election crises of the type witnessed in Kenya in 2007 when accusations of electoral fraud precipitated mass violence and prompted the successful UNSC-authorized R2P mediation by Kofi Annan (Halakhem, 2013). In the way of conflict prevention and also R2P's timely and decisive response to atrocities, the OIC is building its own mediation unit to settle disputes, and it also created a Humanitarian Emergency Response Fund to provide humanitarian assistance as soon as man-made and natural disasters arise (OIC, 2013a). Once these recent changes are fully implemented and new organs are fully operational, the OIC will be better equipped to aid in conflict prevention as well as timely and decisive responses, and thereby meet the expectations set forth in Ban Ki-Moon's report on regional organizations and R2P.

It should be noted, however, that the OIC did not undertake these changes with the specific purpose of meeting R2P expectations, nor has the organization officially endorsed R2P per se, especially its third pillar. Furthermore, many of its members, in spite of their support for R2P action in Libya and elsewhere, have expressed reservations about R2P at UN Informal Interactive Dialogues on R2P (Negrón-Gonzales, 2014). In addition, the new Charter has some elements that do not bode well for the OIC's advancement of R2P-related activities. For example, the Charter states that promotion of human rights is implemented "in accordance with [members'] constitutional and legal systems," (OIC, 2008, p. 1) many of which are authoritarian. In fact, like the Charter it replaced and the overall ethos of the OIC, the new Charter is profoundly state-centric and unequivocally upholds the sanctity of state sovereignty. For instance, it qualifies member-states' obligation to comply with international law by adding, "while strictly adhering to the principle of non-interference in matters which are essentially within the domestic jurisdiction of any State" (OIC, 2008, p. 2) Indeed, the principles of sovereignty and non-interference in the internal affairs of member-states are emphasized repeatedly in OIC resolutions and bylaws (Bicak, 2011).

It comes as no surprise, then, that R2P pillar three intervention, especially military intervention, remains highly controversial in the OIC, similar to other regional organizations in the Global South. Yet, the OIC was willing to compromise the principle of non-interference in 2011 in the face of imminent atrocities in Libya. This is arguably because Libya lacked strong allies in the OIC and military intervention appeared to have a good chance of success. The presence of a strong and influential Syrian ally (Iran) in the OIC and divergent views concerning the likelihood of success of a military intervention have caused OIC members to be more hesitant to follow the same course of action in Syria. This will be discussed further in the next section. First, it is necessary to explore in finer detail the OIC's infrastructure for promoting, monitoring and enforcing principles associated with the Responsibility to Protect. Three broad areas covered in the OIC's Ten Year Program directly relate to R2P: human rights/ good governance, humanitarian assistance and conflict resolution.

Human rights-related activities

The OIC has not historically emphasized international human rights. In 1991, it adopted the Cairo Declaration of Rights, an abbreviated version of the UN Declaration of Human Rights that has been criticized for circumscribing universal rights. For instance, one glaring omission in the Cairo Declaration is the right to freedom of association. The subtext seems to be that the Muslim world follows a different set of principles, which explains the need for a separate document. However, reformists at the OIC and in the Muslim world more generally have challenged those who advocate for a different set of principles, arguing that Islam and international standards of human rights are indeed compatible.[3] The ongoing debate concerning the compatibility of Islam and human rights is beyond the scope of this chapter. However, it should be noted that even if freedoms, such as speech and religion, are deemed to be limited under Islam, the crimes which trigger an R2P response are certainly not sanctioned by Islam.

Indeed, Islam does not permit the mass slaughter of civilians under any circumstance. Thus, Islamic precepts do not serve as a serious impediment to R2P endorsement by OIC (Muslim-majority) states.

In the past decade, the OIC has more readily embraced international standards of human rights, in part because prominent members such as Turkey and Indonesia, which are now more democratic than they were during the early decades of the OIC, have advanced a more pro-human rights agenda. Although the OIC's efforts to step up its work in good governance and human rights are of recent provenance, much groundwork has been laid. For instance, to promote good governance, the OIC created an election-monitoring outfit that participated in training conducted by the United Nations Electoral Assistance Division (OIC, 2014). Moreover, the organization established in June 2011 an Independent Permanent Human Rights Commission (IPHRC). The Commission is the OIC's principal organ addressing human rights, and it consists of 18 members with a mandate to "advance human rights" and "support the member states' efforts to consolidate civil, political, economic, social and cultural rights" (OIC, 2011; Petersen, 2012). Its first meeting was in January 2012, almost a year after both the R2P intervention to protect Libyans and the uprising in Syria. By that point, the OIC Secretariat and other OIC agencies had been actively addressing the crises in Libya and Syria, albeit in rather different ways; and as a new subsidiary organ, the IPHRC was rather ill-equipped to address such complex crises. Still, it is currently developing the institutional capacity to prevent such crises in the future.

Secretary-General Ihsanoglu outlined five principles for the IPHRC in the inaugural speech at IPHRC's first session in Jakarta, Indonesia in 2012:

> First, the commission will complement rather than replace other national and international human rights mechanisms. Second, it will follow an introspective approach, helping OIC member states improve human rights practices. Third, it will fulfill a guidance function, providing member states with services like human rights training for the police. Fourth, it will take an incremental approach, building its credibility and mandate over time. And finally, the commission will prioritize the most pressing human rights problems.
>
> (Kayaoglu, and Petersen, 2013)

These objectives dovetail with R2P's first and second pillars. Insofar as regional organizations encourage states to improve human rights practices, they are advancing R2P's first pillar. The "guidance function" mentioned above fulfills R2P's second pillar, as it involves capacity-building of state institutions (e.g., police training), especially those designed to facilitate the rule of law, the protection of human rights and the peaceful resolution of conflicts before they escalate into violence. These are lofty goals even for highly complex regional organizations, such as the European Union (EU) and the OIC does not yet have the resources to carry out these objectives among its 57 members.

There are other shortcomings that merit attention. Although the IPHRC in theory is independent, it must operate under the watchful eye of the Council of Foreign Ministers (CFM), and many of its commissioners are in fact government officials rather than independent human rights experts (Kayaoglu, 2013). However, there are signs that some stakeholders would like to see a genuinely independent commission. State and civil society representatives from more democratic member-states, such as Indonesia, have already called for greater independence and more inclusion of civil society in the IPHRC's work (OIC Human Rights, 2012). Yet, even if the IPHRC contains more independent officials, it lacks resources to monitor abuse and mechanisms of enforcement. In addition, Kayaoglu explains that:

> [R]ather than emphasizing 'human rights advocacy,' as other international systems do, the Commission is equipped to take an approach of 'human rights diplomacy.' It aims to advance rights by reasoning with governments rather than by applying moral pressure. In essence, its function will be more consultative than prescriptive.
>
> (Kayaoglu 2013, p. 4; See also Inhsanoglu's statements about this in OIC Human Rights (2011)

The IPHRC, as a new commission, must not spark the ire of members, and consequently does not enjoy the same freedom to monitor abuse by member-states. Hence, the atrocities occurring in Syria were not a top agenda item at its 2014 annual forum. The IPHRC's agenda, set by the CFM, prioritizes the rights of women and children, the right to development and the right to education, and the commission's reports tend to focus on rights violations in non-member states. For instance, the agenda items set for the IPHRC by the Council of Foreign Ministers which were discussed at the 2014 annual forum include: Islamophobia, the negative impact of unilateral economic sanctions on member-states, the situation of Rohingya Muslim minority in Myanmar, the human rights situation in Central African Republic, and the creation of a mechanism for monitoring human rights violations against Muslim minorities. The ongoing crisis in Syria was not a focal point, although the Israeli occupation of Palestine was emphasized. All of the aforementioned agenda items involve rights violations carried out by non-member states, which may explain why the crisis in Syria was not prioritized.

Despite constraints, there are signs that some stakeholders would like to see a genuinely independent IPHRC (OIC Human Rights, 2012). Moreover, even if the IPHRC does not carry out closer scrutiny of member-states, addressing discrimination and violence against Muslim minorities in non-member states is profoundly important work in the service of atrocity prevention. Indeed, UN Secretary-General Ban Ki-Moon deemed this a critical area and called on regional organizations to "stem discrimination and xenophobia" and carry out "quiet diplomacy" to ease tensions among groups within societies (UN Secretary-General, 2011). The OIC has heeded the call by creating Contact

Groups to address conflicts in various hot spots, such as Myanmar (OIC, 2013b) and Central African Republic, where violence against Muslim minorities escalated to "massive ethno-religious cleansing" according to the UN Humanitarian Council for Refugees (UNHCR, 2014). A Contact Group has not been created for Syria, however.

Despite the OIC's attentiveness to these matters, it has little influence on non-member states, such as Central African Republic or Myanmar. In fact, the OIC has little influence over the behavior of its own members, and this stymies its ability to promote human rights and good governance. Hence, despite the recently expanded mandate and the creation of new departments, there have not been major changes implemented to strengthen the organization vis-à-vis member-states. The OIC's incapacity to compel compliance with organizational principles, laws and norms appears to be the deliberate work of the states that designed the institution. In essence, OIC countries jealously guard their national sovereignty and have created an organization that lacks the ability to strip them of it (Kayaoglu, 2013; Bicak, 2011; Halliday, 2005; Hinnebusch, 2003; Telhami and Barnett, 2002; Fawcett, 2009). Consequently, OIC resolutions are non-binding, and it does not have the authority or instruments to sanction states that do not abide by the principles enshrined in its Charter. Furthermore, membership in the organization does not require much more than a majority Muslim population and does not come with meaningful privileges, so there is little incentive for members to heed organizational dictates when doing so bestows no real benefits (Bicak, 2011). In short, as Bicak contends, "without strong executive organs, the OIC, at most, comes out as a weak confederation. The obligations on its members are few, and it has no enforcement facility" (Bick, 2011, p. 608).[4]

International assistance

The OIC is actively expanding its capacity to provide international assistance to both member and non-member states as part of its Ten Year Program of Action. Specifically, international assistance advances R2P in two ways, through "operational prevention" and "structural prevention." The former includes "mediation, facilitation and dialogue in crisis situations" (and may also be considered part of third pillar action), whereas the latter involves addressing the roots of conflict and may include activities that generally fall under the rubrics of socio-economic development or good governance (UN Secretary-General, 2011). The OIC engages in both types of conflict prevention, and works closely with other international organizations, especially UN agencies. Former OIC Secretary-General Ihsanoglu underscored the importance of socio-economic development for defeating radicalism in the Muslim world, and the OIC has concentrated on assisting states, such as Somalia and Afghanistan, whose institutions are severely underdeveloped (Ihsanoglu, 2010).[5] Capacity-building projects are aimed at poverty-alleviation and the development of physical infrastructure.

The OIC has several mechanisms for providing international assistance. Its Islamic Development Bank, created in 1973, provides economic and social development grants and loans to member-states (Islamic Development Bank, 2014). In 2008, the OIC created the International Cooperation and Humanitarian Affairs Department, which serves to coordinate efforts between the OIC and development and humanitarian civil society organizations around the world. The OIC has sought to strengthen its relations with global humanitarian NGOs, such as the London-based Humanitarian Forum, with which it co-hosted coordination meetings to address the humanitarian crisis in Syria (Humanitarian Forum, N.D.). The OIC is also a co-facilitator, with several other international organizations (IO), of the Syria Humanitarian Forum, which serves as a platform to coordinate fund-raising and humanitarian assistance.[6] It is unclear how much financial assistance the OIC has contributed, but prominent OIC members such as Saudi Arabia and United Arab Emirates have provided significant aid to ongoing humanitarian efforts in Syria (Oxfam Briefing Note, 2013; Revised Syria Humanitarian Response Plan, 2013). In 2014, the OIC also created the Humanitarian Emergency Response Fund, so that funds will be readily available when humanitarian catastrophes emerge. The Secretariat is currently working on the proposed rules and regulations for the fund, so it is not expected to be fully operational until sometime after 2014 (OIC, 2014).

Conflict resolution

The OIC engaged in conflict resolution even before it was prioritized in the Ten Year Program, although its accomplishments to date are limited due to its intuitional weakness. The organization has, of course, remained focused on the Israeli-Palestinian issue since its inception, and its leaders have consistently maintained that the Israeli occupation of Palestinian territory is the most central issue in the Muslim world. Accordingly, the organization created the al Quds Standing Committee which has held numerous meetings and international conferences to discuss a resolution to the conflict, and has also held activities to raise funds for the Palestinian cause (OIC, N.D.; see also Reiter, 2008). However, the OIC has not been a key player in the peace process (primarily due to its rather dormant state until the past decade), and its work has largely been overshadowed by other regional organizations, such as the League of Arab States (LAS).

The OIC's experience with conflict resolution in the southern Philippines is also a showcase of its political will to facilitate peace in a protracted conflict. In fact, the OIC has been tangentially and at times directly involved in conflict resolution between separatist Muslims and the Philippine government since 1972. Nevertheless, although the OIC was able to facilitate dialogue between the relevant parties, Ozerdem contends that its intervention has been "ad hoc, politically charged and ineffective" (Ozerdem, 2012). The OIC also responded to atrocities in Bosnia-Herzegovina (1992–95), a non-member state,[7] primarily by encouraging its members to financially support the Bosniaks. It was not a major player in the international effort to address atrocities and it did not have a representative at the Dayton peace talks (Karcic, 2013). The OIC has also been ineffectual in resolving conflict in member-states, such as Iraq. For example, although it successfully facilitated dialogue between Sunni and Shia Islamic clerics, culminating in the Makkah Declaration, which prohibited sectarian violence, this did little to stem the tide of sectarian attacks (OIC, 2005).

Despite its patchy success, the OIC has demonstrated its willingness to serve as mediator in numerous conflict-resolution initiatives in countries such as Iraq, the Philippines and Somalia (Sharqieh, 2012). Its *modus operandi* is to facilitate dialogue, and the new Secretary-General, Iyad Madani (January 31, 2014–present), continues to develop the organization's infrastructure for conflict resolution. In fact, the OIC has worked closely with the United Nations Department of Political Affairs since 2012 to strengthen its capacity to carry out mediation. As a result, the OIC created the Peace and Security and Mediation Unit (UN Departmental of Political Affairs, 2012), although the unit will not be fully operational until sometime after 2014.[8]

In sum, although the OIC has not explicitly endorsed all of the principles of the Responsibility to Protect, it clearly has the will to expand its role in promoting human rights, good governance and international peace through conflict resolution, all of which advance R2P. Moreover, its foray into hitherto unchartered territory has been welcomed by the UN Secretary-General, who for the first time in 2010 referred to the OIC as a "strategic and crucial partner of the United Nations" (UN Secretary-General, 2010b). The UN Security Council (UNSC) has also taken note of the OIC's importance, and held its first ever meeting on the role of the OIC in maintaining peace and security in 2012 (UN Secretary-General (2010b)).

Nevertheless, notwithstanding the aforementioned reforms and modest success in some areas, the OIC does not yet have the capacity to effectively meet the expectations set forth by proponents of R2P. The OIC remains weak vis-à-vis member-states, and OIC leadership has tended to tread lightly when attempting to shape the behavior of its members. OIC secretary-generals follow a strategy of "preventive diplomacy"[9] to encourage member-states to behave according to the dictates of the OIC Charter and the UN Declaration on Human Rights. Of course, without resources to monitor human rights abuses in member-states or enforcement mechanisms to compel compliance, the organization's ability to shape behavior remains limited. The OIC's agenda is driven by its most powerful members,[10] and it is unlikely that leaders from powerful autocracies, such as Saudi Arabia, will surrender some of their authority to an international organization.

The crises in Libya and Syria, however, offer compelling reasons to further strengthen the institution, considering that international peace is in the national interest of OIC member-states. These humanitarian crises did not lead to the wave of reforms in the OIC—many of them were approved years before the recent conflicts escalated. Nonetheless, the atrocities in Libya and Syria illustrate the need for a regional organization that can prevent atrocities and resolve ongoing crises. Consequently, these crises may actually engender further strengthening of the OIC, perhaps even more than its Ten Year Program envisions.

OIC's response to the crisis in Syria

The ongoing civil war in Syria has brought untold misery for much of the country's civilians. The crisis erupted in March 2011, following the successful toppling of dictators in Tunisia and Egypt and during global discussions to invoke R2P in Libya. The OIC's response to Syria's civil war cannot be understood without first examining the international community's and OIC's actions in Libya in 2011. Hence, it is necessary to juxtapose the Libyan and Syrian cases in order to highlight the complexities and contradictions of the OIC's responses to these crises.

The OIC's swift response to the crisis in Libya in 2011 stands in sharp contrast to its dithering on Syria. In this respect, it greatly resembles other states and organizations, such as its regional partner, the LAS. The international response to violence in Libya was exceptionally quick, and organizations such as the Arab League and the OIC, with reputations for being rather impotent in the face of conflict, were unusually proactive. Both the LAS and the OIC made early calls for action in Libya, imploring the UNSC to meet its responsibility to protect civilians. Throughout the lead-up to military intervention, both organizations were in lock step with one another. The two organizations have overlapping memberships, with all 22 LAS members represented in the OIC, and they have collaborated on the crises in Libya and Syria (LAS, N.D.; OIC, N.D.).

Only one month after peaceful protests were met with violence in Libya, the UNSC, with the blessing of the LAS and OIC, referred several Libyan leaders, including Gaddafi, to the International Criminal Court (ICC) on allegations of crimes against humanity. Calls for a no-fly zone subsequently grew louder when it became clear that the ICC referral and UNSC sanctions had not compelled Colonel Gaddafi to end the violence. The LAS and Gulf Cooperation Council were the first regional organizations to call for a no-fly zone over Libya, but shortly thereafter Secretary-General Ihsanoglu announced that the OIC "aligned with those calling for a no-fly zone over Libya with a view to protecting civilians from air strikes [and] called on the Security Council to assume its responsibility in this regard" (OIC, 2011b). Nine days later, the UN Security Council, citing endorsement by the OIC, issued Resolution 1973 which authorized NATO to implement a no-fly zone to protect Libyan civilians.

Regional endorsement of external intervention in Libya was considered a precondition for action by the UNSC and NATO (International Coalition for R2P, 2012); hence, the OIC's (and LAS's) approval for action was critically important. Although the OIC and its member-states, like its regional partners, tended to avoid explicit references to R2P, their full-throated endorsement of the international community's first R2P *military* intervention certainly legitimated R2P principles. Of course, the OIC's unprecedented authorization of military intervention in Libya can be attributed in part to Gaddafi's international isolation (Thakur, 2013). After implementation of the no-fly zone was underway, however, some OIC member-states joined the international chorus claiming that North Atlantic Treaty Organization (NATO) exceeded its mandate by targeting Gaddafi's forces (Kuperman,

2013; Hehir, 2013; Morris, 2013). Indeed, the NATO intervention compounded fears of great power abuse, and critics claimed NATO used R2P as a pretext to pursue regime change in Libya (Thakur, 2013). The subsequent lack of international support for a no-fly zone in Syria is a product of these criticisms.

In part because of the alleged mission creep by NATO, international intervention into the Syrian civil war has been a highly divisive issue in the OIC. The organization's stance has not changed much over the course of the three-year Syrian civil war. From the time peaceful protests were met with state violence, the OIC has issued statements condemning violence by both rebels and state forces, and has called for negotiations to reach a political settlement that respects Syria's sovereignty and territorial integrity. Although the OIC has condemned both sides for human rights violations, it has echoed R2P's first pillar by singling out the Syrian state as the party that bears primary responsibility for maintaining law and order and protecting civilians (OIC, 2012b). Moreover, its public statements implore the UNSC to meet its responsibility to protect the Syrian people (OIC, 2013c).

Unlike Libya, Syria was not seen as an international pariah and generally enjoyed good relations with its neighbors, which resulted in a much longer wait-and-see period after violence escalated. Indeed, the presence of strong Syrian supporters in the OIC, particularly Iran, has made reaching agreement on how to respond especially difficult. Iran has served as Syria's voice in the OIC since Syria's membership was suspended in August 2012 (Abdelaziz *et al.*, 2012) and has propagated Syria's narrative that it is fighting ruthless terrorists and needs time to adequately address the security threat. The geopolitics at play within the OIC is clear. Iran and Syria, the so-called resistance block to Western encroachments in the Middle East, have an adversarial relationship with pro-Western regional powers, especially Gulf monarchies and Turkey.[11] Not only have these competing blocks impeded consensus within the OIC, they have turned the Syrian civil war into a proxy war, with Iranians arming Syrian government forces and also sending troops to support them, and Gulf monarchies and Turkey arming various rebel groups.

In contrast to the Libyan case, the OIC has never advocated for R2P pillar three *military* intervention, and has in fact repeatedly argued against it. Moreover, the acute anxiety on the part of regional powers that the intervention in Libya set a dangerous precedent of legitimate Western intrusion in the region comes through in OIC statements, which underscore the importance of non-interference in a sovereign state's internal affairs. For example, Secretary-General Ihsanoglu stated at the third meeting of the Friends of the Syrian People in July 2012:

> Since the onset of this crisis, we made a point of abiding by the principle of non-interference in the internal affairs of a Member State of the OIC, and of respecting its sovereignty and territorial integrity, a principled stand which was coupled by our keenness to preserve Syria's safety, security and stability.
> (OIC, 2012a)

A statement in the OIC Journal further explains the strategy of the OIC in dealing with Syria:

> Since the ongoing crisis in Syria first erupted, the Organization for Islamic Cooperation (OIC) embraced an approach of quiet diplomacy based on its principled commitment to shun any intervention in the Member states' internal affairs and to respect the sovereignty, independence and territorial integrity of every Member State.
>
> (*OIC Journal*, 2012, p. 14)

Quiet diplomacy involves dialogue and non-coercive techniques. Hence, the OIC's approach has differed from other organizations that have employed more coercive diplomacy. For instance, even the Arab League imposed sanctions on Syria, an unprecedented action against a member-state, which underscores the gravity of the situation (Iran is not a member) (BBC News Middle East, 2011). By contrast, the OIC has not called on its members to impose sanctions against Syria. The extent of its punishment for Syria's non-compliance with international humanitarian law and internationally agreed-upon ceasefires and peace plans was suspension of Syria's membership in August 2012, over a year after fighting began. Perhaps the goal was to keep Syria in the fold in order to coax its restraint, but using membership as a stick or a carrot is ineffectual when membership confers so few benefits that its absence generates no disadvantage. The OIC also has not followed the Arab League and Gulf Cooperation Council in recognizing the National Coalition of the Syrian Opposition as the legitimate representative body of the Syrian people.[12] To date, there is no indication that the OIC will allow the Syrian Coalition to take Syria's seat at the OIC, a move that Iran and a few others would surely block.

Bearing few tools with which to cajole or coerce member-states to comply with its Charter or international law, the OIC has not been highly successful in its conflict resolution efforts, although it has sought to facilitate peace. For instance, Secretary-General Ihsanoglu sent a special envoy to Damascus as early as May 2011, who delivered a personal plea to President Assad to end the violence (OIC, 2012a). However, violence continued unabated. New OIC subsidiary organs, such as the mediation unit, tasked with carrying out the OIC's conflict resolution initiatives are not operational. Hence, the Secretariat has had to leave serious mediation efforts to better-equipped and more experienced international actors, such as the UN.

Initially, both the OIC and Arab League wanted to see the Syrian crisis resolved regionally, without the need for Western involvement in particular. The OIC continually supported the LAS's initiatives to bring about negotiations and a cessation of fighting (Global Centre for the Responsibility to Protect, 2012; see also Küçükkeleş, 2012). The LAS's August 2011 peace plan was finally accepted by President Assad in November, but was not implemented, and the LAS suspended Syria's membership shortly thereafter. The OIC then stepped in and called an emergency meeting on November 30, 2011, which Syria attended as a member, "as a 'last chance' to resolve the crisis 'within the broader Islamic family'" (Küçükkeleş, 2012, p. 11). However, after the OIC's meeting did not culminate in a resolution, the OIC (and LAS) increasingly called on the UN to take action.

The UN and the LAS then appointed, in February 2012, former UN Secretary-General Kofi Annan to act as Joint Special Envoy of the UN and the LAS to Syria. Annan and his team drew up a six-point plan for peace, presented to the UNSC on March 16, 2012 (Annan, 2012). The OIC publicly supported Annan's proposal (Fawzi, 2012) and the following month, on March 16, 2012, the OIC embarked on a joint ten-day observer mission with the UN to assess the humanitarian situation (*OIC Journal*, 2012). The UN-OIC joint observer mission coincided with a UN delegation sent to Damascus to discuss ways to implement Annan's six-point proposal. Hence, with respect to involvement of regional actors, there was a division of labor between the OIC and the LAS, with the OIC taking the lead in the humanitarian dimension of the war and the LAS working with the UN to address the political dynamics.

The Annan plan was ultimately accepted by Syria, but like the LAS's proposal, was not fully implemented by the Syrian government. Syria's lack of compliance and a mounting death toll served as an impetus to suspend Syria's OIC membership in August 2012. By that time, some OIC members (e.g., Turkey) had urged President Assad to step down and some had already imposed bilateral sanctions. The OIC, however, has to date refrained from explicitly calling for President Assad to abdicate power. In spite of this, Secretary-General Ihsanoglu expressed his *personal* opinion in a January 2013 *Chicago Tribune* opinion article. He stated, "It is time for President Bashar Assad to step down from power and for peace to come again to Syria" (Ihsanoglu, 2013). Several months later, he expressed his *personal* opinion during an interview that a no-fly zone should be implemented in Syria in order to set the conditions necessary to reach a political settlement. He rejected, however, the funding of Syrian rebels as a solution to the conflict (Rogin, 2013)—a tactic being employed by prominent OIC members, including Qatar, Saudi Arabia and Turkey.

Although the Syrian crisis continues to confound many would-be interveners and a viable political solution remains elusive, the international community, and the OIC specifically, have indeed taken numerous measures to scale the tide of human suffering. These humanitarian actions fall under R2P's third pillar, timely and decisive response to atrocities. Various organs of the United Nations have been highly pro-active, despite the Security Council's inability to authorize meaningful action;[13] and the OIC has worked diligently alongside the UN and other international partners to address the humanitarian dimension of the civil war. OIC appeals for action are generally rooted in Islamic notions of justice and charity rather than explicit references to international humanitarian law or the Geneva Conventions (Ahmad, 2012, p. 3).

In the first year of the crisis, the OIC Humanitarian Affairs Department was engaged in negotiations with the Syrian government to open an OIC humanitarian relief office in Damascus. To date, however, the OIC has not received authorization from the Syrian government to conduct humanitarian activities and does not have a presence in the country. As a result, the OIC's Humanitarian Affairs Department has focused its efforts on providing assistance to the various agencies and state governments of neighboring countries (e.g., Turkey) that are hosting Syrian refugees.[14] For instance, the OIC partnered with the LAS and the Humanitarian Forum to host the Second Humanitarian Conference on Syria in March 2012 at which 110 participants from over 70 non-governmental organizations and UN agencies discussed the humanitarian situation in Syria and its impact on neighboring countries (Global Centre for the Responsibility to Protect, 2012, p. 18). The OIC has also helped to coordinate fundraising for the international humanitarian effort, and has been involved in the Friends of Syria group, which includes representatives from states and international organizations, and meets regularly to discuss coordinated action in Syria (Syria in Crisis, 2012).

To summarize, the OIC has taken a cautious approach to atrocities in Syria. It has not issued statements calling for President Assad to step down or for R2P military intervention. In addition to the complexity of the Syrian conflict (which has stymied international action by even great powers and robust international institutions), the conflicting national interests of OIC members and the OIC's institutional weakness vis-à-vis member-states have hampered the OIC's efforts to play an effective role as peacemaker. It has consistently rejected an R2P third-pillar intervention resembling the no-fly zone it endorsed for Libya in 2011. However, the OIC has frequently condemned the violence in Syria and has assiduously and consistently supported efforts to facilitate dialogue for a political solution to the civil war (e.g., Geneva Conferences I and II), all of which constitute non-coercive R2P pillar three action. The most drastic measure to punish Syria for its actions was the suspension of its membership in the OIC after it refused to comply with agreed-upon ceasefires and peace plans. Although it does not generally explicitly reference R2P in its statements, relying instead on moral persuasion rooted in Islamic values, its efforts to mediate and provide humanitarian assistance are fully in line with R2P's third pillar. Because it lacks the tools to serve as an effective interlocutor between warring parties, it has supported the mediation efforts of other international actors, but it has positioned itself as a key player in the provision of humanitarian assistance.

Conclusion

The OIC has not been a champion of R2P in terms of its rhetoric. Indeed, many of its member-states have expressed concerns that great powers may use R2P as a pretext to carry out regime change. More generally, the organization's firm commitment to non-interference and national sovereignty precludes both deeper institutionalization of the OIC and full acceptance of the principles associated with R2P's third pillar. Nevertheless, recent reforms illustrate the OIC's deeper commitment to promote human rights, resolve and prevent conflict and provide humanitarian assistance during crises, all of which help to advance R2P principles by encouraging and assisting states to meet the requirements of R2P. Moreover, the OIC has responded to crises in Libya and Syria by consistently advocating for external involvement to protect civilians from mass slaughter. Specifically, the organization supported military intervention in Libya and has supported non-military intervention in Syria's ongoing civil war. Although it appears unlikely the OIC will endorse a Libya-style R2P intervention in Syria, the OIC has been at the forefront of the global effort to aid the Syrian people, especially refugees in Syria's neighboring states. The creation of new organs, such as a formal mediation unit to settle disputes before they escalate to mass violence and an Independent Human Rights Commission, will enhance the OIC's capacity to prevent conflict and address humanitarian crises in the future.

Notes

1 The name of the organization was changed in 2011 from the Organization of the Islamic Conference to Organization of Islamic Cooperation, and with that came a name change from the Islamic Conference of Foreign Ministers to the Council of Foreign Ministers.

2 For info on R2P's three pillars, see UN Secretary-General (2012), which addresses third pillar action. It was the fourth report on R2P issued by UN Secretary-General Ban Ki-moon. He has prepared annual reports on different aspects of R2P since 2009. In 2009, he presented the three-pillar framework to operationalize R2P in the report, "Implementing the Responsibility to Protect" (UN Secretary-General (2009). The report was then discussed by the General Assembly in an informal interactive dialogue on July 23, 2009 and in a formal debate on July 23, 24 and 28, 2009. In 2010, the Secretary-General issued a report "Early Warning, Assessment and the Responsibility to Protect" (UN Secretary-General, 2010). It was discussed at an informal interactive dialogue in the General Assembly on August 9, 2010. In 2011, the third report "The Role of Regional and Sub-regional Arrangements in Implementing the Responsibility to Protect," (UN Secretary-General, 2011) was discussed on July 12, 2011.

3 The question itself is rather problematic considering the numerous interpretations of Islamic precepts (see Mayer, 2006). The OIC IPHRC has been tasked with clarifying the status of the Cairo Declaration in light of recent OIC reforms that oblige OIC members to meet minimum standards of international human rights (OIC Human Rights, 2014).

4 Bicak (2011) argues the International Islamic Court of Justice can be seen as the most promising body for rule enforcement. If ratified, it would be the highest judicial organ of the OIC, given that Article 38 of the OIC Charter declares IICJ's judgments to be binding (only upon the parties to the dispute), and Article 39 affirms that those judgments are final and cannot be appealed. The IICJ, however, was never ratified by the requisite two-thirds majority of member-states after its statute was accepted by the Council of Foreign Ministers in 1987, and there is no indication it will be ratified anytime soon. Even if it were ratified, the court would operate like an Islamic version of the International Court of Justice and would not address human rights violations against individuals.

5 For a consideration of the developmental roots of human security and how R2P fits into this framework, see Thakur (2006, pp. 72–73).

6 The Forum is chaired by OCHA and co-facilitated by the Organization of Islamic Cooperation (OIC), the European Commission (ECHO) and the League of Arab States (LAS).

7 Bosnia-Herzegovina currently has observer status in the OIC.
8 Personal correspondence with official at the Permanent Observer Mission of the OIC to the United Nations, August 15, 2014.
9 Secretary-General Ban Ki-Moon has identified dialogue and preventive diplomacy to be tools in the R2P toolkit. Summary of the United Nations Secretary-General's Report on the Responsibility to Protect: Fulfilling our collective responsibility: International assistance and the responsibility to protect, Global Centre for the Responsibility to Protect (2014).
10 The top contributors to the OIC's budget are: Saudi Arabia (10 percent), United Arab Emirates (9 percent), Libya (6 percent), Iran (5.5 percent), Malaysia and Turkey (5 percent each). See (Petersen, 2012, pp. 46–47).
11 Syria and Turkey enjoyed close relations until President Assad's violence to civilians led Turkey to take a principled stance against its erstwhile ally.
12 The Syria National Coalition was officially recognized by the Arab League and the GCC in November 2012, and it assumed Syria's seat in LAS in March 2013.
13 There have been many high-level UN discussions concerning Syria. UN Security Council action includes the following: Votes were cast on October 4, 2011 (Res. S/2011/612) and February 4, 2012 (Res. S/2012/77), and both were vetoed by Russia and China. In response to the joint Russia-China veto on February 4, 2012, the General Assembly issued a nonbinding resolution on February 16, 2012 (Res. A/RES/66/254). The first draft to pass the Security Council was Resolution 2042 S/RES/2042 (2012) on April 14, 2012. The second, Resolution 2043 S/Res/2043 (2012), was passed on April 21, 2012. A third resolution was vetoed on July 19, 2012.
14 Personal correspondence with official at the Permanent Observer Mission of the OIC to the United Nations, August 15, 2014.

References

Abdelaziz, S., Paton-Walsh, N. and Sterling, J. (2012, August, 15). *Organization of Islamic Cooperation suspends Syria*. Retrieved from: www.cnn.com/2012/08/15/world/meast/syriaunrest/index.html. (accessed June 30, 2014).

Ahmad, I. (2012, December). The Organization of Islamic Cooperation's position on the protection of civilians in armed conflicts. *NOREF Policy Brief.*

Annan, K. (2012, March). *Annan's peace plan for Syria, Council on Foreign Relations. Primary Sources*. Retrieved from: www.cfr.org/syria/annans-peace-plan-syria/p28380 (accessed June 30, 2014).

BBC News Middle East (2011, November 27). Syria unrest: Arab League adopts sanctions in Cairo. BBC News Middle East. Retrieved from: www.bbc.co.uk/news/world-middle-east-15901360 (accessed June 30, 2014).

Bicak, G. (2011, December). The Genesis, history, and functioning of the Organization of Islamic Cooperation (OIC): A formal-institutional analysis. *Journal of Muslim Minority Affairs*, 31(4), 594–614.

Fawcett, L. (2009). *International relations of the Middle East* (2nd edn). Oxford: Oxford University Press.

Fawzi, A. (2012, April 15). Briefing by Ahmad Fawzi, spokesperson for United Nations And Arab League joint special envoy. *UN Forum*. Retrieved from: www.unforum.com/UNheadlines805.htm (accessed June 30, 2014).

Global Centre for the Responsibility to Protect (2012, October 18). *Timeline of international response to the situation in Syria*. Retrieved at: www.globalr2p.org/publications/135. (accessed February 15, 2014).

Global Centre for the Responsibility to Protect (2013, June). *Third meeting of the Global Network of R2P focal points: Accra report and recommendations*. Retrieved from: www.globalr2p.org/publications/268 (accessed February 15, 2014).

Global Centre for the Responsibility to Protect (2014, August 13). *Summary of the United Nations Secretary-General's report on the responsibility to protect: Fulfilling our collective responsibility: International assistance and the responsibility to protect*. Retrieved from: www.globalr2p.org/media/files/summary-of-the-r2p-report-2014-1.pdf (accessed August 20, 2014).

Halakhem, A. B. (2013, December). R2P in Practice: Ethnic violence, elections and atrocity prevention in Kenya. *Global centre for the responsibility to protect occasional paper series, No. 4*. Retrieved from: www.globalr2p.org/media/files/kenya_occasional-paper_web.pdf (accessed May 15, 2014).

Halliday, F. (2005). *The Middle East in international relations: Power, politics and ideology*. Cambridge: Cambridge University Press.

Hehir, A. (2013). The Permanence of inconsistency: Libya, the Security Council, and the responsibility to protect. *International Security*, 38(1), 137–159.

Hinnebusch, R. (2003). *The international politics of the Middle East*. Manchester: Manchester University Press.

Humanitarian Forum (n.d.). I. Retrieved from: www.humanitarianforum.org/pages/en/syria.html (accessed August 12, 2014).

Ihsanoglu, E. (2010). *The Islamic world in the New Century: The Organization of Islamic Conference, 1969–2009*. New York: Columbia University Press.

Ihsanoglu, E. (2013, January 24). Syrian president Assad must step down. *Chicago Tribune*. Retrieved from: http://articles.chicagotribune.com/2013-01-24/opinion/ct-oped-0124-syria-20130124_1_syrian-revolutionary-syrian-government-islamic-cooperation (accessed August 12, 2014).

International Coalition for the R2P (2011, August). *Interactive dialogue of the UN General Assembly on the role of regional and sub-regional arrangements in implementing the responsibility to protect*. Retrieved from: www.responsibilitytoprotect.org/ICRtoP%20Report%20on%20RIGO%20GA%20dialogue%20on%20RtoP%20FINAL(1).pdf (accessed March 8, 2014).

International Coalition for R2P (2012). *Crisis in Libya*. Retrieved from: www.responsibilitytoprotect.org/index.php/crises/crisis-in-libya#initial (accessed March 8, 2014).

Islamic Development Bank (2014). *About IDB*. Retrieved from: www.isdb.org/irj/portal/anonymous?NavigationTarget=navurl://24de0d5f10da906da85e96ac356b7af0 (accessed August 12, 2014).

Karcic, H. (2013). In support of a non-member State: The Organization of Islamic Conference and the war in Bosnia, 1992–1995. *Journal of Muslim Minority Affairs*, 33(3), 321–340.

Kayaoglu, T. (2013, January). A rights agenda for the Muslim world?: The evolving framework of Islamic Cooperation's evolving human rights framework. *Brookings Doha Center Analysis Paper No. 6* (January 2013). Retrieved from: www.brookings.edu/~/media/research/files/papers/2013/1/08%20oic%20human%20rights%20kayaoglu/turan%20kayaoglu%20english.pdf (accessed February 12, 2014).

Kayaoglu, T. and Petersen, M. J. (2013, November 19). Human rights experts' recommendations to Independent Permanent Human Rights Commission. *OIC Human Rights*. Retrieved from: https://oichumanrights.wordpress.com/2014/03/11/human-rights-experts-recommendations-to-independent-permanent-human-rights-commission/ (accessed August 5, 2014).

Küçükkeleş, M. (2012, April). Arab League's Syrian policy. *SETA foundation for political, economic and social research, Brief No. 56*. Retrieved from: http://setadc.org/pdfs/SETA_Policy_Brief_No_56_Arab_Leagues_Syrian_Policy.pdf (accessed August 5, 2014).

Kuperman, A. J. (2013). A model humanitarian intervention?: Reassessing NATO's Libya campaign. *International Security* 38(1), 105–136.

LAS (n.n.). *League of Arab States*. Retrieved from: www.lasportal.org.

Mayer, A. E. (2006). *Islam and human rights: Tradition and politics*. New York: Westview.

Morris, J. (2013). Libya and Syria: R2P and the spectre of the swinging pendulum. *International Affairs* 89(5), 1265–1283.

OIC (n.d.). *About OIC*. Retrieved from: www.oicun.org/2/23/ (accessed August 2, 2014).

OIC (n.d.). *Member States*. Retrieved from: www.oic-oci.org/oicv2/states/ (accessed June 18, 2014).

OIC (2005, December 8). *Makkah Declaration of the third extraordinary OIC summit, Third Session of the Extraordinary Islamic Summit Conference December 7–8, 2005*. Retrieved from: www.saudiembassy.net/archive/2005/statements/page3.aspx. (accessed June 18, 2014).

OIC (2005, December 7–8). *Ten year action program, Third extraordinary session of the Islamic Summit Conference*. Retrieved from: www.oic-oci.org/ex-summit/english/10-years-plan.htm (accessed June 18, 2014).

OIC (2008). *Charter of the Organization of the Islamic Conference*. Retrieved from: www.oic-oci.org/is11/english/Charter-en.pdf (accessed June 18, 2014).

OIC (2011a, June 28–30). *Statute of the OIC independent permanent commission on human rights*. Retrieved from: www.cfr.org/human-rights/statute-oic-independent-permanent-human-rights-commission/p26377 (accessed June 18, 2014).

OIC (2011b, August 3). *Ihsanoglu supports no-fly decision at OIC meeting on Libya, calls for an Islamic humanitarian program in and outside Libya*. Retrieved from: www.lcil.cam.ac.uk/sites/default/files/LCIL/documents/arabspring/libya/Libya_15_Ihsanoglu_Support.pdf (accessed June 22, 2014).

OIC (2012a, July 20). *Statement of H. E. Prof. Ekmeleddin Ihsanoglu, Secretary General of the OIC at the 3rd meeting of the group of friends of the Syrian people. OIC human rights*. Retrieved from: http://oichumanrights.wordpress.com/category/oic-member-states-and-un-human-rights-mechanism/syiria/ (accessed August 4, 2014).

OIC (2012b, August 30). *Statement for the IPHRC's second session on August 30, 2012. OIC human rights*. Retrieved from: https://oichumanrights.wordpress.com/tag/syria/ (accessed June 28, 2014).

OIC (2013a, April 14). *Final communiqué of the OIC contact group on Myanmar Muslim Rohingya minority*. Retrieved from: www.oic-oci.org/oicv2/topic/?t_id=7964&ref=3219&lan=en&x_key=rohingya (accessed June 25, 2014).

OIC (2014, April 17). Newsletter. Issue 14. www.oic-oci.org/oicv2/newsletter/?lan=en (accessed August 5, 2014).

OIC (2013b, May 20). *The biennial UN-OIC general meeting on cooperation commences in Istanbul*. [Permanent Observer Mission to the UN in New York]. www.oicun.org/9/20140528055342287.html (accessed August 4, 2014).

OIC (2013c, October 28). *Security Council meeting on UN-OIC cooperation*. [Permanent Observer Mission to the UN in New York]. Retrieved from: www.oicun.org/oic_at_un/79/20131104041141564.html (accessed August 4, 2014).

OIC (2014, May 20). *The biennial UN-OIC general meeting on cooperation commences in Istanbul*. [Permanent Observer Mission to the UN in New York]. Retrieved from: www.oicun.org/9/20140528055342287.html (accessed August 4, 2014).

OIC Human Rights (2011, December 12). *Opening session of the preparatory meeting OIC human rights commission.* Retrieved from: http://oichumanrights.wordpress.com/2011/12/12/opening-session-of-the-preparatory-meeting-oic-human-rights-commission/ (accessed August 7, 2014).

OIC Human Rights (2014, March 11). *Archive for the 'regional mechanism of human rights' category.* Retrieved from: http://oichumanrights.wordpress.com/category/oic-human-rights/regional-mechanism-of-human-rights/ (accessed August 5, 2014).

OIC Human Rights (2012, March 12). *OIC body told to engage civil groups.* Retrieved from: http://oichumanrights.wordpress.com/2012/03/15/oic-body-told-to-engage-civil-groups/ (accessed August 5, 2014).

OIC Journal (2012, January–March). Syria accepts peace plan to resolve crisis: OIC active in the political and humanitarian fronts. *OIC Journal*, No. 20, pp. 14–15. Retrieved from: http://issuu.com/oic-journal/docs/oic_journal_issue_20_english (accessed August 5, 2014).

OIC Statute (2011). *Statute of the OIC Independent Permanent Human Rights Commission.* [OIC/IPCHR/2010/STATUTE]. Retrieved from: http://oichumanrights.files.wordpress.com/2011/08/resolution-oic-iphrc-and-statute.pdf (accessed June 18, 2014).

Oxfam Briefing Note (2013, April 13). *Overtaken by need: The world's failure to meet Syria's escalating humanitarian crisis.* Retrieved from: www.oxfam.org/sites/www.oxfam.org/files/file_attachments/bn-overtaken-by-need-syria-crisis-300413-en_3.pdf (accessed August 2, 2014).

Ozerdem, A. (2012, September). The contribution of the Organization of the Islamic Conference to the peace process in Mindanao. *Civil Wars* 14(3), 393–413.

Petersen, M. J. (2012). Islamic or Universal Human Rights? The OIC's Independent Permanent Human Rights Commission. *Danish Institute for International Studies* (2012). Retrieved from: http://subweb.diis.dk/graphics/Publications/Reports2012/RP2012-03-Islamic-human-rights_web.pdf (accessed August 5, 2014).

Reiter, Y. (2008). *Jerusalem and Its Role in Islamic Solidarity.* New York: Palgrave Macmillan.

Revised Syria Humanitarian Response Plan (2013, January–December) [SHARP]. Retrieved from: http://reliefweb.int/sites/reliefweb.int/files/resources/Revised%20SHARP%2006June2013.pdf (accessed August 5, 2014).

Rogin, J. (2013, June 4). Exclusive: Top Islamic leader call for no-fly zone in Syria. *Daily Beast.* Retrieved from: www.thedailybeast.com/articles/2013/06/04/exclusive-top-islamic-leader-calls-for-no-fly-zone-in-syria.html (accessed August 12, 2014).

Sharqieh, I. (2012, Fall). Can the Organization of Islamic Cooperation (OIC) resolve conflicts? *Peace and Conflict Studies*, 19(2), 162–179.

Syria in Crisis (2012). Group of friends of the Syrian people: 1st conference. *Syria in crisis.* Retrieved from: http://carnegieendowment.org/syriaincrisis/?fa=48418 (accessed June 28, 2014).

Telhami, S. and Barnett, M. (2002). *Identity and foreign policy in the Middle East.* Ithaca, New York: Cornell University Press.

Thakur, R. (2006). *The United Nations, peace, and security: From collective security to the responsibility to protect.* Cambridge: Cambridge University Press.

Thakur, R. (2013, Spring). R2P after Libya and Syria: Engaging emerging powers. *Washington Quarterly* 36(2), 61–76.

UN Departmental of Political Affairs (2012, January–March). Mediation support quarterly update. Retrieved from: http://peacemaker.un.org/sites/peacemaker.un.org/files/MSUQuarterlyUpdate_JanMarch2012_1.pdf/ (accessed August 5, 2014).

UN Secretary-General (2009, January 12). Implementing the responsibility to protect (UN Doc. A/63/677). Retrieved from: www.refworld.org/docid/4989924d2.html (accessed March 5, 2014).

UN Secretary-General (2010a, July 14). *Early warning, Assessment and the responsibility to protect (UN Doc. A/64/864)*. Retrieved from: www.unrol.org/files/SGReportEarly-WarningandAssessmentA64864.pdf (accessed March 5, 2014).

UN Secretary-General (2010b, September 24). *Secretary General, in message to headquarters meeting, highlights importance of crucial strategic partnership between United Nations, Islamic Conference (UN Doc. SG/SM/13143)*. Retrieved from: www.un.org/News/Press/docs/2010/sgsm13143.doc.htm (accessed February 15, 2014).

UN Secretary-General (2011, June 27). *The role of regional and sub-regional arrangements in implementing the responsibility to protect* (UN Doc A/65/877-S/2011/393). Retrieved from: www.un.org/en/ga/president/65/initiatives/Report%20of%20the%20SG%20to%20MS.pdf (accessed February 15, 2014).

UN Secretary-General (2012, September 5). *Responsibility to protect: Timely and decisive response* (UN Doc. A66/876-S/2012/578). Retrieved from: www.responsibilityto-protect.org/UNSG%20Report_timely%20and%20decisive%20response(1).pdf (accessed February 15, 2014).

UNHCR (2014, February 12). UNHRC chief decries "humanitarian catastrophe" in CAR, including massive ethno-religious cleansing. *UN High Commission for Refugees*. Retrieved from: www.unhcr.org/52fbc6e96.html (accessed August 5, 2014).

7 League of Arab States (LAS)

Alan Patterson and Craig McLean

The Syria crisis has exercised the minds of policymakers, diplomats and the general public at large for several years now. As the country descends ever further into a seemingly bottomless pit of violence, the parallels between the situation in Syria at the time of writing and the disintegration of Bosnia and Herzegovina during the 1990s are all too clear—despite worldwide condemnation, the slaughter is continuing. And just as in the former-Yugoslavia, the international community appears to be hamstrung as how best to end the crisis in Syria, let alone resolve it. As Bosnia and Herzegovina imploded, the relative powerlessness of the European Union (EU) became all-too apparent; a conflict started in its own backyard could not be halted by the European powers despite all the then optimism of an ever-closer union within Europe. With startling echoes of the Bosnian experience (at least in terms of a new political beginning for the region; albeit one of uncertainty), the League of Arab States, more commonly called the Arab League (LAS), has been unable to resolve the Syria crisis despite an earlier success within Libya, although the current situation in Libya shows that the early success in deposing President Gaddafi and the beginnings of a new democratic republic have not gone well with opposing militias causing much strife throughout the country. In an attempt to understand why the Arab League has been so relatively ineffective in the case of Syria, this chapter draws upon the theoretical literature from International Relations (IR), and specifically the literature on European Integration. Noting the institutional and organizational similarities between the European Union (EU) and the LAS, the chapter argues that the current impasse within the League can be explained by the divergent foreign policies of its member-states within an area traditionally labeled as "high politics". Had their foreign policies on Syria converged, a more effective League response could have been anticipated, as apparently was the case recently within Libya.

Of course, the problem with writing a case study on contemporaneous events, in this case the Syria crisis can be problematic. Even at the time of writing this chapter the situation in the Middle East is changing and military actions and civil war are spilling over borders into other states, most notably the relative success of jihadist groups, which have merged under the name of ISIS in Iraq. The authors have, therefore, borne in mind these constant changes while attempting to analyze the LAS's role in these events.

Formal responsibilities of the LAS

Generally

In discussing the effectiveness of multinational organizations one must consider the diversity of views and attitudes held by member nations as well as the structure and decision-making processes of the organization. In terms of the LAS in particular, one must consider "the prevalence of political authoritarianism and societal illiberalism and the consequent schism between state and society in the Muslim world" (Saikal, 2006, p. 188). At the time of writing, it is still fair to argue that these issues have not yet been resolved. During the 1940s the idea of rallying Arab countries against colonial rule was growing. A further important regional issue was preventing the Jewish community in Palestine from creating a Jewish state. However, the formation of the League of Arab States did not come into being until just before the end of the Second World War, in March 1945, with six original members: Egypt, Iraq, Lebanon, Transjordan, Syria and Saudi Arabia. The LAS now has 22 members: Algeria, Bahrain, Comoros, Djibouti, Egypt, Iraq, Jordan, Kuwait, Lebanon, Libya, Mauritania, Morocco, Oman, State of Palestine, Qatar, Saudi Arabia, Somalia, Sudan, Syria (at present suspended) Tunisia, United Arab emirates and Yemen.

According to Article 2 of the Pact of the League:

> [T]he purpose of the League is to draw closer the relations between member states and co-ordinate their political activities with the aim of realizing a close collaboration between them, to safeguard their independence and sovereignty, and to consider in a general way the affairs and interests of the Arab countries.
>
> (Pact of the League of Arab States, March 22, 1945, Article 2)

The League now has 22 member-states, although Syria has been suspended since November 2011 because of "its failure to end bloodshed caused by brutal government crackdowns on pro-democracy protests" (Batty and Shenker, 2011). The Council is the highest body of the League and is composed of representatives of the member-states. A secretary-general within the general secretariat (Pact of the League of Arab States) undertake the day-to-day running of the League.

Arrangements for mutual defense and economic cooperation were embedded in a Treaty of Joint Defense and Economic Cooperation among the States of the Arab League in June 1950. The purpose was:

> [T]o maintain their independence and their mutual heritage; in accordance with the desire of their peoples, to cooperate for [the] realization of mutual defense and the maintenance of security and peace according to the principles of both the Arab League Pact and the United Nations Charter ...
>
> (Treaty of Joint Defense and Economic Cooperation Between the States of the Arab League, 1950)

For the purposes of defense, Article 6 of the Treaty created a Joint Defense Council to draw up plans for joint defense and the implementation of these plans. Proposals reaching the Council are today voted upon with each member-state having one vote. Article 7 of the Pact states that the decisions of the Council taken by a unanimous vote shall be binding on all Member-states of the League; those that are reached by a majority vote shall bind only those that accept them. Thus, decisions resulting from Council votes are binding on only those states that voted for them.

The effectiveness of the League's decision-making is severely hindered by Article 7, and by the very diverse types of nations belonging to the League. It is important, therefore, to discuss the many political, ethnic and religious differences that exist within the Arab League countries. First, politically, there are several monarchies (in Saudi Arabia, Jordan, UAE and Morocco); a relatively new parliamentary republic in Libya which held its first parliamentary election in 2012; Egypt, nominally a presidential republic, is currently in a state of revolution and at the time of writing, is under the control of its armed forces; Iraq is a federal republic; while Syria, Tunisia, Algeria and Yemen are presidential republics. Second, there are many ethnic and religious differences. Morocco is an Islamic country with Arab and Berber populations. In Iraq there is an autonomous Kurdish region, while the remaining Arab part of the country is split between the Sunni and Shia movements. Iraq under Saddam Hussein was characterized, amongst other things, by a Sunni minority dominating a majority Shia country. Since the toppling of the Baathist regime in 2003, however, these positions have been reversed, with sectarian violence emerging in the country. Saudi Arabia is predominantly Sunni Islam, of the ultra-conservative Wahhabi sect, while Lebanon has Christian, Eastern Orthodox and Muslim populations. Syria, at the time of writing is in a state of turmoil, has a large Alawite population, a branch of Shia Islam, but also has Druze and Christian minorities. Enmity between Sunnis and Shias and in general among Christians, Jews and Muslims plays a large part in some of the unrest in the region. Egypt has encountered its own difficulties with protest and violence finally toppling the military dictatorship of Hosni Mubarak, followed by the election and subsequent overthrow of the Muslim Brotherhood's Mohamed Morsi as president. President Morsi was then arrested, further elections held, and the head of the Egyptian armed forces, General al Sisi, became president. Protest and unrest, nevertheless, have continued. There have also been many incidences of Christian persecution. The problems in Syria have been exacerbated by support and arms from Saudi Arabia and Qatar to the Syrian rebels. All of this diversity and turmoil makes it difficult for an international organization that covers Southwest Asia and North Africa to arrive at clear, decision-making capabilities—either diplomatically or militarily. At levels below such areas as economic development and defense, the Arab League has been modestly successful. It has created regional telecommunications union, helped shape school curricula and has been involved in the translation of modern technical terminology. In other words, the Arab League has seen some integration across the member-states but only in the realms of what would usually be described as "low politics" (BBC, 2013).

The LAS—a comparison with the EU

Given that the LAS is an attempt by sovereign nations to pool or delegate some areas of policymaking to an international organization, it is useful at this juncture to compare it to another, arguably more advanced, example of international institutions that has emerged through a series of not-too-dissimilar political pressures. The case in point here is the EU. Europe has experienced dreams of unity similar to that of the Arab peoples. European intellectuals dreamt for centuries of bringing some kind of political order to a fragmented continent. It was, however, not until 1945, as in the Middle East, that renewed interest in unity emerged; in particular, the division of Europe between East and West after the Second World War, resulting in the Cold War, created fears in the West over the ambitions of the USSR. This ideological division helped Western Europe move towards defining common interests. This did not happen at once, as there were large debates as to what a united Europe should be.

On the one hand there was the federalist idea of "a once and for all 'big bang' solution, an instantaneous and all-embracing transformation into a federal European state" (Cini, 2003). On the other hand, there was a more cautious, slow moving strategy of integration of economies with inputs from national governments. The EU therefore, "is the product of a complex interaction of centripetal and centrifugal pressures of ideas, principles, and *realpolitik* skepticism" (Cini, 2003). From an integrated coal and steel community to a common market, the following decades have witnessed the emergence of an EU as an international organization that is unique in that has not just economic and cultural institutions, but is part supranational and part intergovernmental in its decision-making. The EU now has a common security and defense policy beyond anything developed by the League. This has allowed the EU to take a prominent part in international negotiations over such issues as Iran's nuclear developments, the Libya and Syria crises, and also what is happening in Ukraine at the time of writing. It is clear from the above that the Arab League is more of an intergovernmental organization in which case matters like foreign policy and defense policy are still largely in the hands of the individual Member-states.

At first glance this might appear to be a bold statement, but a theoretical examination of the two organizations (as opposed to one based strictly on policymaking) demonstrates that through the process of "spillover", the EU has begun to assume competence in certain sectors, albeit not all. Moreover, by pursuing a theoretical examination of the EU, it quickly becomes apparent that the lessons learned from the European experience are potentially applicable to the LAS.

The rich history on EU scholarship need not be examined in too much depth, here, but it is important to highlight how the manner in which debates on integration within the communities can actually help to better understand how the League has reacted to events in Syria (discussed later in this chapter) (and indeed Libya, though that is not our purpose in this chapter). Although scholarship on the EU has mushroomed in recent years to draw on the theoretical insights of comparative politics, epistemic communities, and policy networks among others, the early scholarship on community integration borrowed from the insights of International Relations in order to explain developments within the European Communities. At the risk of gross oversimplification, the works of scholars such as Ernst Haas (Haas, 1958) and Leon Lindberg (Lindberg, 1963) argued that integration in one specific policy sector would create pressures for further integration elsewhere. This became known as "functional spillover". According to this logic, the creation of a single market, for example, would lead to pressures for integration in other policy sectors (i.e., the removal of internal borders, the need for a single transport policy, and perhaps even a common currency as cross-border trade increased). Such theoretical insights stressed the importance of supranational institutions (the European Commission etc.) in pushing the integration process and, for that reason, became known as supranational theories of integration.

The main theoretical school, which challenged this view, developed from the Realist school of International Relations. Scholars from this school included Stanley Hoffmann (Hoffmann, 1966) and, sometime later, Andrew Moravcsik (Moravcsik, 1999), who proposed the theory of Liberal Intergovernmentalism. These scholars conceded that European states might integrate in certain policy sectors of relatively little import, for instance matters relating to trade, but would only do so if it matched their national interests. In other words, according to the Liberal Intergovernmentalist argument, states will essentially pool sovereignty in areas of mutual interests, but will only do so if there is a clear material benefit to them, and will do so only on the basis of lowest common-denominator bargaining (Moravcsik, 1999). As a result, integration tends to take place within areas that would normally be classed as "low politics" policy sectors (telecommunications, trade and the like), whereas the member-states would jealousy protect their sovereignty in what might be termed areas of "high politics" (Rosamond, 2000, pp. 78–79) (defense, foreign policy and the like (McLean, 2008, p. 35). In reality and as if to confirm this point, the EU actually represents its member-states in matters pertaining to trade, through negotiating at the WTO on their behalf, for example, whereas the member-states retain their own separate and distinctive foreign and defense policies (not to mention their own armed forces).

Why the scholarship on IR mentioned earlier is important is because it can be used as a heuristic device to help to better understand the nature of the LAS. This can be achieved by asking the following question: is the Arab League constructed along the lines of the EU? A cursory glance at the respective organizations quickly demonstrates that whereas the Arab League has at least attempted to integrate in certain policy sectors and is an international organization of sorts; it lacks the institutional and legal instruments of the EU (an activist court, a supranational national parliament with co-decision in certain areas and so on). The purpose of Pact of the Arab League (1945) is to strengthen ties among the member-states and coordinate their policies. Among its aims are closer cooperation in economics, trade, agriculture, transport, industry, health and social welfare. There are two councils to deal with these matters. The Joint Defense and Economic Council, mentioned earlier, assisted by a Military Commission that draws up plans to deal with anticipated dangers, makes proposals for military training and development. In the event of war, the Commission organizes a joint forces command to be given to the state possessing the largest military force taking part in field operations (see the military annex of the Pact). The second council is the Economic Council set up in Article 8 of the Pact: "consisting of Ministers in charge of economic affairs to submit recommendations for the realization of all such aims as are set forth in the previous Article" (Pact of the League of Arab States 1945). Meanwhile, the League does not have an equivalent of the EU's Court of Justice. Viewed from a theoretical perspective, the organizational structure of the League is intergovernmental in nature. For that reason, the Arab League more closely resembles the type of organization that Realist scholars of IR would identify: an organization that has been created with the aim to further pursue the interests of its member-states, albeit on the world stage. To put it another way, the Arab League much more closely fits into the theory of Liberal Intergovernmentalism that seeks to preserve national sovereignty proposed by scholars such as Hoffmann and Moravcsik than it does of furthering integration as forwarded by Haas and Lindberg.

Because the LAS is constructed more along the lines of the more intergovernmental parts of the EU outlined earlier, it might be assumed that some foreign policy issues will result in joint action with a comparative minimum of objection, whereas others can lead to apparent inaction. This is due to the preferences of the member-states. Where these tend to converge, it might be speculated that the LAS would speak to the world stage with an apparent united voice and take decisive action. Alternatively, where the interests of the member-states are not in alignment, or indeed diametrically opposed, it might be expected that the Arab League will essentially end up hamstrung with regard to a specific issue. With this in mind, the actual events on the ground within the Arab League will be considered.

R2P and the LAS

The mutual defense principles laid down in the 1945 Arab League Pact and the 1950 Treaty, discussed earlier, do not mention anything approaching the principles contained within the Responsibility to Protect in the context of genocide or crimes against humanity. Yet Arab League nations are also UN members and the 1950 Treaty specifically invokes the UN Charter. Further, as it is made explicit in the 2005 World Summit Outcome document there is:

> [C]lear, unambiguous acceptance by all UN members of individual state responsibility and collective international responsibility to protect populations from genocide, war crimes, ethnic cleansing and crimes against humanity, and a willingness to take timely and decisive collective action for this purpose, through the Security Council, when peaceful means prove inadequate and national authorities are manifestly failing to do it.
>
> (Thakur, 2006, p. 465)

Article 11 of the Treaty of Joint Defense states that:

> No provision of the Treaty shall in any way affect, or is intended to affect, any rights or obligations devolving upon the Contracting states from the UN Charter or the responsibilities borne by the UN Security Council for the maintenance of international security.

The League, therefore, has signed up to R2P whether knowingly or not. Therefore, given the alleged crimes against humanity that have occurred in Syria, the League has legitimate reasons for action upon its responsibility.

Existing capabilities for implementation of R2P

Just like the UN and the EU, the LAS does not have a standing army, but early in the Syrian crisis the Arab League called for a joint Arab-UN peacekeeping force to tackle the problem in Syria. The LAS proposed a ceasefire and the mission was to oversee this ceasefire (CNN, 2012). This was rejected by Syria. But in any case no pre-conditions existed (no ceasefire or UN mandate) for a peacekeeping force, although one journalist observed that there is an historical precedent for this in the deployment of an Arab Deterrent Force between Israel and southern Lebanon in 1976. This was a Syrian initiative and was mainly composed of Syrian troops (Bari Atwan, 2012).

Moreover, although the Treaty of Joint Defense and Economic Cooperation is fairly explicit about "armed aggression made against any one or more" of the contracting countries (Treaty of Joint Defense), and that such aggression will be repelled and peace restored. It is not clear as to what happens when this occurs within one of the contracting nations, i.e., civil war, as the Arab League Pact and the Treaty of Joint Defense are silent on this point.

Actual abilities to address R2P challenges

Before, during and after mass atrocities have occurred

Peaceful protests against the government of Syria in March 2011 were to prove to be the beginning of a conflict that by the middle of 2012 saw large numbers of people fleeing to Jordan, Iraq, Lebanon, Turkey and Egypt. By September 2013 the UN High Commissioner for Refugees (UNHCR) estimated that the number of Syrian refugees had passed the two million mark (UN Refugee Agency, 2013).

In October 2011, in the UN Security Council, France, Germany, Portugal and the UK made a Draft Resolution 612 in which they expressed that they were "deeply concerned by the continuing deterioration of the situation in Syria" and reaffirmed "the need to resolve the current crisis in Syria peacefully" (UN Security Council, 2011). The Draft Resolution also demanded that the Syrian authorities cease violations of human rights, cease the use of force against civilians and ensure the safe and voluntary return of those who have fled the violence to their homes. In this regard the Draft Resolution encouraged the Arab League states to use their influence to end the violence. When the Resolution eventually came up for discussion in the Security Council it was opposed by several states, with nine members voting in favor, four abstained and Russia and China voted against it.

On November 2, 2011 a League peace plan was agreed upon with the Syrian government that would see tanks withdrawn from cities, political prisoners released and the Syrian army would no longer deploy violence against peaceful demonstrators. However, as demonstrators continued to be killed, the Arab League declared this a breach of promise by Syria. In late November, Syrian opposition groups calculated that 300 demonstrators had been killed since the start of the peace plan. The Arab League then suspended Syria's membership in the League (Batty and Shenker, 2011) with economic sanctions also resulting.

In December 2011, Syria agreed to a further peace plan with the Arab League that, among other things, agreed to the admittance of Arab League peace monitors to Syria and for talks to begin between the Syrian government and dissident groups. This was a non-interventionist mission on the part of the Arab League, with the sole duty of observing events and reporting back to the organization. However, at an emergency session in January 2012, the Arab League decided to exclude Syria until it implemented the terms of an earlier agreed peace deal to stop the violence (Ibid). The Syrian government criticized the appropriateness of the choice of the Sudanese general who led the mission, while the Syrian opposition said the mission was a farce and had not achieved anything. On January 31, 2012 a Security Council draft resolution on Syria commended the Arab League on its efforts and:

> regretting that, due to the escalation in violence, the observer mission was not in a position to monitor the full implementation of the League of Arab States action plan of 2 November 2011 and noting the subsequent decision of the League of Arab States to suspend the mission.
>
> (*Guardian*, January 31, 2012)

On August 21, 2013, thousands of Syrian civilians were killed or seriously injured in chemical weapons attack in Ghouta, a district of Damascus. The Syrian government claimed that the Syrian opposition used the weapons, while the opposition blamed government troops for the attack. In response, many countries, including the US, UK, France and Germany, and the Arab League called publicly for UN chemical weapons inspectors to investigate the attack. In September the UN Security Council Resolution 2118 was adopted unanimously with regard to this incident. This resolution dealt with the destruction and disposal of Syria's arsenal of chemical weapons (BBC, 2014).

It might be argued that the LAS's actions (discussed in the next section) in Libya had set a precedent, and that the Arab peoples in future might look to the League for action against member governments to protect citizens. However, the problems the League encountered in Syria have probably dampened that thought. It has been argued that the Arab League effectively excluded Syria and included Saudi Arabia in the 2011–12 peacemaking efforts, and thus this lack of procedural fairness undermined the potential of mediation of this process (Gartner and Premack, 2014, pp. 785–817).

As applied to the case of Syria

The problem for the League is that any force of "foreign" troops that enter Syria, even for peacekeeping purposes, would likely be interpreted by the Assad regime as a declaration of war. So, given the lack of agreement internationally (international proposals for some form of intervention, or for President Assad to stand down, which have been continually opposed by Russia and China, for example), the League has found it extremely difficult to find an effective diplomacy, or any determined efforts amongst its member countries to look for ways to implement any R2P plan.

By contrast the League's handling of the Libyan situation some years ago is as important as it is illuminating. The League's decision to impose a no-fly zone over Libya eventually led to NATO intervention. This is significant as it demonstrated that member nations of the League could reach a consensus on important military issues. As one observer noted:

> The League's decision lent legitimacy to NATO's intervention, inadvertently creating a new standing and position for the League. With bodies like NATO and the United Nations looking for its guidance, the League is beginning to be taken seriously in the international arena.
>
> (Jedea, 2011, p. 2)

Herein lies the theoretical issue outlined above, however: where the preferences of the member-states of the League converged on the issue of Libya. The League was able to take a decisive leadership role in the crisis but was only able to do this because of a consensus amongst the leading members of the LAS. In other words, action was taken when member-states' preferences converged—as the theory of Liberal Intergovernmentalism would predict.

In a not too dissimilar manner to events in Libya, the LAS has attempted to play a mediating role throughout the Syrian conflict, and, on the surface, appears to have had some success, even going so far as to bring the matter to the United Nations. Unfortunately for the standing of the LAS, however, any UNSC resolution demanding President Bashir al-Assad to stand down would be rejected by China and Russia. Nevertheless, this veto should not be interpreted to mean that Damascus can entirely dismiss the thoughts of the LAS. In 2012, it seemed like the regime in Syria acknowledged the peace plan developed by Kofi Annan, the UN and the LAS representatives. In addition, although the UNSC member-states disagreed on resolutions to be determined on Syria, Syria continued to be on the agenda. After the proposed resolution was rejected:

> [T]he General Assembly took the opportunity provided by Human Rights Commissioner Navi Pillay's report on the situation in Syria to vote on the issue. On Feb. 16. [2012] it overwhelmingly passed a resolution … 137 to 12 to support the Arab League's position on Syria".
>
> (Williams, 2012, p. 26)

Yet despite this, the fighting continues with more disparate groups becoming involved. These groups have not formed a single coalition against the Syrian Government, however, as they each have their own agenda. The LAS has continued to work steadfastly, albeit in the apparent background, to help bring hostilities to an end. The LAS has stressed an urgent need for the international community to take actions against the Syrian brutality and to demand the UNSC to respond to the systematic abuses of the norms and values in the UN Charter. The LAS clearly spoke out that the Syrian regime of President Assad has the main responsibility for the escalation of violence and the use of chemical weapons, which must be lead to a trial for those responsible for these criminal acts (Aljazeera, 2013).

At first glance, this stand on the Syrian regime could be interpreted to mean that the League is presenting a united front to bring hostilities within Syria to a swift conclusion. Beneath the surface, however, there are wider geopolitical interests at stake. For example, arguably the two most powerful nations in the region, Egypt and Saudi Arabia, disagree over how best to resolve the crisis. On the one hand, Egypt has taken the stance that the crisis ought to be resolved by the domestic powers within Syria. As has been stated elsewhere, for instance, "Egypt's foreign minister on Sunday [September 1, 2013], said that his nation objected to 'any aggression in Syria'" (Aljazeera, 2013). On the other hand, Saudi Arabia appears to prefer a more interventionist solution. The Saudis in particular has tried to persuade the US to act in a way to get rid of President Assad in Syria and to support the opposition to stop the tyranny in Syria. The Saudis has openly financed the Syrian rebels and argued for the importance to counterbalance primarily Iranian negative influence in the region, but also the destabilizing effects of other actors.

The kind of conflict that is causing so much chaos and bloodshed in Syria cannot be confined within its borders. The Syrian opposition forces consists of a variety of groups, not all of them Syrian citizens that simply oppose the Assad regime, but many jihadist militias. At the time of writing, a particularly strong militia, the Islamic State of Iraq and the Levant (ISIS), that was active in Syria, has moved into Northern Iraq, having successfully taken several cities. On June 15, 2014 the permanent delegates of the Arab League met in Cairo and condemned the terrorist acts carried out by ISIS in Iraq (Middle East Monitor, 2014).

Conclusion

The issues surrounding international politics have been brought into evidence by the recent resignation of the UN Syria envoy, Lakhdar Brahimi. This was the second defeated UN diplomat in Syria after the resignation of Kofi Annan; both diplomats found the Assad regime and the divisions within the UNSC impossible to overcome (Bryant, 2014). The UNSG regretfully had to accept the resignation of both and declared that this was a failure for the international community (Black, 2014).

At first glance it might appear that the League is ideally suited to resolve the Syrian crisis given that it is a conflict being prosecuted within its own region. Yet, in terms of the capability of this multinational institution to use R2P to protect the citizens of the Middle East, the Arab League has a very difficult task. It is very clear from our analysis that because of the longstanding rivalry between Shia and Sunni sects and the diverse political systems of the member-states of the League that much has to change before this institution can speak with one voice for the peoples of the region.

Unfortunately, the delicate balance of geopolitics has ensured that any attempts to resolve the crisis by the Arab League, especially with reference to the Responsibility to Protect, have thus far been rebuffed. The situation is perhaps best encapsulated by Ian Williams:

> The danger of the Russian and Chinese veto is that it takes the Security Council out of the equation and thus removes direction and immediacy from any response. That, after all, is the Council's function. The passed General Assembly resolution mentioned above could just prolong the agony, with the attendant dangers of a replay of Lebanon, as Kurds, Palestinians, Christians, Druze, Alawites and Sunnis run for the cover of their kind.
>
> (Williams, 2012)

The problem for the League in respect of the R2P is that unless it further enhances its reputation for standing up for the Arab peoples, as it did in the Libyan crisis, it is not going to have much standing as a multinational organization. But internal divisions within the Arab League (such as those between Egypt and Saudi Arabia with respect to the Syrian crisis) make such a scenario unlikely.

In that regard, the League is indicative of many international organizations that are intergovernmental in nature (the UN being but one prime example of this). Where the preferences and interests of the member-states converge and align, then there is a possibility of action and a coordinated response. A useful historical case of this is the relative success of the League with regard to the Libyan crisis. However, where the preferences and interests of the member-states do not converge—never mind align—it becomes very difficult for the international organization in question to actually present a united front. Using the literature on integration within the EU as a heuristic device, the League is an intergovernmental organization whose member-states jealously hold onto their sovereignty in this most important area of "high politics"—foreign, defense and security policy. In order to enable the Arab League to become more effective in this area of "high politics," it would seem appropriate for its member-states to cede more powers to it, in a manner not too dissimilar to the European Union (albeit in different policy sectors). At a time when the region is gripped by a state of political turmoil and a quasi-arms-race, however, such a scenario seems unlikely, thereby adding to the many frustrations of the Arab population. Nevertheless, the Arab League continues to explore avenues for a peaceful settlement of the crisis by attempting to involve Iran in regional and international conferences, and indeed those of the League itself.

Therefore, in terms of the capability of this multinational institution to use R2P to protect the citizens of the Middle East, and the citizens of Syria in particular, the League has a very difficult task. It is very clear from this analysis that because of the longstanding rivalry between Shia and Sunni sects and the diverse political systems of the member-states within the Arab League that much has to change before this institution can speak with one voice for the peoples of the region. However, in view of the cautionary note made above about analyzing contemporaneous events, it is clear that as the situation in Syria continues without an end in sight, one can only hope that the Arab League can eventually speak with one voice and influence international opinion on the Syrian crisis.

References

Aljazeera (2013, September 2). *Arab League urges UN-backed action in Syria: Foreign ministers seeks "necessary deterrent measures" against Syrian regime in line with international law*. Retrieved from: www.aljazeera.com/news/middleeast/2013/09/20139118235327617.html (accessed April 15, 2014).

Bari Atwan, A. (2012, February 13). The Arab League has misjudged its actions on Syria. *The Guardian*.

Batty, D. and Shenker, J. (2011, November 12). Syria suspended from Arab League. *Guardian*. Retrieved from: www.theguardian.com/world/2011/nov/12/syria-suspended-arab-league (accessed June 14, 2014).

BBC (2013). *Profile: Arab league*. Retrieved from: www.bbc.co.uk/news/world-middle-east-15747941? (accessed January 19, 2014).

BBC (2014). *Destroying Syria's chemical Weapons*. Retrieved from: www.bbc.com/news/world-middle-east-25810934 (accessed July 27, 2014).

Cini, M. (ed.) (2003). *European Union politics*. Oxford: Oxford University Press.

CNN (2012). *Arab League proposes peacekeeping force, support for Syrian rebels*. Retrieved from: http://edition.ccn.com/2012/02/12/world/meast/syria-unrest/ (accessed July 28, 2014).

Gartner, S. and Premack, B. (2014). Mitigating conflicts of interest in regional governmental organization civil war mediation. *Wisconsin International Law Journal*, 31, 785–817.

Guardian (2013, January 31). *UN Draft Resolution on Syria*. Retrieved from: www.guardian.co.uk/world/2012/jan/31/un-security-council-draft-resolution-syria (accessed July 18, 2014).

Haas, E. B. (1958). *The uniting of Europe: political, social, and economic forces, 1950–1957*. Stanford: Stanford University Press.

Hoffmann, S. (1966). Obstinate or obsolete? The fate of the nation-state and the case of western Europe. *Daedalus*, 9, 862–915.

Jedea, H. (2011). *The Arab League's Evolving Role in the Restless Middle East.* The Stimson Centre: Washington, D.C. Retrieved from: www.stimson.org (accessed March 3, 2014).

Lindberg, L. (1963). *The political dynamics of European economic integration.* Stanford: Stanford University Press.

McLean, C. (2008). *The common fisheries policy of the European Union: Diverging responses in Germany and the United Kingdom.* New York: The Edwin Mellen Press.

Moravcsik, A. (1999). *The choice for Europe: Social purpose and state power from Messina to Maastricht.* London: UCL Press.

Pact of the League of Arab States (1945, March 22). Article 2. The Avalon Project: Documents in Law, History and Diplomacy, Yale Law School. Retrieved from: http://avalon.law.yale.edu/20th_century/arableag.asp#art6/ (accessed January 10, 2014).

Rosamond, B. (2000). *Theories of European Integration.* Basingstoke: Macmillan.

Saikal, A. (2006). Reactions in the Muslim world. In Rajeev Thakur and Waheguru Pal Sing Sidhu (eds.). *The Iraq crisis and world order.* New York: United Nations University.

The Spectator (2012a, February 11). London. (accessed February 5, 2014).

The Spectator (2012b, March 31). London. (accessed February 5, 2014).

Treaty of Joint Defense and Economic Cooperation Between the States of the Arab League, Military annex (1950, June 17). *The Avalon Project: Documents in Law, History and Diplomacy.* Yale Law School: Yale. Retrieved from: http://avalon.law.yale.edu/20th_century/arabjoin.asp (accessed January 10, 2014).

Thakur, R. (2006). The responsibility to Protect and the war on Saddam Hussein. In Rajeev Thakur and Pal Singh Sidhu Waheguru (eds.). *The Iraq War and World Order.* New York: United Nations University.

UN Refugee Agency (UNHCR) (2013). *Syrian Crisis Fact Sheet: Timeline and figures.* Retrieved from: www.uncr.org/5245a72e6.pdf (accessed June 24, 2014).

UN Security Council (2011, October 4). France, Germany, Portugal and United Kingdom of Great Britain and Northern Ireland [draft resolution] UN Doc. S/2011/612.

Williams, I. (2012, March–April). No uniting for peace after Russia and China veto Security Council on Syria. *Washington Report on Middle East Affairs*, 31, 26–27.

8 Gulf Cooperation Council (GCC)

Daniel Silander

In December 2013, the Gulf Cooperation Council (GCC) (also referred to as the Cooperation Council for the Arab States in the Gulf), with six member-states in Saudi Arabia, Bahrain, the United Arab Emirates, Oman, Qatar and Kuwait, declared at a two-day summit in Kuwait that Syria's President Bashar al-Assad must be removed from power. The GCC member-states also declared that the Syrian regime had committed genocide and must be punished accordingly. As argued, "Pillars of the Syrian regime whose hands had been stained by the blood of the Syrian people must have no role in the transitional government or Syria's political future" (*Cairo Post*, 2013). The Syrian foreign minister accused the GCC of intervening in Syrian domestic politics (*Cairo Post*, 2013). In March 2014, the GCC member-states continued to condemn the Syrian regime for the humanitarian disaster created in the country. All member-states called for "deterrent action" (Arab News, 2014) to halt the ongoing slaughter of civilians and once again charged the regime with committing genocide. It was further declared that the UN had the responsibility for protecting civilians against the regime. After three years of ongoing regime brutality, the GCC statements urged the international community to refer the "perpetrators of such crimes" (Arab New, 2014) to the International Criminal Court (ICC); meanwhile, Gulf member-states and the international community have had to assure the delivery of major humanitarian aid to civilians in the war-torn society.

This chapter explores the role of the GCC in the quest to resolve the civil war in Syria. It addresses the position of the GCC on the Syrian regime and assesses the capabilities and abilities of the gulf organization to follow through on its strong statements against President Bashar al-Assad and the Syrian regime. While the first section of the chapter addresses the nature and developments of the GCC, the second section discusses in particular the limited capabilities of the GCC to deal with military- and security-related challenges. As the GCC member-states have agreed that the Syrian regime is conducting genocide in Syria, calling for urgent intervention by the UN, the final section explores the GCC's role with the challenges presented by Syria. It is argued that the GCC military and security abilities are challenged by internal political differences on what the GCC objectives should be and—in the case of Syria—also challenged by the member-states' different relationships to Iran. This leaves the GCC as a political actor pushing for Responsibility to Protect (R2P) with the international community and the United Nations Security Council (UNSC), albeit with limited ability to remove President Assad from power without regional and UNSC support.

Formal responsibilities and objectives: economic integration

The Shia revolution in Iran in 1979 was the starting point for the development of the regional organization soon to become the GCC. Worries that the revolution would spill over to neighboring states and encourage Shia minorities to revolt against Sunni regimes led to intensified talks. The war between Iran and Iraq in 1980 was another triggering factor for regional cooperation (Utrikespolitiska institutet, 2006, p. 18). The GCC, with headquarters in Riyadh, Saudi Arabia, was founded in Abu Dhabi on May 25, 1981, based on a common decision by the Foreign Ministers' Summit in Riyadh on February 4, 1981 of Bahrain, Kuwait, Oman, Qatar, Saudi Arabia and the United Arab Emirates (Askari, 1982). The participating states agreed on establishing an intergovernmental organization with member-states bordering the Persian Gulf. The six member-states, of approximately 35 million people, had as an objective to counterbalance the politically stronger states of Iraq (about 26 million inhabitants) and Iran (about 70 million) by establishing deeper economic and political collaboration based on shared cultural and historical traits. Since 1981, the number of member-states has been consistent, but current negotiations continue with Yemen with an objective to enlarge the organization in 2016 or 2017 (Legranzi, 2011).

The GCC is formally structured as set out in Articles Six and Seven of the charter with a Supreme Council as the highest body comprising the six heads of member-states, a rotating presidency and one regular meeting each year if no member-states requested extra meetings. The overall responsibility of the Council is to assure the implementation of the objectives of the GCC or to assess common interests, set policies and relations to other states and organizations, approve rules and procedures for the Commission for Settlement and Disputes, appoint the secretary-general of the GCC and approve the overall budget of the Secretariat General (GCC Charter, 1981, Article 8). In short, the role of the secretary-general is to prepare for recommendations, plans and programs as well as to draft resolutions on cooperation requested by the Supreme and/or Ministerial Council (GCC Charter, 1981, Article 15). The Supreme Council also decide amendments to the GCC charter. Article Nine sets out the voting procedures among the six member-states. It is clearly stated that "[e]ach member of the Supreme Council shall have one vote" and that "[r]esolutions of the Supreme Council in substantive matters shall be carried by unanimous approval of the member-states participating in the voting, while resolutions on procedural matters shall be carried by majority vote." (GCC Charter, Article 9). This means that in all substantive matters concerning the organization, the decision-making procedure is intergovernmental with an ultimate veto right, as stated in the request for unanimous approval, for each of the six member-states. Structurally attached to the Supreme Council is a second body of the GCC, the Commissioner of the Settlement of Disputes. Article Ten sets out the role of the Commission to deal with disputes within the Supreme Council and/or the Ministerial Council on how to interpret and implement the objectives of the Charter. The Ministerial Council develops recommendations and reports on what the Supreme Council is advised to do regarding further integration and cooperation. The Ministerial Council consists of the foreign ministers of the member-states with assigned meetings every third month plus potential extra sessions (GCC Charter, 1981, Article 11). As is the case in the Supreme Council, the voting procedures within the Ministerial Council are based on one vote per member-state with an intergovernmental approach to substantive matters in the unanimous vote for member-states (GCC Charter, 1981, Article 13).

The GCC Charter set out that the main goal in providing closer cooperation is based on shared norms and values rooted in Islam. It was stated that with "faith in a common destiny and sharing one goal … cooperation among these states would serve the sublime objectives of the Arab nation" (GCC Charter, 1981, Concept and Foundations). Since its founding, the GCC has foremost been an economic, intergovernmental organization. The economic roots of the organization are visible in the objectives set out in Article Four of the Charter:

> To effect co-ordination, integration and inter-connection between member states in all fields in order to achieve unity between them. To deepen and strengthen relations, links and areas of cooperation now prevailing between their peoples in various fields. To formulate similar regulations in various fields including the following: Economic and financial affairs. Commerce, customs and communications. Education and culture. Social and health affairs. Information and tourism. Legislative and administrative affairs. To stimulate scientific and technological progress in the fields of industry, mining, agriculture, water and animal resources: to establish scientific research: to establish joint ventures and encourage cooperation by the private sector for the good of their peoples.
>
> (Colombo and Committeri, 2014)

In 1983, the GCC member-states agreed on a free trade area with freedom of movement and common rules and regulations on customs being implemented. In addition, the member-states also agreed on the Gulf Investment Corporation, an investment bank to provide for loans to new developments. These first steps of economic integration were in the mid-1980s followed by further harmonization regarding rules and regulations on commerce and trade. The GCC economic reforms halted, however, in the 1990s. This was due to the regional war between Iraq and Kuwait, the destabilization of the region at large and the economic recession. However, on December 31, 2001, the member-states of the GCC agreed on the Economic Agreement. The new agreement called for a GCC Free Trade Area with one common external custom rate toward third states as well as common laws and regulations on commercial, industrial and trade issues. The discussions in 2001 and onward were about providing for a common market (Article Three), a customs union (Article One) and an economic and monetary union (Article Four) and the ability to become a coherent international economic actor (Article Two). In January 2008, the GCC member-states finally implemented a common market, aiming at removing all national barriers for trade and investments. In December of 2009, four member-states—Bahrain, Kuwait, Qatar and Saudi Arabia—institutionalized a Monetary Council aiming at a future unified central bank system with one common currency. In 2005, the GCC member-states also agreed to engage the Greater Arab Free Trade Area (GAFTA) (Sturm and Siegfried, 2005).

Regime security and military integration?

Although the founding ideas of the GCC were primarily economic in nature, the GCC also emphasized in the 1981 charter other dimensions of integration in security and military integration as essential pillars to economic collaboration. The following was explicitly stressed:

> Recognizing that the economic development and prosperity of the GCC States can only be achieved within a safe and stable environment, and Inspired by the firm belief that the security of the GCC States is an integral entity, Their Majesties and Highnesses, leaders of the GCC States, have instructed Their Highnesses and Excellencies, the Interior Ministers of the GCC States to make contacts and coordination for holding a meeting to discuss and examine the mechanisms and requirements of the security cooperation among Member States.
>
> (GCC Secretariat General, 1981)

The negotiations that ended up in the GCC Charter of 1981 included discussions on regime security as a requirement for economic collaboration (Ramazani, 1988). The member-states commonly argued that their shared Arabic identity and their geographical closeness, embedding a common historical and religious heritage, should include a military/security commitment. At the very first meeting in Riyadh on February 23–24, 1982, principles and objectives for future developments within the GCC on security was identified. It was stressed that, “the GCC security is an integral whole, and any attack on any Member State means an attack on all Member States, and the responsibility of confronting the attack on any Member State is a collective one.” Further, “the interference by any entity whatsoever in the internal affairs of any member State means an intervention in the internal affairs of all Member States” (GCC Secretariat General, 1981).

The very first meeting on military cooperation was held at the first meeting in Riyadh on September 21, 1981 with explicit recommendations on military objectives to be commonly met by the member-states. These recommendations were further discussed at the second meeting in November 1981, leading up to the late January 1982 approval by all six defense ministers on how to address military collaboration. The first and perhaps most important decisions on military cooperation were made in October 1982, agreeing on the *Peninsula Shield Joint Forces*. The shared forces were to be located in Saudi Arabia with the mission to be launched swiftly in an event of an external attack. It was argued that the main objective was to uphold regime security while waiting for external military support from the US and/or UK. The expected help from these Western states was due to long-term cooperation between the US and most GCC member-states (*Kuwait Times*, 2013). As has been argued:

> Since the 1970s international involvement in the region has been dominated by the US in a drive initially to secure oil supply, and more recently to ensure security and stability by advocating political reform. To protect its interests in the region the US sought to ensure the stability of the oil producing countries by extending security guarantees to the Gulf states.
>
> (Echagüe, 2007, p. 6)

The overall ambition among the GCC member-states was to agree on developing one common army and to coordinate all weapons imports by the member-states. In the early 1990s, the GCC joint forces were limited to 7,000 soldiers, suggesting low capacity and credibility in the event of war. Despite decisions in the early 2000s on redeveloping the joint forces to reach a number of about 22,000 soldiers, few reforms were seen. It was not until late 2013 that the joint forces reached a number of about 30,000 soldiers. In 2003, when the US decided to invade Iraq, the GCC member-states agreed on moving the joint forces to Kuwait to secure Kuwait borders (Utrikespolitiska institutet, 2006, p. 19).

The war in Iraq and the September 11 attacks resulted in 2002 in the adoption by the GCC of a security strategy on terrorism, in 2004 a counter-terrorism agreement and in 2006 a permanent anti-terrorism committee was established with annual meetings held. Other security-related areas of collaboration have been cooperation against nuclear and radioactive risks, on drug control, on criminal investigations and inquiries, on border and coast guards, and in the field of penal and corrective institutions (GCC Secretariat General, 1981). The GCC supported the American invasion of Iraq in 1991, backed by a UN mandate, and the former President George W. Bush's declaration of the war on terrorism after the September 11 attacks of 2001 (Youngs, 2006; Utrikespolitiska institutet, 2006, pp. 18–25). The US military presence intensified with growing security dependence between the GCC and the US regarding oil exports to the US and US military bases in the GCC region (Echagüe, 2006, p. 7). In December of 2000, at the Twenty-first Session of the Supreme Council, the GCC member-states signed the GCC Joint Defense Agreement, including enhancing individual capacities to be coordinated efficiently to boost the quality of the Peninsula Shield Force. Other military areas of strategic importance for the GCC have been said to be the interconnection of the operations centers of the air forces and the air defense to improve the joint air defense and the regular implementation of joint land/air/sea exercises to assure high quality and coordinated GCC military missions (Baabood, 2005, p. 156).

GCC and R2P in Syria

The GCC member-states have individually intensified their international actions in the region, but more and more often, they have also used the organization as a legitimate platform to have a stronger say in regional disputes and conflicts. It should, however, be stressed that the GCC member-states have traditionally been conservative in their security efforts within the organization. The main focus has been on regime security and regime stability, rather than on human security and political reforms. The creation of the GCC was also a direct effect of regional instability and growing insecurity. It was the challenge to domestic security and stability that forced the six member-states to discuss how to defend their regimes from regional spillover effects from conflicts and wars. The founding principles are said to be maintaining amicable policies with member-states, respecting sovereignty and the principle of non-intervention, seeking peaceful settlements of disputes, and collectively supporting Arab and Islamic issues as well as enhancing peace processes in the Middle East. The tough stand on Syria should be viewed in light of a historical concern over regional insecurity and instability due to regime failure. The GCC had been engaged in the Iraq–Iran war of the 1980s (Ramazani, 1988, pp. 60–69). This long-term war destabilized the GCC region and caused insecurity and military threats to all neighboring states in the region, forcing GCC member-states to act diplomatically to halt the war. In the 1990s, the GCC strongly condemned the Iraqi invasion of Kuwait, declaring that Iraq needed to obey the demands set out in the various UN resolutions. As a consequence, the GCC member-states initiated talks with Egypt and Syria calling for closer collaboration. This was due to their support of the US-led UN mission to liberate Kuwait and the common stand that these states have had on the Iraqi occupation. In March 1991, the GCC member-states Egypt and Syria agreed on the Damascus Declaration with the objective to develop a regional peace force, forbid weapons of mass destruction in the region and seek a final solution to the Palestine–Israel conflict. Despite these ambitions, political disagreements on how to finance and compose the common peace force undermined the implementation of the Damascus Declaration (Utrikespolitiska institutet, 2006, p. 19). The GCC was also occupied by its political support of the United Arab Emirates (UAE) to regain sovereignty and political control over the three islands of the Greater Tunb, the Lesser Tunb and Abu Musa, which had been occupied by Iran. The GCC continuously worked on improving the diplomatic relations with Iran to find security and economic agreements with the country that could benefit the GCC individual member-states and the region at large (Pinfari, 2009).

The Arab Spring led the GCC to push for improved security in the region. It should be stressed that although the GCC regimes have been critical to how many regimes have treated their population, the main GCC concern has continued to be regime security and regional stability. The GCC member-states have shared concerns that regime abuses against civilians could trigger mass mobilization and riots against the regimes, which eventually could spill over and jeopardize the whole region, including GCC member-states. The escalation of violence in Syria was noted early by the GCC. The Syrian government's actions from 2011 onward have jeopardized regional stability, and the abuse of power against its civilians is a symbol of how President Assad has failed to provide for security within Syria and in the region. As a consequence, both Saudi Arabia and Qatar have stepped up efforts on security challenges and have used the GCC as a regional tool to develop a greater voice (Legranzi, 2011). The civil war and the obvious brutalities from both sides were acknowledged by the GCC, as they sought an immediate solution to the war through diplomatic talks.

The GCC's first step was to call for political reforms and for the Syrian regime to initiate peace talks with anti-government forces and reorganize the political and civil society systems. The GCC member-states initiated a series of diplomatic talks with Syria in Damascus asking for a political solution to the rising crisis. The GCC governments also conditionally offered economic assistance to the Syrian regime to see political measurements taken in the country. In spring 2011, after violent deterioration in Syria, King Abdullah of Saudi Arabia took the lead to initiate discussions with President Assad to convince him of the importance of implementing political reforms linked to external economic assistance and to halt the regime's brutal treatment of civilians. Within about half a year, the GCC stated that the Syrian regime seemed to be uninterested in a peaceful solution and that the regime's promises of seeking political reforms rang false. Meanwhile, the international community hoped for peace talks; the GCC stated that the Syrian regime delayed all political talks just to find time to mobilize military forces to be used against civilians. The GCC member-states also agreed that the harsh position taken by the regime only led to further demands from the population on reforms and that the GCC diplomatic approach was met by false promises from the regime (Sager, 2012).

A second step by the GCC was, due to the failed diplomatic talks with President Assad, to call for greater regional attention to increase the political pressure on the regime. The GCC acknowledged the common stand on Syria among the six member-states and agreed to reach out to other Arab states to commonly put pressure on President Assad to initiate political reforms, including constitutional changes and diplomatic talks with the opposition. One immediate step by the GCC was to discuss with the Arab League a wider Arabic diplomatic initiative on Syria. With the hope that they could successfully convince President Assad to launch political reforms, based on the greater legitimacy for the GCC in cooperation with the Arab League, the member-states were soon faced with another diplomatic failure, as the Syrian regime refused to follow through on the political demands arranged by the GCC member-states with others (Batty and Shenker, 2011). In November 2012, the Arab League decided to suspend Syria due to its unwillingness to obey a previously negotiated peace deal. The member-states also, to add pressure on President Assad, imposed economic and political sanctions. In agreement with all of the GCC member-states, the Qatari prime minister argued, “We are calling all Syrian opposition parties to a meeting at the Arab League headquarters to agree to a unified vision for the transitional period” (Batty and Shenker, 2011). The GCC and the Arab League mutually requested the loyal forces of the regime to cease attacks on civilians and to stop supporting President Assad. The Syrian National Council applauded the decision, acknowledging that the suspension of the Syrian regime from the Arab League was a decision favoring the popular revolution by isolating President Assad and the Syrian regime. Approximately one year after the decision to suspend Syria from the Arab League, the GCC member-states approved the new national coalition of the Syrian opposition as the representative body of Syria. The decision was made to emphasize the illegitimacy of President Assad and his regime as well as to push for a transfer of power in Syria. The GCC, with support from the Arab League through its recognition of the national coalition with granted observer status, aimed at convincing other regional organizations and individual states to demand a new Syrian regime. In March 2013, the Arab League allowed the coalition to replace Syria’s seat in the organization to represent the Syrian people (Aljazeera, 2012).

A third step taken by the GCC was to approach the UN Security Council and demand military action. The GCC called upon the Security Council to take immediate actions to halt the ongoing civil war and to take actions to protect civilians. The GCC argued that it was the legal and moral obligation of the Security Council to intervene, and it defined the regime’s brutal actions as genocide. The tough stand on Syria from the GCC member-states were undermined by the Russian and Chinese veto, leaving without any affirmative response the GCC’s demand to act upon the genocide in Syria (Sager, 2012). In December of 2013, the GCC member-states finally, after years of ambitions to promote military integration, also agreed on how to develop a shared military command structure. When the agreement was announced, the member-states stated that a new Syria had to be supported and that President Assad was responsible for growing insecurity in the region by using chemical weapons and causing genocide. The GCC announced its military command structure as a direct reply to what GCC member-states saw as foreign military support to the illegitimate Syrian regime. While approving the new development in Iran, which led to somewhat better diplomatic relations to the GCC, GCC member-states accused Iran and other regional powers of backing up President Assad, despite obvious evidence that he had committed atrocities against civilians (*Al Arabiya News*, 2013; *Daily News*, 2013).

The tougher stand by the GCC on Syria over time has led to hostile reactions from the Syrian regime. In December 2013, the Syrian regime accused the GCC of “inflammatory rhetoric” (*Kuwait Times*, 2013) and of interfering in Syrian domestic politics. The Syrian foreign minister responded to the explicit call from GCC member-states that President Assad could not have any future in Syria and specifically accused Qatar and Saudi Arabia of sponsoring terrorism in Syria and of escalating the violence in Syria by backing the anti-government forces, undermining the security and stability of the country. The harsher tone from the Syrian regime was the direct consequence of GCC statements on genocide and massacres by the Syrian regime and on how the Syrian regime had lost all legitimacy.

On January 23, 2014, the UN initiative in Geneva for peace talks on Syria began, and it included representatives of the Syrian regime and the opposition. During the first day of talks, however, the GCC member-states demanded an exclusion of Iran, which had been invited to the talks. The GCC contended that Iran was destabilizing the region with its nuclear projects, its support to Hezbollah and its systematic military support of President Assad. The GCC had explicitly charged President Assad with committing genocide; thus, any state providing military assistance to such a leader would not have anything to offer in fruitful negotiations for a peaceful future in Syria. The GCC's demand to exclude Iran was fulfilled, creating further tension between the Syrian regime and its allies with the GCC member-states and Western actors supportive of GCC's stance on Syria. The GCC consistently argued for a new, liberated Syria. The GCC also argued that President Assad had committed war crimes leading to the obvious risk of destabilizing spillover effects into Lebanon and Iraq. The GCC, however, also addressed the danger of Al-Qaeda in Styria and how the international community had to be determined to promote a new Syria (Karasik, 2014; Black, 2013).

With a divided Security Council, the GCC has continued to push for immediate actions on President Assad. Both Saudi Arabia and Qatar explicitly argued for assisting the opposition with military equipment, accusing both Iran and Hezbollah in Lebanon of providing military assistance to the Syrian regime. The GCC member-states had, in discussions with the North Atlantic Treaty Organization (NATO) member-states, declared the importance of providing the opposition with military means. Although the GCC stated that supplying weapons to anti-government forces in Syria was not an ideal solution to halting the violence in the country, it agreed that all other viable solutions had been halted by the Syrian regime or by the Russian and Chinese stance on Syria in the Security Council (Sager, 2012). Both the Qatari Prime Minister Hamad bin Jassim al-Thani and the Saudi Arabia Foreign Minister Saud al-Faisal argued in favor of arming the Syrian opposition. Such assistance would consist of military training, equipment, and strategic planning as well as, perhaps, direct engagement on Syrian territory with foreign specialized troops assisting the opposition.

Saudi Arabia has an active track record on unconventional warfare operations and in supporting oppositions against regimes. It was engaged in the north Yemen civil war and in providing support to jihadi forces in Afghanistan against the Soviet occupation. In 2009, Saudi forces were also engaged in northern Yemen against rebel forces. Both the UAE and Qatar have also had experience in providing foreign military support. The UAE has been involved in funding and training operations to develop Jordanian forces to be used against rebels. The UAE has, over the last eight years, developed a special force launched in Afghanistan with the capacity to implement combat operations against the

Taliban. In addition, the UAE has also supplied Lebanon with large amounts of military equipment, from vehicles and helicopters to anti-riot gear for security forces to use. There is also a historical record of peacekeeping forces deployed in Lebanon, Somalia and the Balkans in the 1990s. It should also be mentioned that the GCC was supportive of military attacks on Libya and Muammar Gaddafi. Both Qatar and the United Arab Emirates provided Special Forces inside Libya to force Gaddafi from power. These two powers were coordinated with the NATO forces and assisted Libyan rebels on the ground. They also deployed aircraft against Libyan aircrafts, tanks and vehicles on the ground.

In sum, based on the security objectives of the GCC, in regime security and regional stability, the GCC member-states all contributed with foreign assistance to one or more states over the last decades. Such military support has been provided to regimes, challenged by rebels or armed oppositions and provided to rebels and opposition forces to facilitate a transfer of power. Although the most recent trend among GCC member-states is to support the established regime to be protected from the transfer of power by rebels or armed opposition, such as in Afghanistan, Bahrain, Lebanon and post-Gaddafi Libya, the recent support to force Gaddafi out of power by Qatar and the United Arab Emirates opened discussions on what the GCC could do to President Assad (Knights, 2012). In June of 2012, both the Saudis and Qatar had decided to arm the opposition in Syria. While such assistance to the opposition also came from the US, the UK and Turkey, President Assad received military assistance from Russia, Iran and Hezbollah. The GCC had gone from soft talks with Syria to convince the regime to halt violence and engage political reforms to direct military assistance to anti-government forces.

Remaining R2P Challenges for GCC on Syria?

The GCC stands on Libya and Syria illustrate that the member-states are in no way unwilling to take robust actions against such states. However, the GCC interference in Syria has so far not progressed beyond diplomatic and economic isolation and military assistance from some of the GCC member-states. A major difference between Syria and Libya is President Assad's regional and international support from strong powers such as Iran, Russia and China with their proclamation of state sovereignty and non-intervention. It appears that the GCC member-states would approve military intervention and a forced transfer of power from President Assad, albeit only with an international mandate from the UN Security Council. The GCC has a strong interest in a change of power in Syria, and there is regional support both within the GCC and within the Arab League to see that such transfer of power occurs. There are other regional powers, such as Turkey and Jordan, which would support the departure of President Assad. Most factors involved in the Libyan case are, therefore, also visible in Syria but with the difference in the implacably divided UN Security Council and the strong ties between Russia and Syria (Knights, 2012). As the Washington Institute stated:

> GCC military intervention in Syria's civil war could provide a significant boost to the opposition Free Syrian Army's viability as a military force. But such intervention will only come about if Saudi Arabia, Qatar, and the UAE receive a mandate from a major international forum, and if a military ally such as Turkey or Jordan strongly commits to the endeavour.
>
> (Knights, 2012)

In addition to the divided UN Security Council and the strong ties between Russia and Syria are the policy consequences of GCC intervention in Syria. Over the years of escalating war in Syria, the opposition, which has been supported by the GCC and others, has become more and more heterogeneous, including radical forces with few common interests with GCC member-states. There is a growing risk that international support of opposition forces includes support of extremist Islamist forces with no interest in a new, liberated Syria. The region has also become very vulnerable to political changes, as the Syrian war has spilled over into other parts of the region in terms of refugee flows and military arms trade and assistance to neighboring states. A GCC intervention does not only have to take into account Russian reactions but also how Iran and the Hezbollah would react, as we know that these states have been very supportive of President Assad, particularly providing diplomatic, financial and military support (Knights, 2012).

The lack of the UN Security Council and, thus, a firm international mandate to intervene in Syria, the strong links between Russia and Syria and the divided opposition forces are three major obstacles for GCC actions on Syria. However, there are also challenges besides these that are determining the GCC actions on Syria. Although the organization today is only composed of six member-states and despite the fact that these member-states in the charter and elsewhere have expressed their geographical and Arabic commonalities, it is obvious that the Syrian case has led to internal disagreements on how far the GCC is ready to go with President Assad. While Qatar and Saudi Arabia have launched military assistance to opposition forces to see a transfer of power, other member-states, such as the United Arab Emirates, Oman and Kuwait, have been less focused on regime change in Syria. Oman has historically cooperated with Iran and has, therefore, been less outspoken on all challenges that have come with President Assad, while Bahrain has felt threatened by potential Iranian attacks, particularly regarding whether it is viewed as being too harsh on Syria (Amal, 2013). There are also recent examples of political tension within the GCC that have challenged the notion of being one coherent player in international politics. Saudi Arabia has shown tendencies to perceive US security commitment in the region as undergoing change. This has worried Saudi Arabia, especially when the US and Iran have worked toward improved diplomatic relations. At the end of 2013, Saudi Arabia also learned that Oman had conducted security talks on nuclear energy with the US and Iran at the same time that Oman had expressed its disinterest in future political integration in the GCC. When the Saudis pushed the GCC for further integration to become a stronger security player in the region,

Oman has stressed a neutral position in security, trying to stay friendly with the GCC member-states and Iran (Black, 2013). Oman has preferred to see military integration with support from the US, while Saudi Arabia has been in favor of developing a GCC military shield that is less dependent on a US security umbrella (Ryan, 2014). It is obvious that the minor GCC member-states have continued to rely on US security guarantees in a time of security challenges, which have included defense pacts with the US as well as military sales packages (Salel, 2006; Cloud and Cooper, 2007). While most integration is found in the economic and social sectors, the collaboration on military and security-related issues has been challenged by the overall different objectives by GCC member-states. For example, all discussions on modernizing the joint forces to increase the number of military training operations and to develop a common warning and surveillance system have led to disagreements on financing and on how the military system to be used. The contemporary political differences among the GCC member-states also have a historical record of disputes.

In the 1980s, diplomatic challenges escalated between Bahrain and Qatar regarding the control of the potential oil sources in Fasht al-Dibal-reven. The International Court of Justice reached a final solution after Qatar decided to find a judicial result to the conflict. Territorial disputes have also existed between Saudi Arabia and Qatar and led to chilly relations between the two in the early 1990s with a final settlement in 1997. In addition, political tensions continued to trouble the GCC in the early 1990s when Kuwait and Qatar refused to sign a GCC agreement on the challenges of criminality and terrorism. Kuwait argued that such an agreement was against its constitution, while Qatar, with territorial disputes in mind, argued that Saudi Arabia was too powerful within the organization.

Conclusion

Although the GCC has primarily been an economic intergovernmental organization, regional instability and the regional hegemonic powers of Iran and Iraq have consistently reminded the GCC member-states of the common interest to develop a coherent regional security arrangement. However, despite historical conflicts and the present destabilizing effects of the Syrian civil war, the GCC member-states have been unable to find common ground on how such a security arrangement should be designed. Within the GCC, Saudi Arabia is the most powerful member-state—both politically and militarily. While Saudi Arabia has pushed for a common military stance on Syria, the minor member-states have tried to limit Saudi influence within the GCC and the region at large. The most problematic challenge to a GCC security arrangement is the unwillingness of member-states to develop a common security and defense policy. The GCC member-states have been outspoken on the atrocities in Syria. Their shared statements on R2P by the international community to stop the ongoing genocide symbolizes that the GCC has improved its capability to speak with one voice about security matters. The historical and contemporary tension between major and minor states within the organization, their different relationships to major regional states and the member-states' different objectives on the core purposes of the GCC, however, leave the GCC with limited abilities to act upon R2P toward the Syrian regime. The diplomatic relationships between the GCC and Syria are today are at a standstill and have deteriorated to such a level that some GCC member-states provide anti-government forces with military assistance. This is a direct consequence of failed bilateral talks between the GCC and Syria, failed economic initiatives to the Syrian regime to promote political reforms, and failed UN efforts to find a common ground for building a new Syria.

References

Al Arabiya News (2013, December 11). *GCC to form unified military command.* Retrieved from: http://english.alarabiya.net/en/News/middle-east/2013/12/11/Gulf-states-focus-on-Iran-Syria-at-summit.html (accessed July 26, 2014).

Al-Mani, S. (2006, July). The Search for an Optimal Gulf Security Regime. *GCC-EU Research Bulletin* 5.

Aljazeera (November 12 2012). *GCC recognises new Syrian opposition bloc – Recognition by the Gulf Co-operation Council comes as Arab foreign ministers deliberate the Syrian crisis in Cairo.* Retrieved from: www.aljazeera.com/news/middleeast/2012/11/20121112175539534504.html (accessed August 5, 2014).

Amal, A. K. (2013, Winter). Regional Upheaval: The Stakes for the GCC. *The Middle Eat Policy Council.* Retrieved from: www.mepc.org/journal/middle-east-policy-archives/regional-upheaval-stakes-gcc (accessed August 5, 2014).

Arab News (2014, March 5). *GCC toughens Syria stance.* Retrieved from: www.arabnews.com/news/535081 (accessed August 5, 2014).

Askari, Hasan R. (1982). Gulf Cooperation Council. *Pakistan Horizon, 35,* 29–38.

Baabood, A. (2005). Dynamics and Determinants of the GCC States' Foreign Policy, with Special reference to the EU. In G. Nonneman (ed.). *Analyzing Middle East Foreign Policies.* New York: Routledge.

Batty, D. and Shenker, J. (2011, November 12). *Syria suspended from Arab League – Member states agree to exclude Syria and impose sanctions over its failure to end government crackdown on protests.* Retrieved from: www.theguardian.com/world/2011/nov/12/syria-suspended-arab-league (accessed July 16, 2014).

Black, I. (2013, December 12). Gulf widens as Iran returns from cold – General view of the opening session of the 34th Gulf Cooperation Council summit held in Kuwait City on 10 December 2013. *Guardian.* Retrieved from: www.theguardian.com/world/on-the-middle-east/2013/dec/12/iran-saudi-gulf-gcc-oman (accessed July 17, 2014).

Cairo Post (2013, December 11). *Syria rejects statement of GCC summit.* Retrieved from: http://thecairopost.com/news/53578/news/syria-rejects-statement-gcc-summit. (accessed August 5, 2014).

Cloud, D. S. and Cooper, H. (2007, April 5). Israel's Protests Are Said to Stall Gulf Arms Sale. *New York Times.* Retrieved from: http://select.nytimes.com/search/restricted/article?res=F40F10FA3D5B0C768CDDAD0894DF404482 (accessed July 21, 2014).

Colombo, S. and Committeri, C. (2014). Need to Rethink the EU-GCC Strategic Relation. In Silvia Colombo (ed.). *Bridging the Gulf: EU – GCC Relations at a Crossroads.* IAI Research Paper. Retrieved from: www.iai.it/pdf/Quaderni/iairp_14.pdf (accessed July 21, 2014).

Daily News (2013, December 12). *Leave Syria, GCC urges foreign forces to leave.* Retrieved from: at www.hurriyetdailynews.com/leave-syria-gcc-urges-foreign-forces-to-leave.aspx?pageID=238&nID=59433&NewsCatID=352 (accessed July 21, 2014).

Echagüe, A. (2007). *The European Union and the Gulf Cooperation Council.* FRIDE – Fundación Para Las Relaciones Internacionales Y El Diálogo Exteriror – Working Paper No. 39. Retrieved from: www.fride.org/descarga/WP39_EU_Persian_Gulf_EN_may07.pdf (accessed July 16, 2014).

GCC Charter Article 5 (1981). *GCC Charter 1981 – Council Membership.* Retrieved from: www.gcc-sg.org/eng/index895b.html?action=Sec-Show&ID=3 (accessed July 16, 2014).

GCC Charter Article 8 (1981). *The Functions of the Supreme Council.* Retrieved from: www.gcc-sg.org/eng/index895b.html?action=Sec-Show&ID=3 (accessed July 16, 2014).

GCC Charter Article 15 (1981). *The Functions of the Secretariat General.* Retrieved from: www.gcc-sg.org/eng/index895b.html?action=Sec-Show&ID=3 (accessed July 16, 2014).

GCC Charter Article 9 (1981). *Voting in the Supreme Council.* Retrieved from: www.gcc-sg.org/eng/index895b.html?action=Sec-Show&ID=3 (accessed July 16, 2014).

GCC Charter Article 11 (1981). Ministerial *Council.* Retrieved from: www.gcc-sg.org/eng/index895b.html?action=Sec-Show&ID=3 (accessed July 16, 2014).

GCC Charter Article 13 (1981). Voting in the Ministerial *Council.* Retrieved from: www.gcc-sg.org/eng/index895b.html?action=Sec-Show&ID=3. (accessed July 16, 2014).

GCC Charter Concept and Foundations (1981). Council Membership. Retrieved from: www.gcc-sg.org/eng/index895b.html?action=Sec-Show&ID=3 (accessed July 16, 2014).

GCC Secretariat General (1981). *Military Cooperation.* Retrieved from: www.gcc-sg.org/eng/index895b.html?action=Sec-Show&ID=3 (accessed July 17, 2014).

GCC Secretariat General (1981). *Security Cooperation.* Retrieved from: www.gcc-sg.org/eng/index895b.html?action=Sec-Show&ID=3 (accessed July 17, 2014).

Karasik, T. (2014, January 23). *GCC reactions to Geneva II are on the right track.* In Al Arabiya News. Retrieved from: http://english.alarabiya.net/en/views/2014/01/22/GCC-Reactions-to-Geneva-II-are-on-the-Right-Track.html (accessed July 20, 2014).

Knights, M. (2012, April 17). Could the Gulf States Intervene in Syria? *The Washington Institute.* Retrieved from: www.washingtoninstitute.org/policy-analysis/view/could-the-gulf-states-intervene-in-syria (accessed July 17, 2014).

Kuwait Times (2013, December 12). GCC *wants militias out of Syria, hails Iran shift.* Retrieved from: http://news.kuwaittimes.net/gcc-wants-militias-syria-hails-iran-shift (accessed July 20, 2014).

Legranzi, M. (2011). The GCC and the International *Relations of the Gulf: Diplomacy, Security and Economic Coordination in a Changing Middle East.* London: I. B. Tauris.

Pinfari, M. 2009. Nothing but Failure? – The Arab league and the Gulf Cooperation Councils as Mediators in Middle Eastern Conflicts. Crisis States Research Center, No. 5—The London School of Economics. Retrieved from: www.lse.ac.uk/internationalDevelopment/research/crisisStates/download/wp/wpSeries2/WP452.pdf (accessed July 17, 2014).

Ramazani, R. K. (1988). *The Gulf Cooperation Council – Records and Analysis.* Charlottesville: The University Press of Virginia.

Ryan, C. (2014, April 15). Jordan, Morocco and an Expanded GCC. *Middle East Research and Information Project.* Retrieved from: www.merip.org/jordan-morocco-expanded-gcc (accessed July 21, 2014).

Sager, A. (2012, November 12). *Arming the Syrian Opposition – The GCC and the Syrian Crisis*. Retrieved from: www.worldsecuritynetwork.com/Syria/Sager-Abdulaziz/Arming-the-Syrian-Opposition-The-GCC-and-the-Syrian-Crisis (accessed July 21, 2014).

Sturm, M. and Siegfried, N. (2005). Regional Monetary Integration in the Member States of the Gulf Cooperation Council. Occasional Paper Series No. 31, June 2005. Retrieved from: www.ecb.europa.eu/pub/pdf/scpops/ecbocp31.pdf (accessed July 22, 2014).

Utrikespolitiska institutet (2006). *Regionala organisationer i Mellanöstern och Nordafrika*. Stockholm: UI.

Youngs, R. (2006). *Europe and the Middle East: In the Shadow of 11 September*. Boulder: Lynne Rienner.

9 NATO

Daniel Silander

The North Atlantic Treaty Organization (NATO) was founded in 1949 based on the principles formulated by Winston Churchill and Franklin D. Roosevelt in the Atlantic Charter of 1941. This Charter emphasized core principles for the national policies of the US and United Kingdom on how to provide security for a recovered world. A changed world was to be based on self-determination, market economy, and transatlantic, collective security (Gudmundsson, 2000, pp. 10–11). In 1949, consisting of Belgium, Canada, Denmark, France, Iceland, Italy, Luxembourg, Netherlands, Norway, Portugal, the UK and the US, NATO was founded as a symbol of transatlantic, political integration (Medcalf, 2006, pp. 1–2).

The Washington Treaty consisted of 14 paragraphs of shared norms and values (Gress, 1998). During the Cold War, NATO expanded to include Greece (1952), Turkey (1952), Germany (1955) and Spain (1982); in the post-Cold War era, the Czech Republic, Hungary and Poland (1999); followed by Bulgaria, Estonia, Latvia, Lithuania, Romania, Slovakia and Slovenia (2004); and finally Albania and Croatia (2009) (Kay, 2011, pp. 27–28; Michta, 1999; Sloan, 2003). Today, the organization consists of 28 member-states. For each new member-state, NATO symbolized not only an important security umbrella but also a political revolution to become a member of the Western community. If the NATO of the twentieth century was an organization to deter communism, the NATO of the twenty-first century has come to focus on a complex set of security challenges beyond NATO territory. Based on this transformation, this chapter explores the normative nature of NATO and its role to protect human security in failed states such as Syria. Although NATO has not officially endorsed R2P, the organization has a normative basis that could lead to a comprehensive human security agenda. The challenges ahead for such development are identified.

Formal responsibilities of NATO

The Washington Treaty expresses how the objectives of the organization "are to safeguard the freedom, common heritage and civilizations of their peoples, founded on the principles of democracy, individual liberty and the rule of law" (Kay, 2011; Michta, 1999; Sloan, 2003). NATO is an exclusive organization by accepting member-states that share the founding norms and values of the organization (Sloan, 1995, p. 220). The cooperation on defense and security among 28 member-states is based on democratic norms and values to assure a common approach to peace and security (Whitehead, 2001). Each member-state is also responsible, under Article 5, to safeguard other member-states. Article 5 stresses that "[t]he parties agree that an armed attack against one or more of them in Europe or North America shall be considered an attack against them all" (The Washington Treaty, Article 5). Based on Article 51 of the UN Charter, Article 5 embeds a commitment to see an attack on a member-state as an attack against NATO. It also sets out the right to collective self-defense and to use necessary means to restore peace and security (The Washington Treaty, Article 5).

All NATO actions must represent the collective will of member-states. NATO refers to the importance of variable geometry, meaning that cooperation and military operations do not necessarily require all member-states to participate. As long as fundamental norms and values are shared among member-states and member-states have equal say, NATO activities may be implemented by a few or a coalition of member-states. Article 9 provides for equal representation from member-states and sets out the North Atlantic Council (NAC) to be the platform for meetings to decide on committees, institutions and missions. NAC is chaired by the secretary-general, and meetings take place between permanent representatives, foreign and/or defense ministers, and heads of governments. NATO is further structured into 39 principal committees that include representatives from all member-states. Article 9 has implied that major changes in organizational structure and performance are authorized without any need for constitutional changes to the Treaty. It has left NATO with great leverage in adapting the organization to the spirit of the time (Edström and Gyllensporre, 2012a, pp. 46–54).

The end of the Cold War highlighted NATO's future responsibilities (Kissinger 1990; Owen 1993; Steel, 1989; Mearsheimer, 1990). NATO continued to exist based on the embedded flexibility provided by Article 9, but also due to its normative basis of shared norms and values (Moore, 2007, pp. 10–11). In the early 1990s, NATO began to redevelop its organization and responsibilities. First, all NATO member-states desired to see NATO continue to exist as a security provider to its member-states. In July 1990, NATO member-states gathered at the London top meeting to develop NATO's future role. The intensive discussions continued with a top meeting in Rome in November 1991. These two meetings set out the new responsibilities for NATO in a post-Cold War context. One responsibility was to continue to protect member-states from military threat (The Alliance New Strategic Concept, 1991). In addition, NATO gained a new responsibility in dealing with neighboring post-communist states. After decades of Soviet oppression, post-communist states longed for a security provider against potential Russian expansionism (Zeliko, 1997, pp. 84–88). Joining NATO was about rejoining Europe. Article 10 set out the possibility to become a member-state, stressing that NATO may "invite any other European state in a position to further principles of this Treaty and to contribute to the security of the North Atlantic area to accede to this Treaty" (The Washington Treaty, 1949). In the early 1990s, NATO became an important norm-promoter in Eastern Europe. By emphasizing its collective strategy, NATO provided instruction activities on democracy, the rule of law, and security to neighboring states (Schimmelfennig, 2002, pp. 1–9). The Washington Treaty of 1949 embedded NATO's normative basis of democracy, liberty and rule of law. The organization was founded by democratically elected regimes and continued to expand its number of member-states based on the requirement of sharing common democratic norms and values. The end of the Cold War was therefore a triumph for NATO. It was argued that peace and security were to be built upon NATO's founding norms and values of democracy, individual liberty, and the rule of law (Solana, 1999) and how the new mission of NATO was to "help build the structure of a more united continent, supporting security and stability with the strength of our shared faith in democracy, the rights of the individual and the peaceful resolution of disputes" (Declaration on a Transformed North Atlantic Alliance, 1990a). At the NATO top meeting in London July 5–6, 1990, member-states declared that:

> Europe has entered a new, promising era. Central and Eastern Europe is liberating itself. The Soviet Union has embarked on the long journey towards a free society. The walls that once confined people and ideas are collapsing. Europeans are determining their own destiny. They are choosing freedom. They are choosing economic liberty. They are choosing peace. They are choosing a Europe whole and free. As a consequence, the Alliance must and will adapt.
>
> (Declaration on a Transformed North Atlantic Alliance, 1990b, p. 273)

At the Rome Summit in 1991, NATO declared the New Security Concept of NATO. It included a helping hand for the security of neighboring and post-communist states while acknowledging Russian interests (Asmus *et al.*, 1997, pp. 107–112; Brown, 1997, pp. 121–131). NATO decided to be a diplomatic liaison and military contact for all interested neighbors and to establish multilateral consultations through the North Atlantic Cooperation Council (NACC), which was replaced in 1997 with the Euro-Atlantic Partnership Council (EAPC). The EAPC aimed at improving the Partner for Peace program (PfP) (Williams, 1997, pp. 221–232) to become an institution for decision-making, planning, and implementation of operative functions (Allin, 1997). The PfP was decided at the Brussels Summit of 1994 and included more than 20 PfP states (Partnership for Peace, 1994, p. 120). NATO also took further steps to approach the Eastern European region; in 2002, the Individual Partnership Action Plan was launched, and special partnerships or relationships were developed with Georgia, Ukraine, and Russia, among others (Edstsröm *et al.*, 2011, p. 3).

Second, NATO also gained new responsibilities to deal with the new type of war in the world. The wars in the Balkans of the early 1990s re-emphasized the conceptual missions that were under development within NATO. With the disappearance of the communist threat, NATO needed a new operative mission to stay alert and relevant. The operations in the Balkans provided for lively debates at NATO on how to address future crises (Medcalf, 2006, p. 40). The dissolution of the former Yugoslavia had forced NATO to respond by pushing for a UN arms embargo on military equipment in the Adriatic Sea (Larsdotter, 2012, 60). NATO also ensured the establishment of a no-fly zone, authorized by the UN Security Council. It assisted UN peacekeepers with supportive airstrikes against Bosnian Serb air forces, Operation Deadeye, and was followed by Operation Deliberate Force aiming at Bosnian Serb command installations and ammunition centers. The pre- and post-events at the Dayton Peace Accord in late 1995 engaged NATO both as an Implementation Force (IFOR) and a Stabilization Force (SFOR). In December 1995, about 60,000 forces were deployed as part of IFOR to oversee the implementation of the Dayton Peace Treaty and in 1997; SFOR was deployed in Bosnia with a more limited military presence of 24 battalions (Medcalf, 2006, pp. 29–31; Moore, 2007, pp. 29–30). NATO was also active in the Former Yugoslav Republic of Macedonia (FYROM) in 2001 when the Macedonian regime invited NATO to operate to disarm Albanian forces. Operation Essential Harvest was followed by Operation Amber Fox, referring to the military protection of international observers in Macedonia to assess the consolidation of the peace plan. The final mission was Operation Allied Harmony, which embedded support for the government institutions to uphold law and order in society (Larsdotter, 2012, pp. 98–100; Moore, 2007, p. 52). In 1999, the Kosovo crisis escalated. On March 23, 1999, Secretary-General Javier Solana authorized air raids. NATO argued that the UN Security Council failed to fulfill its duties to protect civilians from ongoing atrocities and that the UN's wait-and-see policy jeopardized regional stability. On June 20, 1999, Serbian forces withdrew from Kosovo and in about a week, a NATO-led multinational peace force for Kosovo (KFOR) was in place. NATO's engagement in Kosovo was unique in the sense that the organization did not act as a subcontractor to the UN Security Council, but independently in the name of humanitarian intervention (Silander, 2009).

Based on the experiences in the Balkans, NATO has profoundly redefined its role in international politics. NATO has gone from being a collective defense organization for state security, based on Article 5, to an organization pursuing non-Article 5 operations of crisis management, peacemaking, and peacekeeping in the name of human security. NATO has also redefined its territorial scope of operations, previously tied to Article 6, defining the treaty area, to become a global actor (Petersson, 2012, pp. 124–125). In 1999, NATO member-states agreed, at the top meeting in Washington, for a new Alliance Strategic Concept. The Alliance Strategic Concept held that although NATO was to continue to provide security and defense to its member-states, the new NATO missions included non-Article 5 duties such as humanitarian operations, conflict prevention, and crisis management outside of the NATO area.

Existing capabilities for implementation of R2P

In 2010, NATO defined for the third time in a post-Cold War context its new Strategic Security Concept. The previous strategy of downplaying the role of conventional forces in favor of rapid reaction forces, crisis management and global commitments to human security and democratic norms and values was highlighted (Petersson, 2012, pp. 125–126). Already in 1994, and as a consequence of the Balkan wars, NATO leaders had decided on the Combined Joint Task Forces (CJTF). This new concept referred to NATO's new ambition to develop mobile and flexible military forces to address new patterns of conflicts and crisis in failing states. CJTF aimed at providing for rapid military force to be launched in the event of a sudden crisis in which peacekeeping and/or peacemaking was necessary. The CJTF has been described as a multinational, task-tailored force of NATO and non-NATO participants aimed at quick deployment in complex security situations.

One such complex security situation involved the September 11 events in 2001. NATO member-states quickly realized that "security could no longer be conceived in purely regional terms" (Moore, 2007, p. xi). An attack on strategic military and economic centers of the US had been due to failing states geographically far from NATO territory (Schreer, 2012, p. 140). As a consequence, NATO developed numerous missions out of its area. These included counter-piracy missions, such as Operation Allied Provider, Operation Allied Protector, and Operation Ocean Shield. NATO also promoted the African Union (AU) in peacekeeping missions throughout Africa, such as in Darfur and Sudan from 2005 to 2007 (Gyllensporre, 2012, pp. 157–161). NATO also stepped in and took command of the International Security Assistance Force (ISAF) to allow the UN to assist the Transitional Authority of Afghanistan to be established (Moore, 2007, pp. 31, 34). In addition, acknowledging the humanitarian catastrophe in Libya, NATO member-states, with support from the AU and the Arab League, requested humanitarian action to stop the regime from committing further atrocities. UN Resolutions 1970 and 1973 applied a no-fly zone, an arms embargo, and the protection of civilians in Libya. In March 2011, NATO enforced the no-fly zone and was soon the sole commander of all military missions in Libya under the name "Operation Unified Protector" (Engelbrekt *et al.*, 2014).

The NATO Summit of 2004 explicitly pointed out the Caucasus and Central Asia as strategic areas resulting in two liaison officers and the employment of one NATO special representative to these regions. In addition, the Summit also highlighted the importance of the Mediterranean Dialogue from 1994 and was now reinforced by intensifying bilateral and multilateral meetings with the NAC within the framework of PFP. The Mediterranean Dialogue countries included Algeria, Egypt, Israel, Jordan, Mauritania, Morocco and Tunisia. Another initiative was the Istanbul Cooperation Initiative (ICI), a program for developing security collaboration between NATO and states in the Middle East such as Bahrain, Kuwait, Qatar and the United Arab Emirates (Moore, 2007, pp. 116–122). In 2008, the Bucharest

Summit emphasized the importance for NATO to continue to develop security collaboration in different regions around the world. It was argued that these types of "partnerships" (Kay, 2011, pp. 18–36) would enhance the political dialogue between NATO and important "Contact Countries" (CC) that share the normative basis of NATO (Edström *et al.*, 2011, p. 4). The partnerships aimed at providing a buffer against potential enemies and to provide NATO with additional military assistance (Matlay, 2011, pp. 60–64). As was argued:

> The Alliance seeks a wider engagement, including political dialogue and practical cooperation, with like-minded nations that do not have a formal partnership arrangement in order to enhance regional security all across the globe.
>
> (Edström and Gyllensporre, 2012b, p. 6)

At the NATO Summit in Chicago of 2012, all 28-member-states agreed that peace and security required three tasks for NATO: providing collective defense, crisis management, and cooperative security. The NATO Defense Planning Process (NDPP) became the operational structure in which individual member-states and the alliance at large were to be integrated. The defense planning included, on a four-year basis, the capacities each individual state had to provide to the organization. The "Chicago Defense Package" of necessary capabilities of the Alliance included capabilities to address nuclear attacks; ballistic, chemical, biological and cyber-attacks from states or terrorist organizations; but also capabilities embedded in CJTF to meet the multidimensional challenges provided by failing states. The NATO Response Force (NRF) included multinational forces capable of missions on land, in the air and offshore. The NRF is a technological advanced force that was to be implemented swiftly and efficiently in the event of any kind of crisis in the world that requires military force or crisis management operations. The NRF has come to be NATO's major symbol of a new political and military alliance of the twenty-first century. The defense package explicitly addressed the importance of developing a Smart Defense. Smart Defense referred to the financial burden to meet technological requirements and challenges and the importance of collaboration among member-states to develop security capabilities. Such security capabilities included strengthened cooperation in assessing security challenges, training military and civilian know-how within the organization, protecting and assisting troops in the field, and developing necessary industrial projects to produce capabilities for the future.

NATO human security and R2P?

The London Declaration of 1990 had visualized NATO's new mission to promote NATO's norms and values beyond NATO areas to secure and stabilize the new post-Cold War world (Declaration on a Transformed North Atlantic Alliance 1990). As argued by the former Supreme Allied Commander of Europe, George A. Joulwan, in 1997, "We want our values to take root in other countries because that is the best way we know to prevent conflicts from exploding into war" (Joulwan in Moore, 2007, p. 2). The debates of the early 1990s on enlargement became a strategy of promoting stability through democratization. By offering potential membership and partnership, democratization could prevail in these fragile states within the security framework provided by NATO (Asmus *et al.*, 1997, pp. 94–96). NATO's prevailing capacity to provide security in the twenty-first century has been argued to be due to its normative basis (Flanagan, 1992, pp. 141–151). Scholars have pointed out that the democratic peace provided among the democratically elected member-states has been a pivotal source of transatlantic stability. NATO has provided an institutionalized and cultural determinant of required expectations and behavior to member-states and non-member-states (McCalla, 1995, pp. 445–475). The normative basis has not only consolidated NATO's existence. It has also guided NATO in its transformation over time and its current policies and partnerships in the world. "The liberal democratic values that NATO safeguarded during the Cold War are now understood to be norms that should govern the whole of Europe and even areas well beyond its borders" (Moore, 2007, p. 35).

In 2000, the US Department of Defense argued, "The security of the Euro-Atlantic Community must spring from the consent of free peoples and must be built upon shared purposes and values that can be defended when the need arises." In the twenty-first century, NATO's mission to promote security and stability has been based on the promotion and protection of democracy and human rights (Edström and Gyllensporre, 2012a, p. 6). NATO spokespersons have continuously argued that by expanding democracy in the world, peace and stability are to be secured. This has been called a "value-based security order" (Moore, 2007, p. 55). For example, NATO's intervention in Kosovo in 1999 was justified without a UN mandate as humanitarian to halt ongoing systematic human rights abuses by Serbian forces on Kosovo Albanians. NATO continued to provide security in Kosovo after the war, aiming to build democratic institutions and implement the rule of law. In addition, in Libya from 2010–11, protecting and promoting human security was ensured through regime change and democratization. Several powerful Western leaders argued in favor of military operations against the Gaddafi regime in the name of democracy, liberty, human security, and humanitarian obligations. The Secretary-General of NATO during the operations, Anders Fogh Rasmusen, concluded afterward,

> For many in Libya, NATO has literally made the difference between life and death. Operation Unified Protector has shown that when the cause is just—when the legal base is strong—and when the regional support is clear, NATO is the indispensable alliance.
>
> (Engelbrekt and Wagnsson, 2014, p. 1)

Several member-states had spoken out on the justness of the cause to deal with Gaddafi. The French government linked the call for freedom in Libya to the regional Arab uprisings and argued for military forces to protect civilians and assist the popular uprisings against the brutal regime. In addition, the UK government agreed with the French statements and stressed the importance of protecting human rights and civil liberties and international law. Both governments argued for a humanitarian position against the illegitimate and brutal dictatorship by focusing on finding support for a humanitarian intervention in the name of R2P. The American side agreed by arguing for humanitarian needs in Libya that had to be promoted by protecting human security and pushing for democracy (Janzekovic and Silander, 2013, pp. 109–116).

NATO, as a normative community of democratic member-states, has adhered to the moral obligation for any regime to represent its population and safeguard citizens. Therefore, the collective identity of NATO as a security provider is strongly linked to the normative foundation of the organization and its policies. However, the NATO bombings in Kosovo and Libya met serious criticism from other states. While the Kosovo bombings occurred without a UN mandate, criticism of NATO in Libya addressed how NATO had overstepped its UN mandate when operating to see regime change and not only establish and oversee a no-fly zone (Keller, 2011). Major states have come to see R2P simply as an extension of Western imperialism. The strong opposition to the notion of humanitarian intervention from major states intensified with the Libyan intervention. The accusation that the West overstepped its mandate has led to both China and Russia using the UNSC veto in the case of Syria. When France, the UK and the US called for actions against President Bashar al-Assad, they were met with accusations of double standards and hidden motives (Okeke, 2012). Instead of protecting civilians from harm's way, the West was criticized for pushing for regime change in Libya. Both China and Russia, and other major states have argued that this will not be allowed to happen in Syria (Davis, 2011).

Protecting universal rights and liberties and safeguarding civilians are embedded in the normative dimension of NATO. The transformation of NATO as an organization and in its responsibilities has also clearly led to a human security perspective. The changes from collective defense of NATO territory to peacemaking and peacekeeping as well as crisis management on a global level have addressed the new type of wars in the world in which civilians are too often abused. However, NATO has not developed a clear-cut strategy on R2P. Although post-Cold War crises clearly indicated that NATO has acted on the notion of R2P both as a moral and strategic imperative, the organization has not developed a comprehensive approach to systematic atrocities or genocide. Despite the numerous of transformations of responsibilities and definitions of NATO's new security concept, it has not formally endorsed R2P. Although several major member-states of NATO have officially accepted R2P, NATO has continued to stress the importance of democracy and human rights, but without embedding R2P in its formal responsibilities. In addition, NATO has only partly transformed its capacities to address human security and is still focusing much of its attention on the defense of NATO territory. By analyzing its efforts in Libya in the name of humanitarian intervention, NATO has an essential platform for discussions and reforms on R2P. It could include assessments on potential threats of ethnic cleansing, genocide and other atrocities, and on capabilities of protection and prevention and what internal adjustments NATO has taken to promote R2P as an "actionable norm" (Davis, 2011). It should be a logical step for NATO to endorse R2P and prepare its capacities and abilities to the ends of humanitarian protection and human security. NATO is a normative organization of embedded democratic norms and values that are strongly linked to the idea of safeguarding individual liberty and safety. It should therefore be an objective to be ready to take action to prevent mass atrocities.

A current development in NATO's work to foster human security through democratization is NATO's reform enshrined in UN Resolution 1325, decided upon in late 2000. It specifically addresses human security from a gender perspective. Acknowledging the serious human security challenges that come with failing states and war-torn societies, NATO focuses on the situation for women and children in failing states. Resolution 1325 requires the international community to focus on women and children in both the prevention stage of conflicts and the protection phase. Since Resolution 1325, the Security Council has further emphasized the importance of protecting women and children in failing states; resolutions 1820, 1888, 1889, 1960, 2106 and 2122 all address a security framework for peace and stabilization to protect women and children in failing states (Nilsö, May 13, 2014).

In November 2010, the Lisbon Summit endorsed all Security Council resolutions on peace, security and gender; in 2014, NATO's Crisis Management Exercise set out a specific objective on gender perspective (Nilsö, May 13, 2014). Based on Resolution 1325, NATO developed in December 2007 a NATO/EAPC policy on peace, security, and women. It included the four pillars identified in Resolution 1325—prevention, protection, participation and relief and recovery—by embedding these pillars into NATO's policies, objectives and missions. NATO also sought to adopt the content of Resolution 1325 in all policies and programs and set up discussions with international organizations and non-governmental organizations to promote a growing awareness of gender issues in war-torn societies. NATO continued to implement structured education and training on gender-related challenges in NATO Training Centers and Centers of Excellence and stressed to Allied states the importance of national initiatives on gender awareness and how NATO in missions is required to follow a conduct of behavior. In addition, NATO has employed gender advisers within its Strategic Commands for Operations and for Transformation, as well as at the headquarters of KFOR and ISAF. NATO also appointed a gender adviser to ISAF—a Special Representative for Women, Peace and Security. In May 2012, NATO leaders decided to review the work on Resolution 1325 in NATO missions around the world. It authorized the Nordic Centre for Gender in Military Operations to assess the practical impact of Resolution 1325 in NATO missions to assure that NATO activities specifically addressed women and children's human insecurity in war-torn societies. The assessment is to assure that NATO acknowledges security threats and peace issues from a gender perspective and is able to develop its capabilities to prevent civilian causalities and protect women and children in the event of conflict (Lackenbauer and Langlais, 2013).

Actual abilities to address R2P challenges in Syria

NATO consists of the most militarily developed groups of allies in the world. Together, NATO's member-states have great leverage on states in the event of conflict and war. In addition to military strength, NATO member-states are also hard powers economically. Being part of the developed world, these allies together are economically powerful in terms of international politics. The alliance also has great soft power in terms of normative strength. As argued earlier in this chapter, NATO member-states share democratic norms and values. This, together with institutional checks and balances inherited in democratic governance, has provided adhesion within the organization, but has also become a political tool against third states. NATO is not only a powerful military power, but also a normative power—a symbol of a democratic community of shared institutions, norms, and values. Altogether, NATO has in a post-Cold War era not only survived, but also revived to become a global actor with multiple humanitarian missions around the world.

Based on NATO's recent actions (e.g., Kosovo from 1998–99, Afghanistan from 2003 and Libya in 2010–11), there are lessons to be learned for the alliance to remain vital in ongoing crises, such as the one in Syria. NATO's inaction in Syria is primarily due to the refusal by China and Russia to use the UN Security Council as a platform for imposing measures on the Syrian regime to halt the ongoing civil war. Compared to the Libyan intervention, Syria has strong ties to both China and Russia that together have stopped all Western ambitions to authorize UN resolutions on the Syrian regime. As in the case of Libya, both China and Russia have stressed the principle of state sovereignty and with less interest to make human rights a core foreign policy issue. This is due to their poor human rights records and an apprehension of internal violent regime resistance at home. Another important factor to Russian protection of the Syrian regime is the developed military links between Moscow and Damascus with Russia's naval base in the Syrian city of Tartus as well as its overall lucrative arms contract with Syria (Crimmins, 2013).

The crisis in Ukraine has further worsened the situation between NATO and Russia. The previous positive signs of Russian/NATO collaboration on coordinating and safeguarding the transportation of Syria's chemical weapons from Syria were recently suspended by NATO. As argued by the Secretary-General of NATO, Anders Fogh Rasmusen, "We have suspended the planning for our first NATO-Russia joint mission.... Let me stress, this will not affect the destruction of chemical weapons, but Russia will not be involved in the escort of the U.S. vessel" (Global Security Newswire, 2014).

Out of area or only within NATO?

Besides international power politics over Syria, NATO and its member-states also face serious internal challenges to be a coherent player on humanitarian crises as the one in Syria. A first challenge to NATO is the internal debate on its responsibilities. NATO has gradually transformed from a regional defense organization of NATO territory to a global actor in peacemaking and peacekeeping operations. The new security context of NATO, with fewer Article 5 challenges to NATO territory, has led to an internal debate among member-states on how to pursue future security strategies. Centrifugal dynamics within the organization are evident due to a broadened security concept and a larger number of member-states. The centrifugal dynamics consist of different security perceptions among member-states and different approaches for when and how NATO is to act. While many new member-states engaged NATO due to its traditional role of defending member-states from external attacks, older member-states, like the US and the UK, have stressed the importance of NATO's new global mission. This has created tension within the organization, and questions whether NATO is pursuing common strategies and gathering sufficient military capabilities (Schreer, 2012, pp. 141–144; Medcalf, 2006, pp. 75–81).

> After all, countries often join military coalitions or an alliance effort because they share common interests. Shared interests, however, do not always equate to agreement as to the best ways to pursue those interests. Too often, individual countries engage in efforts that either distract from or undermine the overall coalition effort.
>
> (Auerswald and Saideman, 2014, p. 2)

Despite the fact that NATO is available for humanitarian intervention, conflict prevention, and crisis management out-of-area, its traditional security concept of protecting member-states at home from external security attacks remains. Since obligations of NATO under Article 5 only refer to security and defense of member-states, there is no obligation within the treaty to act upon human security abuses elsewhere in the world. Although NATO has opened up to out-of-area responses to human rights abuses, several member-states have argued against future interventions. Although NATO decided to intervene in Kosovo in the name of humanitarian crisis and following the intervention secured Kosovo to build democratic institutions and the rule of law, NATO member-states still disagree on the status of Kosovo. While many member-states have approved the sovereignty of Kosovo, some member-states refuse to see Kosovo as independent from Serbia. In addition, NATO's military raids on Gaddafi's Libya in 2011 led to internal disagreement on motives behind engagement. While some member-states such as Denmark and the UK have been globalists, arguing for NATO missions out of area, members such as the Baltic States, France and Germany have at times stayed more regional in terms of security policy (Engelbrekt and Wagnsson, 2014, pp. 8–9). Several member-states of NATO have questioned the motive to push for regime change in Libya. This criticism was shared by China and Russia, which accused NATO of misusing the UN mandate to protect civilians. When Russia and China abstained in 2011 from using the veto on Resolution 1973 concerning Libya, this happened based on the perception that the Resolution would only allow forces to protect civilians. NATO member-states have disagreed on what to do with Syria. Based on the disagreement on how to perceive NATO responsibilities on security, few actions have been taken. One action is the Turkish call for the deployment of Patriot missile inceptors along Turkish borders after a Syrian bomb killed five civilians close to Syrian borders. Such a system had been debated for some time within Turkey as a tool to secure Turkey from missiles launched from Syria (NATO Watch, September 11, 2012). Another action involving Syria came when its forces shot down a Turkish aircraft. This led to NATO consultations based on Article 4 of its Treaty as Turkey called for a meeting due to jeopardized territorial integrity and security (NATO Watch, June 26, 2012).

One alliance or multi-tier NATO?

A second challenge to NATO's ability to respond to human insecurity in the name of R2P is the intergovernmental nature of the organization. NATO consists of 28 member-states with veto authority. This implies that NATO seeks consensus on all phases in potential missions abroad. It includes finding agreements on where in the world to act, why to engage, when such engagement is needed, and how to implement the mission (Auerswald and Saideman, 2014, pp. 34–36). The Treaty explicitly sets out the right of any member-state to have an equal voice. Achieving consensus within NATO requires common ground on where and why to take common action, when such agreements are made, and how to plan and implement missions. It is the right of any individual member-state to opt out from engagement or to supply any capability. The increasing number of states has raised concerns over the ability of NATO to reach consensus under the time pressure of a humanitarian crisis. Even if all member-states do agree to engage in a crisis or conflict, each member-state can select certain activities and decide on capacities (Auerswald and Saideman, 2014, pp. 34–36).

The new member-states of NATO have argued for safeguarding member-states' safety and security against external risks, such as Russia. This perception on the role of NATO has been in sharp contrast to the ones in the US and the UK, among others (Kay, 2011, p. 30). In fact, the Kosovo crisis of 1998–99 provoked an intense debate within the organization on what to do—if anything at all. The lack of UNSC authority resulted in several member-states opposing NATO engagement. Belgium, France, Germany, Greece, Italy and Spain all opposed NATO engagement, referring to Article 1 in the NATO Treaty, which could be interpreted as a requirement for a UNSC mandate for NATO to act (Larsdotter, 2012, pp. 85–86). In the case of Libya, NATO member-states agreed on engagement to protect civilians under the UN mandate, but member-states engaged differently. Some member-states fully engaged in the military operations, some did not at all, and some only sporadically, in ad hoc operations. Other states were engaged in Libya, but without participating in air attacks or acting in controversial aspects of the mission (Auerswald and Saideman, 2014, pp. 199–200). In addition, while non-NATO member-states such as Sweden were involved militarily, Germany as a powerful NATO member-state was not militarily involved in the operation at all. NATO's role in Libya was therefore complex due to the intergovernmental nature of the organization and the high number of member-states. "As NATO continues to gain members and takes on a broader set of challenges, differences in opinion on 'out-of-area' operations will no doubt remain and most likely increase" (Olsen, 2014, p. xvi).

Debate within NATO has called for the introduction of constructive abstention in the decision-making procedure (Medcalf, 2006, pp. 67–68). It has implied that member-states that are less willing to act upon a crisis or a security challenge around the world should be able to abstain as long as they do not use their veto and stop other member-states from taking action. The constructive abstention provides skeptical member-states a chance to wait and see while NATO acts based on those member-states' readiness to act. This is what was happening in Libya (Auerswald and Saideman, 2014, pp. 5–13). This could also be an important remedy to potential challenges during the operations in the field. Since NATO consists of few organizational forces beyond the capacities provided by each member-state, national commanders in operations may at times act upon national interests rather than the common interests of NATO. This has happened in Kosovo, Afghanistan and Libya and created a less efficient military operation in the air and on the ground than what had been planned. The main objective in Syria would be to safeguard civilians, but also to aim for regime change which would require long-term engagement in building democratic institutions and the rule of law; missions that prove to be hard to do in Iraq and Afghanistan (Crimmins, July 10, 2013). As argued in a study on NATO in Libya in 2011,

> Looking behind the curtain clearly reveals that the 28 NATO heads of state were far from unanimous about how to deal with the Libyan situation. Despite agreeing to "answer the call" of resolution 1973, they had different opinions and interpretations of ends, ways and means.
>
> (Olsen, 2014, p. xvii)

Unilateral or transatlantic burden-sharing?

A third challenge to NATO's ability to provide and protect human security is to solve the long-term transatlantic debate on internal burden-sharing. The debate has foremost been triggered by America, which has blamed Europe for doing too little in terms of military spending and engagement in NATO operations. Although the crisis in the Balkans in the 1990s was a European problem, most operations were led by the US military due to its superior military capacity and political and diplomatic strength. The debate on unfair burden-sharing existed throughout the Cold War. As it ended, the US took for granted that Europe would step up to its obligations and start to spend more money on European security and defense. After the Cold War, a European security pillar developed within NATO. It was argued from both sides of the Atlantic that it was time for Europe to provide for European security to a larger extent than had been possible during the Cold War.

In January of 1994, NATO decided on the European Security and Defence Identity (ESDI) within the NATO structure. It refocused on burden-sharing and the role of European partners, which implied that it would increase its share in operating for peace and security. One ingredient of ESDI was the Combined Joint Task Force (CJTF), referring to the possibility of two or more European states to act in the name of NATO when willing to do so (Medcalf, 2006, pp. 84–85). In 1998, the European Security and Defence Policy (ESDP) was established, stressing the importance of European member-states having the capacity to act autonomously from the US and provide for security and defense without transatlantic support. In December 1999, the European Council in Helsinki declared a Rapid Reaction Force (RRF), consisting of about 60,000 troops to be deployed within 60 days. This force was to be deployed when NATO was not to be engaged, when Europe needed forces to be deployed and with the specific purpose to be implemented on humanitarian, peacekeeping and crisis management missions.

Despite these efforts, however, the post-Cold War context showed the superior power of the US regarding intelligence, planning, and implementation both by land, sea and in the air (Clark and Cornish, 2012, p. 778). The capability gap has created serious tension in the US regarding why American soldiers should be deployed to solve a European crisis, as well as between the US and its allies in Europe. Although some estimations point at 60 percent being spent on the military for European defense compared to that in the US, such figures tend to hide that Europe is not one cohesive actor in security and defense. Each European NATO member-state must provide substantial military expense to cover all aspects of national defense. This has implied that a lower total budget on security and defense on the European side of the Atlantic also should be subtracted from national defense spending for all military branches. This has had a negative effect on the European ability to act upon human security challenges. Further on, it is also possible to see how the European side is lagging behind in technology and investments in new military equipment adjusted to human security operations.

While the European governments invest less money in security and defense compared to America, a larger share of investments is made in conventional and personal weapons. Europe has invested in military equipment and technology that seem less and less usable in a new security context. In 2010, NATO involvement in Afghanistan created a debate on both sides of the Atlantic on how the European side was unable to provide capable troops on the ground, but also how these troops lacked necessary tools for deployment (Michaels, 2014, pp. 27–31; Kay, 2011, p. 30). While European powers have continued to provide NATO with traditional forces, the new wars require swift and flexible missions with sufficient troops as well as mobile planning, strategic centers and high-tech forces in the air and on the ground (Moore, 2007, pp. 106–107). In sum, NATO is in dire need of the specialization of capabilities provided by each member-state (Moore, 2007, pp. 88–89).

The debate on burden-sharing has intensified with the global financial crisis and NATO being heavily engaged in Afghanistan. NATO member-states on both sides of the Atlantic have greatly suffered due to the economic recession and the ongoing operations in Afghanistan, which has resulted in less popular support for military operations out of area (Michaels, 2014, pp. 18–22). The crisis in Afghanistan and Libya may also have led to a fatigue among member-states to engage abroad. The lengthy operations in Afghanistan followed by the complexity to stabilize a post-war Libya may very well have negative effects on NATO's willingness to engage Syria. In addition, another debate concerning burden-sharing has been the imbalance of capability among European member-states. While Germany, Spain and Turkey were heavily criticized by other member-states for not providing NATO sufficient capabilities, Canada, Denmark and Estonia invested the most money per capita (Auerswald and Saideman, 2014, p. 3). In sum, the different investments in capabilities from member-states have led to debate on how some member-states are warrior states and others are ration-consumers. Analysis of NATO in Libya shows clear examples of how some member-states lack capabilities as efficient military actors in out-of-area crises. In mid-April of 2011, seven out of 28 member-states alone were conducting military strikes on Gaddafi's Libya. These were Belgium, Canada, Denmark, France, Norway, the UK and the US (Michaels, 2014, p. 25).

Conclusion

NATO is an important military and political actor in international politics. Due to its high number of member-states, their shared democratic norms and values, and the existing capabilities, there is no other international organization that has the capacity to develop, deploy and operate in large multinational missions (Moore, 2007, pp. 104–105). NATO has transformed from a regional defense organization into a global peacemaker and peacekeeper ready for crisis management operations. NATO has engaged in missions in Africa, Europe and the Middle East, providing support to the UN and regional organizations. At times, however, NATO member-states have perceived security crises inconsistent with the UN Security Council. Although the UN Security Council has appealed for NATO support for peacekeeping missions, NATO and the UNSC have not always agreed on when humanitarian intervention is legal and legitimate. This has created tension over Syria. However, there is also disagreement within NATO on what to do, when to do so, and with what capacities. The transformation of NATO from a regional to a global actor has raised debate on what security NATO should defend—state security among member-states or human security globally—and how to share the costs of such missions. The humanitarian interventions in Kosovo and Libya intensified an internal debate on these issues, questioning NATO ability and willingness to act upon R2P. It also highlighted that NATO is transforming and how member-states capacities to act on R2P is limited, due to the imbalance in burden-sharing across the Atlantic. Despite the normative basis of NATO on democracy, human rights, and human security, member-states continue to disagree on where, when and how NATO is to pursue humanitarian intervention. The fact that NATO still has not officially endorsed R2P as part of its responsibility is a sign of how NATO should develop a comprehensive agenda on R2P to meet future humanitarian crises and relate to disagreements within the UN Security Council.

References

The Alliance New Strategic Concept (1991). *Decided on by NATO member states at the NAC meeting in Rome, November 7–8, 1991*. NATO Handbook: Chronology.

Allin, D. H. (1995). Can Containment Work Again? *Survival: Global Politics and Strategy*, 37, 53–65.

Asmus, R. D., Kugler, R. L. and Larrabee, F. S. (1997). NATO enlargement: a framework for analysis. In P. H. Gordon (ed.) NATO's *transformation—the changing shape of the Atlantic Alliance* (pp. 107–112). Lanham, BO; New York; London: Rowman & Littlefield Publishers, Inc.

Auerswald, D. P. and Saideman, S. M. (2014). *NATO in Afghanistan—Fighting together, fighting alone*. Princeton and Oxford: Princeton University Press.

Brown, M. E. (1997). The flawed logic of NATO enlargement. In P. H. Gordon (ed.) *NATO's Transformation—The Changing Shape of the Atlantic Alliance* (pp. 121–131). Lanham, BO; New York; London: Rowman & Littlefield Publishers, Inc.

Clarke, M. and Cornish, P. (2002). The European Defence Project and the Prague Summit, *International Affairs* 78, 777–788.

Crimmins, D. (2013, July 10). *NATO would go into Syria if it Could – Here's why it can't. PolicyMic*. Retrieved from: www.policymic.com/articles/53823/nato-would-go-into-syria-if-it-could-here-s-why-it- (accessed April 7, 2014).

Davis, I. (2011, September 8). How Good is NATO After Libya? *NATO Watch – Briefing Paper No. 20*. Retrieved from: www.responsibilitytoprotect.org/index.php/crises/190-crisis-in-libya/3658-how-good-is-nato-after-libya (accessed April 7, 2014).

Declaration on a Transformed North Atlantic Alliance (1990a). *The London Declaration, July 6, 1990*. Retrieved from: www.nato.int/docu/basictxt/b900706a.htm (accessed April 9, 2014).

Declaration on a Transformed North Atlantic Alliance (1990b). Issued by the Heads of State and Government participating in the Meeting of the North Atlantic Council, July 6, 1990. NATO Handbook: Chronology.

Edström, H. and Gyllensporre, D. (eds.) (2012a). *From strategy to operations—or the other way around? In pursuing strategy—NATO operations from the Gulf War to Gaddafi*. Houndmills/New York: Palgrave Macmillan.

Edström, H. and Gyllensporre, D. (2012b). Painting the theoretical landscape. In H. Edström and D. Gyllensporre (eds.). *Pursuing Strategy—NATO operations from the Gulf War to Gaddafi* (pp. 46–54). Houndmills and New York: Macmillan.

Edström, H., Matlay, J. H., and Petersson, M. (eds.) (2011). *Utility for NATO—Utility of NATO? In NATO: The power of partnerships*. Houndmills and New York: Palgrave Macmillan.

Engelbrekt, K. and Wagnsson, C. (2014). Introduction. In K. Engelbrekt, M. Mohlin and C. Wagnsson (eds.). *The NATO intervention in Libya—Lessons learned from the campaign* (pp. 1–14). London and New York: Routledge.

Engelbrekt, K., Mohlin, M. and Wagnsson, C. (eds.) (2014). *The NATO intervention in Libya—Lessons learned from the campaign*. London and New York: Routledge.

Flanagan, S. J. (1992). NATO and Central and Eastern Europe: From Liaison to Security Partnership. *The Washington Quarterly*, spring, 141–151.

Global Security Newswire (2014, March 6). *NATO 'Suspends' Russia Security Collaboration on Syria Chemicals*. National Journal. Retrieved from: www.nti.org/gsn/article/nato-drops-plan-team-russia-guard-syrian-chemicals/ (accessed April 24, 2014).
Gress, D. (1998). *From PLATO to NATO*. New York: The Free Press.
Gudmundsson, U. (2000). *Nato i närbild* (pp. 1–245). Lund: Studentlitteratur.
Gyllensporre, D. (2012). NATO engagement in Africa: Is there a strategy for the continent? In H. Edström and D. Gyllensporre (eds.). *Pursuing strategy—NATO operations from the Gulf War to Gaddafi* (pp. 157–161). Houndmills and New York: Macmillan.
Janzekovic, J. and Silander, D. (2013). *Responsibility to Protect and prevent—Principles, promises and practicalities*. London, New York and Delhi: Anthem Press.
Kay, S. (2011). Partnerships and power in American grand strategy. In H. Edström, J. H. Matlay and M. Petersson (eds.). *NATO: The Power of Partnerships* (pp. 18–36). Houndmills and New York: Palgrave Macmillan.
Keller, C. (2011, October 12). The End of the responsibility to protect? In *Foreign Policy Journal*. Retrieved from: www.foreignpolicyjournal.com/2011/10/12/the-end-of-the-responsibility-to-protect/ (accessed April 24, 2014).
Kissinger, H. (1990). The End of NATO? *Washington Post*, July 24.
Lackenbauer, H. and Langlais, R. (eds.) (2013). *Review of the practical implications of UNSCR 1325 for the conduct of NATO-led operations and missions – Full report*. Stockholm: Swedish Defence Research Agency (FOI).
Larsdotter, K. (2012). The Development of a NATO strategy in Bosnia-Herzegovina. In H. Edström and D. Gyllensporre (eds.). *Pursuing strategy—NATO Operations from the Gulf War to Gaddafi* (pp. 60–81). Houndmills and New York: Macmillan.
Matlay, J. H. (2011). Partnerships to the East and South: A 'win–win' policy. In H. Edström, J. H. Matlay and M. Petersson (eds.). *NATO: The power of partnerships* (pp. 60–64). Houndmills/New York: Palgrave Macmillan.
McCalla, R. (1995). NATO's persistence. *International organizations*, 50, 445–475.
Mearsheimer, J. J. (1990). Back to the future: Instability in Europe after the Cold War, *International Security*, 15, 5–56.
Medcalf, J. (2006). *NATO*. Oxford: Oneworld Publications.
Michaels, J. H. (2014). Able but not willing—A critical assessment of NATO's Libya intervention. In K. Engelbrekt, M. Mohlin and C. Wagnsson (eds.). *The NATO intervention in Libya—Lessons learned from the campaign* (pp. 17–40). London and New York: Routledge.
Michta, A. A. (ed.) (1999). *America's new allies. Poland, Hungary, and the Czech Republic in NATO*. Seattle ands London: University of Washington Press.
Moore, R. (2007). *NATO's new mission—Projecting stability in a post-Cold War world*. Westport: Praeger Security International.
NATO Watch (2012, June 26). *NATO Watch media briefing*. Retrieved from: www.natowatch.org/node/733 (accessed April 26, 2014).
NATO Watch (2012, September 11). *Turkish request still pending for NATO missile inceptors near Syria*. Retrieved from: www.natowatch.org/node/802 (accessed April 26, 2014).
Nilsö, B. (2014, May 13). *Presentation at the mission of Sweden to NATO*. Brussels, May 13, 2014.
North Atlantic Council at Istanbul Summit Communiqué (2004, June 28). Paragraph 8.
Okeke, J. M. (2012, April 12). *Why NATO intervention in Libya is not a victory for responsibility to protect*. Retrieved from: www.issafrica.org/iss-today/why-nato-intervention-in-libya-is-not-a-victory-for-responsibility-to-protect (accessed April 24, 2014).

Olsen, J. A. (2014). Foreword. In K. Engelbrekt, M. Mohlin and C. Wagnsson (eds.). *The NATO intervention in Libya—Lessons learned from the campaign* (p. xvii). London and New York: Routledge.

Owen, H. (1993). The Collapse of the West. *Foreign Affairs* 72. Retrieved from: www.foreignaffairs.com/articles/49202/owen-harries/the-collapse-of-the-west. (accessed April 7, 2014).

Partnership for Peace: Framework Document (1994, January 10). NATO Handbook: Chronology.

Petersson, M. (2012). The Forgotten dimension? NATO and the security of member states. In H. Edström and D. Gyllensporre (eds.). *Pursuing strategy—NATO operations from the Gulf War to Gaddafi* (pp. 122–138). Houndmills and New York Macmillan.

Schimmelfennig, F. (2002). Introduction: The impact of international organizations on the Central and eastern European States—Conceptual and theoretical issues. In R. H. Linden (ed.). *Norms and nannies—The Impact of International Organizations on the Central and East European States* (pp. 1–9). Lanham, BO; New York; Oxford: Rowman and Littlefield Publishers, Inc.

Schreer, B. (2012). The evolution of NATO's strategy in Afghanistan. In H. Edström and D. Gyllensporre (eds.). *Pursuing strategy—NATO operations from the Gulf War to Gaddafi* (pp. 139–157). Houndmills and New York: Macmillan.

Silander, D. (2009). *United Nations interim mission in Kosovo—Standards before status: a policy of catch 22*. Saarbrücken: VDM Verlag.

Sloan, S. (1995). US perspectives on NATO's future, *international Affairs*, 71.

Sloan, S. R. (2003). *NATO, The European Union, and the Atlantic Community: The transatlantic bargain reconsidered.* Lanham: Rowman & Littlefield.

Solana, J. (1999). *NATO in the 21st century: An agenda for the Washington Summit.* Congressional Digest April.

Steel, R. (1989). NATO's last mission, *Foreign Policy*, 69, 83–95.

US Department of Defense (2000). *Strengthening transatlantic security: A U.S. strategy for the 21st century*. Washington DC: Department of Defense.

The Washington Treaty (1949). *Article 5*. Retrieved from: www.nato.int/cps/en/natolive/official_texts_17120.htm.

Whitehead, L. (2001). *The international dimensions of democratization: Europe and the Americas*. Oxford: Oxford University Press. pp. 1–496 (accessed April 7, 2014).

Williams, N. (1997). Partnership for peace: Permanent fixture or declining asset? In P. H. Gordon (ed.). *NATO's transformation—The changing shape of the Atlantic Alliance* (pp. 221–232). Lanham, BO; New York; London: Rowman & Littlefield Publishers, Inc.

Zelikow, P. (1997). The Masque of Institutions. In P. H. Gordon (ed.). *NATO's transformation—The changing shape of the Atlantic Alliance*. Lanham, BO; New York; London: Rowman & Littlefield Publishers, Inc.

10 G8

Niall Michelsen

The Group of 7/Group of 8 (G7/G8) is an unusual international actor occupying an odd position within the international political system. It is unusual because it has no specific legal justification for its existence, although it is generally recognized as a Track 1 organization, in this way being akin to customary international law (they exist, but they are not founded on formal treaties) (Yamashita, 2013). It resides in political space between the individual states and the universal international organizations such as the United Nations. This chapter will address the roles played by the G7/G8 in Responsibility to Protect (R2P) cases and with respect to the humanitarian situation in Syria. It first looks at the institution itself and then analyzes its position and role in the international system.

Depending on what particular time one is considering, the membership of the G7/G8 may vary. The original members of the G7 are: Canada; France; Germany; Italy; Japan; United Kingdom; United States, with the European Community (now the EU) having one seat and sometimes two, at the table. In 1998 Russia joined, creating the G8. In 2014, Russia was at least temporarily suspended from the group, reverting back to the G7 (Wilson and Morello, 2014). A note on terminology: "G7/G8" will be used when discussing the institution generically or over its history; "G7" will refer to the institution prior to accepting Russia as a member; "G8" refers to the institution during Russia's membership; and, "G8–1: denotes the institution after it effectively exiled Russia in response to the 2014 Ukrainian political and military conflicts.

The formal responsibilities of the G7/G8 in dealing with situations such as the contemporary situation in Syria are shaped by the very nature of the institution. The G7 was born in the mid-1970s in the midst of numerous questions about the ability and willingness of the United States to manage the increasingly complex and interdependent global economy. There are three reasons for creating a new, informal institution each of which has a bearing on the performance of the institution in Responsibility to Protect (R2P) situations (Bayne, 2005). First, the summits allow face-to-face interactions of political leaders who might be able to fashion agreements where lower bureaucratic efforts had failed. The leaders would be less constrained than lesser bureaucrats and thus freer to craft new proposals. The personal dynamics that could emerge during one, or over the course of several summits, could also yield a level of trust that would create opportunities for compromise.

Second, the political instincts of the G7/G8 allow it to better reconcile domestic and international pressures. The domestic impact of the G7/G8 summits was always a part of the enterprise because of the sense of legitimacy it conferred on a policy recommendation made by a leader. Instead of the proposal being attached to a particular partisan political figure, it now had the imprimatur of the leading Western democracies. In reality however, the positive domestic benefit has limited the impact upon high-level political elites. The impact of G7/G8 pronouncements on the American public has certainly been negligible. It is much more common to hear the G7/G8 decried as the managers of globalization, sparking anti-globalization demonstrations as in Genoa, 2001 (Hajnal, 2007, pp. 108–110).

Third, burden-sharing enabled the US to regain its domestic and foreign policy equilibrium while also acknowledging the elevated status of the other members. One specific political purpose was helping to anchor Japan into the broader Western security system rather than remaining strictly in a bilateral US–Japanese security arrangement. The acceptance of Russia into the organization in 1998 served a similar anchoring purpose (Hajnal, 2007, pp. 40–45).

The essence of the G7/G8 is the annual summits that have been held since 1975 (Hajnal, 2007). The agendas for each summit are a product of cross-national bureaucratic bargaining under the direction of the host country. So, while the host did not have the freedom to adopt an agenda all of its own, it did have significant input on the final shape of the agenda. Naturally these are preceded by planning meetings among the relevant national bureaucracies (foreign ministry, finance ministry, etc.). These meetings generate the substantive materials, which the leaders discuss at the leaders' summits. Initially each leader appointed a personal representative who would take the lead in summit preparations (Bayne, 2004). These representatives are selected for their personal connection to the leader rather than their position within a particular bureaucracy. This served to further personalize the summits. This format has strengths and weaknesses. One of the strengths is that the agendas could shift quickly as warranted by changes in the international landscape. Conversely, the brief, once-a-year summits mean the institution is not suited to deal with crises. A global crisis could erupt three weeks after a summit, with the result that the group would not be able to address the issue for another 11 months. Even in cases where the crisis precedes the summit, the lack of any institutional structures distinct from those associated with the summits means there is no mechanism for monitoring the crisis and making adjustments as appropriate. The case of the Rwanda genocide in 1994 is instructive here. Within a period of 100 days from April to July, 800,000 people were slaughtered and by time the Naples Summit of July 8–10 was held the G7 was limited to making a call for uninterrupted continuation of the humanitarian action carried out by France. Another related weakness is that the limited institutional memory reduces the continuity between summits. This is especially true whenever there is a change in the leadership in either a number of members or in the most important leaders between summits. This can be offset by the advantages of personalized diplomacy in that leaders interacting face-to-face can build levels of trust that open the ground for imaginative compromises.

While the G7/G8 is embedded in a complex international institutional network, it can be seen as a return to the earlier European great power concerts that characterized the nineteenth century (Penttila, 2003). The original membership illustrates that it was not created as a means of reconciling adversaries by providing a forum where they could split the difference between their opposing positions. Rather, it was created by allies to be a forum where "the leaders of the great powers can meet collectively to discuss common approaches to key economic and political issues" (Barkin, 2013, pp. 114–115).

The focus of the G7/G8 has evolved from being overwhelmingly economic to increasingly political, to significantly security. Born with the goal of coordinating economic policies and managing the growing interdependence of the global economy, the focus quickly shifted to political and even security issues. The record of the shift into politics and security matters can be traced through the series (termed for the 7–8 summits that rotate through all the members). Although political matters were never entirely absent from the summits, a prominent analyst (Bayne, 2005) identifies the Third Series (1983–88) as the Rise of Politics, with terrorism being central on the agenda during this period. The 1983 Summit agenda was focused on the issues of nuclear missiles in Europe. This was a clearly East-West situation and typified the early incarnation of this institution. Subsequent series (4th 1989–93; and 5th 1994–97) dealt with the end of the Cold War and the integration of Russia into the institution itself. Integrating Russia into the post-Cold War international order was one of the most important political acts of the G7/G8 even though this recently collapsed (Cooper, 2014).

G7/G8 power and influence

The international system contains both formal and informal institutions. A formal international institution can be defined as: "entities created with sufficient organizational structure and autonomy to provide formal, ongoing, multilateral process of decision-making between states, along with the capacity to execute the collective will of their members" (Volgy *et al.*, 2008, p. 839). With the exception of multilateral decision-making, the G7/G8 has none of these attributes. As one British diplomat observed "it has neither a restaurant nor a pension plan" (cited in Penttila, 2003, p. 5). According to Barnett and Duvall, "Institutional power highlights how actors are able to guide, steer, and constrain the actions and circumstances of others through the rules that exist in structural positional differences in formal and informal institutions" (Barnett and Duvall, 2014, p. 54.). This captures the best way to envision the power of an institution like the G7/G8. It is insufficient to count up the number of airplanes and tanks the members have. Thus, the G7/G8 does not act in direct fashion, but it does have significant influence in many other fora. So attention must shift to the apparent influence the institution has on the behavior of other institutions. The G7/G8 has no standing military and has no binding authority beyond what its own members agree to.

According to a former Canadian diplomat "In examining the G7/G8 Summit's contributions to conflict prevention, clearly the most effective role it can play is through the act of consensus that the leaders agree to take to the other relevant bodies" (Fowler, 2004, p. 40). He goes on to say the G7/G8 works "simply because these summit agreements are promoted by this uniquely powerful set of governments in whatever other forums deal with such matters" (Fowler, 2004, p. 40).

Barkin (2013, p. 163) warns that, "it is important not to confuse the power of the IOs with the power of member states." While the power of an institution's members does not equate to the power of the institution itself, the combined power of the members does lend weight to the decisions and actions of the institution. When the G7/G8 addresses global issues its statements carry weight because of two factors. One is that the member-states are among the most powerful in the international system. In 2005 its members controlled nearly 50 percent of votes in the International Monetary Fund (IMF) and nearly 46 percent of votes in the World Bank (Hajnal, 2007, p. 86) and their economies amounted to 49 percent of the global total in 2013 (Economy Watch, 2014).

The second source of the G7/G8 authority resides in the characteristics of its members. Being self-appointed and unaccountable to anyone else, G7/G8 legitimacy comes from either the members' democratic nature, or their representativeness. As Hajnal (2007, p. 4) points out, some of the G7/G8 successes are attributable to its "democratic legitimacy (given that the leaders are dependent on their electorate)." It is the inability of these institutions to satisfy both of these criteria simultaneously that renders its ability to authorize intervention so problematic. To become genuinely more globally representative it must become less democratic by bringing in leaders who are not accountable to their electorates.

As impressive as the G8 statistics are, they also indicate that with more than 180 states as non-members, and half the global economy excluded, the G7/G8 is constantly vulnerable to charges of being illegitimate (Smaghi, 2004). It is seen as a "sideshow" by one analyst because "it is too elitist to be the source of effective multilateral cooperation" (Barkin, 2013, p. 115). In particular, the absence of China is especially debilitating. Its economy is on track to becoming the largest in the world, its military presence is growing, and its population is nearly 20 percent of the world total (US Census, 2014). China's rise in power raised the prospect of it following Russia into the body. China did not wait for an invitation and moved forward with forming a parallel and rival informal institution along with Brazil, Russia, India and South Africa in what is commonly referred to as BRICS. These rival institutions still exist independently but have also joined in the 2008 creation of the G20, which includes them all as members (Cooper, 2014). Not only does the G20 have more members and therefore a greater share of global resources but it also consists of a diverse range of political and economic systems. This gain in legitimacy from global representativeness comes at the cost of the shared values and compatible political systems that have been characteristics of the G7/G8.

Informal institutions can interact with formal institutions in complementary or competitive ways (Helmke and Levitsky, 2004, p. 728). The United Nations Security Council (UNSC) is the G7/G8's most important formal institutional counterpart when dealing with security or R2P issues. The two have a relationship that contains both elements and the relationship has taken different shapes through time. A rough sketch of the history suggests the variety of forms the relationship has experienced:

- Stage One—Cold War (1975–98) UNSC was frequently paralyzed by the veto and threat of veto—Competitive.
- Stage Two—Post-Cold War (1998–2001) G8 was able to craft an agreement that was then approved by UNSC on Kosovo—Complimentary.
- Stage Three—War on Terrorism (2001–2009) US unilateralism sidelined both G7/G8 and UNSC.
- Stage Four—Back to Normal (2009–2014) G8 and UNSC work together in Libya—Complimentary.
- Stage Five—East-West tensions (2014–) TBD.

The twists and turns in the relationship reflect the shifting geopolitical landscape. But they also indicate that the two institutions have different strengths and weaknesses and do not have a fixed position relative to the other. But does it matter if the two institutions cooperate or if sometimes the G7/G8 seems to usurp the UNSC authority?

We can compare the two in terms of the criteria used to evaluate the power of the G7/G8: total capabilities of the members; legitimacy of the institution based on its claim to authority and on the democratic nature and the representativeness of the members. The UNSC matches or exceeds the G7/G8 in terms of the resources and capabilities of their members. The memberships overlap considerably, with the major difference being that Japan is in the G7/G8 and rotates on and off of the UNSC; and China is in the UNSC and not in the G7/G8. The UNSC is based on a multilateral treaty and it has gained the tacit acceptance of the majority of states who have voluntarily joined the United Nations. While the UNSC is legitimate, it is also unrepresentative. Dissatisfaction with the composition of the UNSC eventually led to the 2005 World Summit, which was not able to effect reforms but merely committed to pursuing them in the future (Pease, 2008). Nonetheless, many of the excluded members see the UNSC, as flawed as it is, as more representative than the G7/G8 (Penttila, 2003, p. 93).

Shifting the decision-making location from the UNSC to the G7/G8 takes the legally sanctioned voice from the rotating, non-permanent members of the UNSC and the PRC. One former diplomat concluded that there are unlikely to be cases where the G8 and the UNSC disagree on security matters involving areas such as Africa and the Balkans (Fowler, 2004, p. 40). This is because four of the Permanent Five members with veto power are also members of the G8 with only China missing. However, that is a big consideration and China's absence creates the possibility of a gap between the G8 and UNSC and particularly so when issues are in a very high stakes area such as the Middle East.

MacFarlane raises questions about identifying the proper expectations when the UNSC does not completely fulfill its primary mission (MacFarlane, 2014,

p. 438). He cites two examples, one where the UNSC fails to act—does this mean that no other international actor has the legal right to act in the face of humanitarian crises? The second example asks what happens if the UNSC acts, but its actions do not come close actually to solving the problem—again, raising the question of what is legal or legitimate for other actors to do in such situations. To sit by impotently is to ignore the heart of the R2P but to act independently, without authorization from a higher body, threatens to undermine the UNSC, which, for whatever its flaws are, is at the center of hopes to create a stable world without genocidal and humanitarian disasters.

This raises the question of why the G7/G8 forum might yield a decision whereas the UNSC with its veto might not. There are two types of explanations. One focuses on how decisions are made, and the second focuses on who makes the decisions. The UNSC can reach legally binding decisions, but it can also be totally paralyzed by the use or threat of a veto by one of the Permanent Five members. That means that in many cases it is incapable of acting. This leaves political space for the G7/G8 and this can work well as in the Kosovo and Libyan cases. The G7/G8 is not hindered by procedures and thus has greater flexibly in finding a consensus on difficult issues. To be specific, the G7/G8 has neither a charter nor a mission statement.

The second type of explanation is that in the Summits the role of the individual politicians expands. Among the implications of how the Summits operate is that the absence of rules of procedure allows for freer, flowing discussions and the private nature of the discussions means that nonconforming, creative ideas could be put forward with little chance that the media would find out who put the ideas forward. This dynamic increased after 1998 when the leaders began meeting separately from the foreign and financial ministers, differences could exist between the UN representative, who is from the Foreign Ministry, and the head of government. This is a symptom of how different bureaucracies can generate a different range of options with different potential ranges of compromises.

It remains an open question of whether the UNSC authority is undercut when the G7/G8 acts in security matters and the outcome will probably vary from case to case. However, when R2P situations arise then in all cases the G7G8 acting in accordance with those principles strengthens those norms. It is not a small thing to have the leading industrial democracies issuing statements clearly addressing the humanitarian crises.

When the G7/G8 chooses to act it has two broad options (Penttila, 2003, p. 33). One is to work as a coordinator of the actions taken by others (states and IGOs primarily), as we shall see in the Kosovo crisis. The second is to work through its members directly in crisis management, which is more characteristic of its behavior in the Syrian civil war. As an informal institution with neither a charter nor a mandate, the G7/G8 can take up any issues the members wish, although spending time on issues that are being effectively handled elsewhere wastes its limited time. In a sense if the G7/G8 does not even take up an issue, it cannot be accused of not meeting its responsibilities. In another sense however, any actor that has undertaken certain actions a number of times, builds an expectation that they will continue to act the next time. These types of implicit expectations should apply to a self-appointed entity of rich states. Moreover, when R2P principles were adopted in 2005 international actors were no longer free to ignore humanitarian crises. Instead, "The international community should, as appropriate, encourage and help States to exercise this responsibility" (ICRtoP, 2014).

In the view of one of the leading experts on the G8:

> In the broadest sense, conflict prevention has been a concern of the G7 since its inaugural 1975 Summit at Rambouillet, France.... Here the leaders publicly declared in their concluding communique that the new institution's central mission was to promote globally the values of open democracy, individual liberty, and social advancement.
>
> (Kirton and Stefanova, 2004, p. 3)

Initially, G7/G8 efforts were limited because of the very heated Cold War atmosphere that was imposed on all conflicts. The end of the Cold War opened the way for this institution especially after adding Russia and thereby transitioning from a Western entity to one that could aspire to global power and influence. Some formidable impediments may hinder the ability of the G7/G8 from playing a leading role in resolving humanitarian crises. One concern raised by critics is that the G7/G8 is too dispersed in its agendas which tend to be heavy on economic matters, so that it is questionable whether or not it is suited to maintain its focus or whether its attention will be so episodic as to be unsuited for handling such issues. Moreover, the institutional limitations, in terms of following up on decisions reached at the summits, are significant (Kirton *et al.*, 2004).

The G7/G8 record in humanitarian crises

The Kosovo crisis of 1999 stands as the single most significant action undertaken by the G8 during the lengthy and bloody wars during the break-up of Yugoslavia. This instance represents the closest example of the G7/G8 behaving like a concert of great powers. In this case the UNSC was not able to reach agreement on a resolution to protect non-Serbians who were widely perceived to be at risk from future Serbian actions nor was it able to prevent NATO from bombing Serbia. The Russians and the Chinese were both opposed to UNSC action with the Chinese wary of supporting a war against a government seeking to keep its territory intact, and the Russians being particularly protective of the Serbians. An alternative to the UNSC had been created to handle earlier Balkan crises, called the Contact Group. This ad hoc group was called into being when existing institutions seemed incapable of rising to the humanitarian challenge. It was comprised of the US, the UK, France, Germany, Italy and Russia. With the United States leading a NATO air war without attaining the approval of the UNSC, Russia saw the G8 as a preferred alternative to the Contact Group. Even though it was a member of the Contact Group, Russia preferred the G8 because its inclusion in the group in 1998 was a more formal acknowledgment of Russia's legitimacy and great power status. That the personalized nature of the G8 summits played a role can be seen in Russian President Yeltsin's comment at the summit "I am among my friends now" (quoted in Bayne 2005, p. 55). The deal reached by the Foreign Ministers meeting on the eve of the Leaders' Summit and was labeled the Stability Pact for South Eastern Europe and was issued on June 8, 1999. It was officially accepted by the UNSC as Resolution 1244 on June 10, 1999 and it brought the bombing campaign to an end (Penttila, 2003).

In evaluating the Kosovo crisis as the first major G7/G8 intervention into humanitarian crises one prominent and experienced analyst concluded, "In this dangerous situation, the G8 framework proved its worth" (Bayne, 2005, p. 54). This crisis marked the worst period of US–Russian relations to that point in the post-Cold War world. The fact that Russia's inclusion in the G8 facilitated its acceptance of the agreement that ended the conflict seemed to augur for a promising role for the G8 in such matters. A more cautious appraisal, directed not only to the hopes resting on the G8 but also on the UNSC, focused on the fact that the NATO bombing attack went forward without the sanction of either of those bodies (Chesterman, 2014, p. 494). That one of the great powers, with seats on all the relevant bodies would act militarily without any authorization indicates that these bodies do not have overarching power, even in cases where the rationale is based on a global concern over humanitarian situations.

After this, the G7/G8 turned its attention to conflict prevention while pursuing a variety of initiatives involving Africa. The G8 Africa Action Plan was the G8 response to the New Partnership for Africa's Development (NEPAD) agreed to by the Organization of African Unity (OAU) in 2001. The G8 plan was worked out in collaboration with several African leaders who were invited to participate in the 2002 Summit in Kananaskis, Canada. This highlights one of the advantages that the institution has compared to some others, in that it has total flexibility and autonomy to invite leaders of non-member states to participate in their meetings when the agenda is better suited (University of Toronto, 2002).

One analyst terms the Kananaskis Summit as a mixed bag in the sense that it did not have the content sufficient to the magnitude of the task at hand, but still

> in approaching conflict prevention at Kananaskis, the Africa Action Plan focused on the doable and the achievable – that is, on strengthening regional and sub-regional institutions dealing with conflict resolution and peace-building training and with disarmament, demobilization, and reintegration, on post-conflict management, and on training in negotiations and peacekeeping.
>
> (Fowler, 2004, p. 42)

So, while achieving the task would require a significant reduction in regional poverty, which the G8 was unwilling or unable to seriously address, there were many more secondary types of actions that the G8 could and did undertake. The

G8 stated its view of the interconnectedness of poverty and humanitarian crises this way in 2000:

> We commit ourselves to work for their implementation particularly with respect to economic development and conflict prevention, children in conflict, and international civilian police. We express special concern that the proceeds from the illicit trade in diamonds have contributed to aggravating armed conflict and humanitarian crises, particularly in Africa.
>
> (University of Toronto, 2000)

These African-centered activities were extended in 2004 at the Sea Island Summit with a focus on poverty and disease in the region. They also announced the G8 Action Plan: Expanding Global Capability for Peace Support Operations (University of Toronto, 2004). One main feature was the training of peacekeeping troops to improve their ability to handle non-state actors. Another feature involved various forms of assistance specifically for African peacekeeping, including coordinating contributions from the G8 members with other IGOs including the UN.

One authoritative assessment of these efforts concluded that the G8 role in conflict prevention in Africa was primarily complementary in relation to other international institutions (Yamashita, 2013). It worked to build peacekeeping capabilities and helped create links between financial donors and national institutions. The analyst concluded, however, that based on the limited follow up efforts by the G8 members that the most important role the G8 would play would be to focus on capacity building rather than more forceful types of intervention. The analyst stressed that one area of comparative advantage for the G8 in support of peacekeeping missions, is in building the capacity of civilian peacekeeping units, once again focusing on heading matters off before they escalate. The founding core document of the R2P, the Report of the International Commission on Intervention and State Sovereignty (ICISS, 2001) identifies prevention as the most important element in the R2P and concludes that, "Root cause prevention may also mean tackling *economic* deprivation and the lack of economic opportunities" (ICISS, 2001, p. 23). A major test of the willingness and ability of the G8 to influence ongoing humanitarian crises came in the Libyan civil war. With political events in Libya unfolding rapidly beginning in February 2011, the May 26–27 Summit allowed the G8 to call for Gaddafi's ouster from office and to use R2P language signaling the intent of the G8 members to use their influence in other institutions to support the rebels and effect regime change:

> We demand the immediate cessation of the use of force against civilians by the Libyan regime forces as well as the cessation of all incitement to hostility and violence against the civilian population. In that regard, we take note of actions undertaken by UN Member States to implement fully UNSCRs 1970 and 1973. We stress the need to hold to account those responsible for

> attacks on civilians. These criminal actions will not go unpunished. We welcome the work of the International Criminal Court in investigating crimes in Libya and note the Chief Prosecutor's request on 16 May for three arrest warrants. Qadhafi and the Libyan government have failed to fulfil their responsibility to protect the Libyan population and have lost all legitimacy. He has no future in a free, democratic Libya. He must go.
>
> We are committed to supporting a political transition that reflects the will of the Libyan people. We recall our strong commitment to the sovereignty, independence, territorial integrity and national unity of Libya. We stress the central role of the Secretary-General's Envoy to Libya, Mr, Al-Khatib, in facilitating an inclusive and lasting political solution, based on the legitimate demands of the Libyan people and taking into account the role of regional organisations, the League of Arab States and the African Union.... We reiterate the central role of the UNSC in accordance with the UN Charter.
>
> (University of Toronto, 2011)

These comments show the G8 making very specific demands and linking its calls to several other international bodies with various types of power and legitimacy: UNSC; ICC (International Criminal Court); League of Arab States; African Union. Their statement was explicit that on matters involving Libya the UN Charter and the UNSC had determinative authority. The G8 statement made explicit reference to two UNSC Resolutions (1970 and 1973), which justified the international community's intervention into the Libyan civil war on a humanitarian basis. Interestingly, UNSCR 1970 which introduced economic sanctions and referred matters to the ICC was passed with unanimous affirmation. On the other hand UNSCR 1973 which established the basis of military action against the Libyan government, passed with five abstentions, including two G8 members (Russia and Germany) and three of the BRICS (Brazil, India and China). The G8 statement also affirmed the roles of regional organizations in these matters, referencing the League of Arab States and the African Union.

The G8 and Syria

The G8 moved as quickly as is possible for an institution that has no secretariat or any active presence between the annual summits. Mass anti-government demonstrations in Syria began in March 2011; the first G8 summit was in Deauville, France, May 26–27, 2011. In its end of summit declarations the G8 condemned the Syrian government for its violent repression of the demonstrations. The statement placed the events within the regional context of the Arab spring, raising the connection between democracy and security and peace, "Only the path of dialogue and fundamental reforms will lead to democracy, and thus to long-term security and prosperity in Syria" (University of Toronto, 2011).

The G8 also sought to leverage its own advice by affirming the IAEA in its effort to investigate Syrian activities that were suspected of being related to a nuclear weapons program. At the same time the G8 statement chided Syria for its uncooperative behavior, "We note with deep concern the lack of cooperation by Syria reflected in the most recent IAEA report." The G8 then went beyond that admonition with its statement that, "We look forward to the IAEA Board of Governors addressing the seriousness of the issue." This is emblematic of the G8 role of using the power of its members to influence other international institutions. In 2011 all of the G8 states were members of the IAEA Board of Governors. Although they did not represent a majority of the 35 members, their weight, when unified behind a consensus document, is significant (University of Toronto, 2011).

Following a year of ineffective international action characterized by mixed signals from the United Nations in the face of the deteriorating situation in Syria, the G8 Summit was held at Camp David May 18–19, 2012 and once again the group issued a strong condemnation of Syrian behavior and placed its weight behind two specific UN based activities. One effort was led by former UN Secretary-General Kofi Annan and the Arab League, and the second was based in the UN Security Council. The G8 issued strong language of condemnation "We remain appalled by the loss of life, humanitarian crisis, and serious and widespread human rights abuses in Syria." The G8 proclaimed, "The Syrian government and all parties must immediately and fully adhere to commitments to implement the six-point plan of UN and Arab League Joint Special Envoy (JSE) Kofi Annan, including immediately ceasing all violence." The statement combined a call for action with a hint of further actions from the UNSC, "We remain deeply concerned about the threat to regional peace and security and humanitarian despair caused by the crisis and remain resolved to consider further UN measures as appropriate." So, rather than just indicating that other bodies might take action (e.g., IAEA) the G8 was saying that the members of the G8, including the four members of the Permanent Five (P5), states with veto power, were ready to use the UN to address the Syrian problems (University of Toronto, 2012).

The following year in Lough Erne, Northern Ireland, June 17–18, 2013, the G8 strongly endorsed a conference to address the "appalling conflict in Syria" that would implement the UN sponsored 2012 Geneva Communique. For the first time, the G8 made specific mention of chemical weapons and its condemnation of their use in Syria. In keeping with the spirit of R2P, which entrusts the international community with the responsibility to use appropriate means to protect populations from "genocide, war crimes, ethnic cleansing, and crimes against humanity," the G8 said:

> We are determined to work together to stop the bloodshed and loss of life in Syria and to support the Syrian people to establish peace and stability through political means. We are gravely concerned at the appalling human tragedy that the UN estimates has cost the lives of over 93,000 people and led to 4.2 million internally displaced persons and 1.6 million refugees.
>
> (ICRtoP, 2014)

In acknowledging the humanitarian tragedy playing out in Syria, the G8 stated "we are resolved to make exceptional contributions commensurate with the scale of the problem". Specifically the leaders of the G8 countries promised to increase their contributions to meet humanitarian needs both inside and outside of Syria, by an amount of $1.5 billion. The G8 remained mindful of earlier themes such as the connection between democracy and stability, "We remain committed to achieving a political solution to the crisis based on a vision for a united, inclusive and democratic Syria." And it strongly endorsed the 2012 Geneva Communique, which outlined a path towards a transitional government to replace the Assad regime. The G8 also raised for the first time the specter of terrorism and trans-border problems arising from the ongoing conflict in Syria, warning of "the growing threat from terrorism and extremism in Syria and also by the increasingly sectarian nature of the conflict." Additional comments raised concerns about chemical weapons and endorsed the work of the IAEA and the WHO in investigating allegations of chemical weapons use by the Syrian government (University of Toronto, 2013a).

In the first meeting after the expulsion of Russia in Brussels, Belgium, June 4–5, 2014, the G8–1 continued its condemnation of the Syrian government, "We strongly condemn the Assad regime's brutality which drives a conflict that has killed more than 160,000 people and left 9.3 million in need of humanitarian assistance." They drew further attention by condemning "the violations of international humanitarian law and human rights." In a statement that was both strong and unimaginable in the G8 "We deplore Russia and China's decision to veto the UN Security Council (UNSC) Resolution draft authorizing referral to the International Criminal Court and demanding accountability for the serious and ongoing crimes in Syria." While it called for implementation of UNSC Resolution 2139 dealing with refugees caused by the conflict, the G7 signaled its shift in budgetary focus away from working through intergovernmental organizations to other actors including non-governmental ones, "In our funding we decide to give particular support to humanitarian actors that can reach those most in need, including across borders" (University of Toronto, 2014). In 2012, the G8 members, including the European Union contributed 46 percent of the total funds dedicated to alleviating the humanitarian crisis generated by the Syrian conflict (Financial Tracking Service, 2014).

The G20 addresses Syria

In the G20 meeting, held in St Petersburg, Russia, September 6, 2013 in the face of what appeared to be an imminent US led attack upon Syria, the G20 strongly condemned the use of chemical weapons by Syria, which by this time was being accepted as undisputed fact, with an attack on August 21, 2013 cited. In a strong diplomatic statement the G20 made explicit reference to the failure of the UNSC:

> Signatories have consistently supported a strong UN Security Council Resolution, given the Security Council's responsibilities to lead the international response, but recognize that the Council remains paralyzed as it has been for

two and a half years. The world cannot wait for endless failed processes that can only lead to increased suffering in Syria and regional instability.

(University of Toronto, 2013b)

The statement goes on to compliment one member of the P5, "We support efforts undertaken by the United States and other countries to reinforce the prohibition on the use of chemical weapons." The naming of the US but not Russia is revealing especially since the summit was being hosted by Russia. In the spirit of the R2P the G20 phrased its statement in the context of humanitarianism rather than geopolitics, although geopolitics was paralyzing the UNSC.

We condemn in the strongest terms all human rights violations in Syria on all sides. More than 100,000 people have been killed in the conflict, more than 2 million people have become refugees, and approximately 5 million more are displaced.... We have contributed generously to the latest United Nations and ICRC appeals for humanitarian assistance and will continue to provide support to address the growing humanitarian needs in Syria and their impact on regional countries.

(University of Toronto, 2013b)

These statements by the G20 contributed to the efforts within the UNSC to fashion an agreement between the US and Russia and the Syrian government to a deal that would remove the chemical weapons from Syria. In September of 2013 this deal was struck, although the political killings continued.

Conclusion

An evaluation of the G8's role in the Syrian civil war must take into account its behavior as a decision-making actor, as well as the impact of its actions on the issue in question. This second part requires an evaluation of the G8 within the international political system in which it is situated. In looking first at the G7/G8 as a decision-making body, it is clear that when confronting humanitarian crises in Kosovo, Libya and Syria, the G7/G8 was vocal and active.

During the 2011 Summit in Deauville, France the G8 moved surprisingly quickly and afterwards the G8/G8–1 used the resources and tools it had available to it:

Naming and Shaming. The summits regularly condemned the Syrian government for its "brutality" and decried the humanitarian crisis. Under R2P, condemnation of the government that is behaving irresponsibility is a central function. It is a precursor to further actions. While some G8 statements referenced the need for both sides to seek a peaceful solution; they always held the Syrian government responsible.

Establishing support for their position via other IGOs and NGOs. These connections are among the most powerful levers the G8 has since its members are typically central players in other IGOs. The groups include the IAEA; UNSC; and JSE, and other unspecified NGOs.

Affirming their own individual commitments. This is most evident in the discussion of funding of humanitarian operations within Syria and in the countries accepting the millions of refugees. Because the G8 has no armies, and because it does not have the legal authority to call for military action that has not already been sanctioned by a legally authorized body (e.g., UNSC) it is limited to underlining the point that its members are ready to act.

Threatening further action. This standard diplomatic technique is designed to build pressure on the target state and also to build pressure on the member states and other states in the international system. In this case the UNSC was identified as the agent of further action.

The G8–1 never overtly called for military action, although it referenced future actions by the UNSC, which implies the possibility of military intervention in Syria. Certainly the presence of Russia, which was acting as the protector of Syria against international action, made it impossible for the G8 to get ahead of the UNSC on this issue.

In the context of a complex network of global institutions with the responsibility and power to deal with humanitarian crises such as has existed in Syria since 2011, the G8 stands as an institution that consistently addressed the situation and directed international attention on the humanitarian dimensions of the problem. It often spoke with admirable clarity and power, but this is a case where the words might not have made a major impact on the ground. Ultimately the responsibility for the lack of international action must reside with the states. Thus, the G8 did its part; however, the members were unsuccessful in swaying other international institutions to adopt its position.

This consistency of G8 action in the face of the Kosovo, Libya and Syria humanitarian crises indicates the extent to which the member-states take seriously the R2P. This is surprising because the G8 is not designed for consistency. Consistency is a rare commodity in international organizations that deal with high value political issues, and the G8 is inherently an inconsistent international actor. It is commonplace to say that states routinely have difficulty reaching strong decisions even when virtually everyone agrees on the decision. International organizations can help overcome these problems in a couple of ways. The essence of bureaucratization is to generate identical responses to similar situations. The G7/G8 with its highly personalized summits fits the description of an idiosyncratic actor. One descriptor involves the rules and procedures that set out the mandate for the organization and sets the framework within which decisions are made. Another is a continuing secretariat and other ongoing enterprises that create a type of bureaucratic memory. The G7/G8 has neither of these, and furthermore, whereas most international organizations are filled with representatives of the respective member-states, the G7/G8 has the actual leaders negotiating. While the national representatives operate in coordination with their respective home bureaucratic masters, which themselves have to work out their positions in typical bureaucratic fashion, the leaders go to the summits with their position papers but without the need to constantly check back home to their bureaucratic masters. This means that once the meetings, formal and informal, begin at the summit and positions are explored and negotiations begin, the outcomes are increasingly dependent on the nature of the individual leaders and on their interpersonal relationships, and less dependent upon the bureaucratically generated national interest.

Moreover, not only is the G7/G8 prone to inconsistent behaviors, it is good that they are. This is because gains in consistency come at the expense of speed and flexibility. Speed means that opportunities can be quickly seized. Flexibility means bureaucracies can be circumvented and imaginative solutions can be brought forward. In contrast to formal international institutions that lack any specific deadline (even politically defined deadlines can be finessed by their extensions) the summits are going to end on a specific time at which time the summit declarations will be announced. Consensus must be reached, as it would be unacceptable to acknowledge that a humanitarian crisis exists in Syria, but be unable to make a declaration on the subject. Nothing limits formal institutions from returning tomorrow and discussing the topic again.

By contrast, the impacts of the actions taken by the G8 in the humanitarian crises in Kosovo, Libya and Syria have been very different. A number of variables could explain the differences in the impact of the G7/G8 to the humanitarian crises in the post-Cold War world. For one, the overall balance of power internationally could play a role. Whereas the collapse of the USSR changed the possibilities for concerted international actions in the name of human security, the rise of China in the world balance of power means that global issues decided without the input of the PRC face a credibility gap.

An important difference between the case of Kosovo and Syria is that for China, the events in the Balkans were not of primary importance with little or no economic links and not primary products of value. The Chinese could comfortably allow the Europeans and Americans handle the Balkans matters. However the Middle East is not as strong a natural area of European-American dominance and is of great importance to the Chinese. Thus, whereas in the Kosovo case the PRC agreed to abstain, it is not likely that China would give the G7/G8 (a body from which it is excluded) a free hand in Syria (Goldstone, 2014, p. 485).

A second variable involves the orientation of the US towards the global community in particular the role that the US sees for itself in managing international processes and its responsibility for upholding (and restraining itself on occasion) international norms of behavior. When the US is either withdrawn, feeling that it is incapable of being the world's police officer, or when it is acting unilaterally then the G8 is not likely to be very productive in generating solutions. In 1999 the US was economically strong, in 2011 it was struggling economically and was war-weary.

A third type of variable is that of the individuals that take part in each summit. One of the advantages the G8 has over other global institutions is its ability to change directions quickly. This is a result of the summit nature of the institution and the centrality of powerful individuals at the center. Other institutions have inertia of sorts that keep outputs consistent over time, regardless of the particular personalities who are the decision-makers. With such a central role of individuals there are both individual and ideological factors at work so that it will be impossible to predict which group of G8 leaders is most likely to generate new ideas and take actionable decisions that were impossible at other levels. It is possible that the foreign policy orientation of the leaders could be related to the likelihood of success, but research has not yet established that.

The G7/G8 was originally conceived as a forum for the coordination of Western economic policies during the bifurcated international system that existed during the Cold War. When the Cold War ended, the G7/G8 undertook the important task of welcoming Russia into its ranks and thereby accelerating the transformation from antagonist to partner. Even as this important and once unthinkable development was unfolding; the rapid rise of China was preventing the G8 from credibly claiming to be representing the major world actors. This tension is exacerbated at this point in 2014 with what is effectively the expulsion of Russia from the G8. Not only were huge geographic areas devoid of any representation (South America; Africa) but also with Russia, China and India all outside the organization, its representative inadequacies were unsustainable. All of this created a movement for a more representative informal institution. This ultimately took the form of the G20, which had begun at the level of Finance Ministers in response to the 1999 Asian financial crisis, and then escalated to the leaders level in 2008 in response to the global economic crisis. In some ways (undefined in any formal way, of course) the G20 has assumed some of the roles of the G7/G8.

If the international community seeks to fully and consistently implement R2P it is likely that the existing institutional arrangements are inadequate. Certainly the G8–1 has a serious legitimacy deficit due to its limited membership. The G20 largely addresses the legitimacy deficit but also lacks the institutional capacity to effect long-term policies.

The actions of the G7/G8 in the Kosovo, Libya and Syria cases show clear evidence that the leaders of those states take R2P seriously even though outcomes differed significantly. In the Kosovo case the G8 successfully crafted a compromise that was then sent to the UNSC where it was adopted. In the Libyan case the G8 vigorously threw its weight behind the UNSC in its ultimately successful efforts to effect regime change. In Syria, by contrast, the strong statements, identifying the crises and suggesting solutions by the G8, G20 and G8–1, have not ended the civil war that is continuing to exact high costs in lives in Syria. Some of the mixed record has to be assigned to the anarchical nature of the international system that decentralizes both power and responsibility. When the actions of one state are so central to the total international responses to these humanitarian crises, an international society has not yet matured.

References

Barkin, J. S. (2013). *International organization: Theories and institutions* (2nd ed.). New York: Palgrave Macmillan.

Barnett, M. and Duvall, R. (2014). International organizations and the diffusion of power. In Weiss, T. and Wilkinson, R. (eds.). *International organization and global governance* (pp. 48–59). New York: Routledge.

Bayne, N. (2004). Concentrating the mind: Decision making in the G7/G8 system. In Kirton, J. and Stefanova, R. (eds.). *The G8, the United Nations, and conflict prevention* (pp. 21–38). Burlington, VT: Ashgate.

Bayne, N. (2005). *Staying Together: The G8 Summit confronts the 21st century*. Burlington, VT: Ashgate.

Chesterman, S. (2014). Humanitarian intervention and R2P. In Kirton, J. and Stefanova, R. (eds.). *The G8, the United Nations, and conflict prevention* (pp. 488–499). Burlington, VT: Ashgate.

Cooper, A. and Thakur, R. (2014). The BRICS in the new economic geography. In Weiss, T. and Wilkinson, R. (eds.). *International organization and global governance* (pp. 256–278). New York: Routledge.

Economy Watch (2014). *Country Statistics*. Retrieved from: www.economywatch.com/economic-statistics/country/ (accessed September 1, 2014).

Financial Tracking Service (2014). *Syrian Arab Republic – Civil Unrest 2012*. Retrieved from: http://fts.unocha.org/pageloader.aspx?page=emerg-emergencyDetails&appealID=974. (accessed September 1, 2014).

Fowler, R. (2004). The intricacies of summit preparation and consensus building. In Kirton, J. and Stefanova, R. (eds.). *The G8, the United Nations, and conflict prevention* (pp. 39–42). Burlington, VT: Ashgate.

Goldstone, R. (2014). The pursuit of international justice. In Weiss, T. and Wilkinson, R. (eds.). *International organization and global governance* (pp. 477–487). New York: Routledge.

Hajnal, P. (2007). *The G8 system and the G20: Evolution, role and documentation*. Burlington, VT: Ashgate.

Helmke, G. and Levitsky, S. (2004). Informal instructions and comparative politics: A research agenda. *Perspectives on Politics*, 2, 725–740.

ICRtoP (2014). *Paragraphs 138–139 of the World Summit Outcome Document*. Retrieved from: http://responsibilitytoprotect.org/index.php/component/content/article/35-r2pcs-topics/398-general-assembly-r2p-excerpt-from-outcome-document (accessed September 1, 2014).

International Commission on Intervention and State Sovereignty (2001). *The responsibility to protect*. Retrieved from: http://responsibilitytoprotect.org/ICISS%20Report.pdf (accessed September 1, 2014).

Kirton, J., Kokotsis, E., Stephens, G. and Juricevic, D. (2004). The G8 and conflict prevention: Commitment, compliance, and systemic contributions. In Kirton, J. and Stefanova, R. (eds.). *The G8, the United Nations, and conflict prevention* (pp. 59–84). Burlington, VT: Ashgate.

Kirton, J. and Stefanova, R. (eds.). (2004). *The G8, the United Nations, and conflict prevention*. Burlington, VT: Ashgate.

MacFarlane, S. N. (2014). Regional organizations and global security governance. In Weiss, T. and Wilkinson, R. (eds.). *International Organization and global governance* (pp. 429–441). New York: Routledge.

Pease, K. S. (2008, 3rd ed.). *International organizations: Perspectives on governance in the twenty-first century.* New Jersey: Pearson Education.

Penttila, R. E. J. (2003). *The role of the G8 in international peace and security.* New York: Oxford University Press.

Smaghi, L. B. (2004). The G8's role in promoting financial stability. In Kirton, J. and Stefanova, R. (eds.). *The G8, the United Nations, and conflict prevention* (pp. 143–155). Burlington, VT: Ashgate.

University of Toronto G8 Information Centre (2000). *G8 Commuique Okinawa 2000, July 23, 2000.* Retrieved from: www.g8.utoronto.ca/summit/2000okinawa/finalcom. htm (accessed July 23, 2014).

University of Toronto G8 Information Centre. (2002). *G8 Africa Action Plan.* Retrieved from: www.g8.utoronto.ca/summit/2002kananaskis/africaplan.html.

University of Toronto G8 Information Centre (2004). *Chair's Summary: Sea Island, June 10 2004.* Retrieved from: www.g8.utoronto.ca/summit/2004seaisland/summary.html (accessed July 23, 2014).

University of Toronto G8 Information Centre (2011). *Declarations: 2011 Deauville Summit.* Retrieved from: www.g8.utoronto.ca/summit/2011deauville/index.html (accessed July 23, 2014).

University of Toronto G8 Information Centre (2012). *Camp David Declaration.* Retrieved from: www.g8.utoronto.ca/summit/2012campdavid/index.html (accessed July 23, 2014).

University of Toronto G8 Information Centre (2013a). *G8 Leaders Communique* (2013 Lough Erne Summit). Retrieved from: www.g8.utoronto.ca/summit/2013lougherne/index.html (accessed July 23, 2014).

University of Toronto G20 Information Centre (2013b). *Joint Statement on Syria.* Retrieved from: www.g20.utoronto.ca/2013/2013-0906-syria.html (accessed July 23, 2014).

University of Toronto G8 Information Centre (2014). *G7 Brussels Summit Declaration.* Retrieved from: www.g8.utoronto.ca/summit/2014brussels/declaration.html (accessed July 23, 2014).

US Census (2014). *International Programs: Country Rank.* Retrieved from: www.census.gov/population/international/data/countryrank/rank.php (accessed September 1, 2014).

Volgy, T., Fausett, E., Grant, K. and Rodgers, S. (2008). Identifying formal intergovernmental organizations, *Journal of Peace Research*, 45, 837–850.

Weiss, T. and Wilkinson, R. (eds.). (2014). *International organization and global governance.* New York: Routledge.

Wilson, S. and Morello, C. (2014, March 24). Obama, allies agree to boycott G8 meeting in Russia, isolating Vladimir Putin. *Washington Post.* Retrieved from: www.washingtonpost.com/world/obama-in-europe-with-ukraine-high-on-agenda-kiev-makes-crimea-withdrawal/2014/03/24/001708a4-b344-11e3-8020-b2d790b3c9e1_story.html (accessed August 15, 2014).

Yamashita, H. (2013). The G8 and global peacekeeping, 2004–2010, *Global Governance,* 19, 333–352.

11 Organization for Security and Co-operation in Europe (OSCE)

Martin Nilsson

> The Syrian conflict has caused one of the worst humanitarian crises in decades. One that directly impacts the OSCE, specifically the participating member states in the region.
>
> (Gueterres, 2014)

The Organization for Security and Co-operation in Europe (OSCE) is often seen as the largest regional security organization around the world. Though its general aim has been to ensure peace, democracy, and stability in Europe, it currently has 57 members across the Northern Hemisphere from Europe, Asia and North America. In the Astana Summit 2010, in Azerbaijan, the member-states reaffirmed that the OSCE's overall ambition is to work for "a free, democratic, common and indivisible Euro-Atlantic and Eurasian security community stretching from Vancouver to Vladivostok, rooted in agreed principles, shared commitments and common goals" (OSCE, 2010).

The OSCE dates back to the early 1970s in the middle of the Cold War between the West (Western democracies in Europe, North America, Oceania and NATO) and the East (Communist Soviet Union, Eastern Europe and the Warsaw Pact). It was founded in the aftermath of the ratification of the Helsinki Final Act (1975) (Helsinki Act, 1975) as the *Commission on Security and Cooperation in Europe* (CSCE) and was primarily an attempt to improve relations between the West and the East (Pourchot, 2011; Nailes and Lachowski, 2010). Though the states were not legally bound to the agreement, it included guiding principles for cooperation between the governments of the member-states, such as respect for sovereignty and territorial integrity, peaceful settlements and non-interventions in international disputes, respect for human rights and fundamental civil and political freedoms, fulfillment of cooperation among states, and faith in international law.

At the same time, the end of the Cold War changed the scope and dynamics of the CSCE. In the early 1990s, the CSCE became one of the main actors to ensure peace and democracy in the newly independent states across Eastern Europe and the former Soviet republics (OSCE, 1990). As a consequence, the organization was renamed with its present title, the OSCE (Pourchot, 2011, pp. 179–195). While the former CSCE had the intention to establish a bridge between the East and the West during the Cold War, the new OSCE had the ambition to have a broader agenda in a new world with different security challenges than before, such as dealing with conflicts or crises, as in Syria (2011–present).

This chapter describes the nature of OSCE and its capacity to deal with failed states, such as Syria. In reality, however, though the OSCE has the capacity to handle some of the issues related to human security and humanitarian intervention, its ability to accomplish such missions seems to be weak, and as a consequence the OSCE has not accomplished any major missions in Syria. Rather, the OSCE can be seen as one among other organizations that support the UN system in its effort to handle the crisis in Syria.

Formal responsibilities of OSCE

Since the early 1990s, when the modern international organization became established, the OSCE has had a general secretariat located in Vienna, where most of the daily dialogues, negotiations and diplomacies take place (Pourchot, 1990; Lynch, 2007). Nowadays, it maintains an annual budget of between €150 and €200 million (OSCE, 2014a). The member-states meet in the permanent council every week in Vienna to consider relevant issues, and the chair's position rotates every year between the member-states and a troika of the former, current and future chairs. The highest decision body is the Ministerial Council, which has meetings once a year and summits in which the heads of state or governments are taking broader directions, mostly held every other year. (Pourchot, 2011). However, the legal status of the OSCE is more of one that demonstrates the political commitments between the governments, as the acts are not legally binding and are implemented in the member-states' national parliaments. All decisions at all levels are taken in consensus, which means that every state has the right to either veto any decision or mission or reject participation in field missions. In addition, there is another important decision-making body, the Forum for Security Co-operation, which deals with military operations, especially issues such as military inspections.

Besides the headquarters in Vienna, there are also other branches, for example, in Copenhagen (The International Secretariat for the OSCE Parliamentary Assembly), in the Hague (Higher Commissioner of National Minorities), and in Warsaw (Office for Democratic Institutions and Human Rights), and in Vienna there is also the Representative of Freedom of Media. In 2013, about 500–600 people were employed by the different OSCE's offices, while about 2,200 were working in 16 different field missions (OSCE, 2014b). The Parliamentary Assembly meets on a regular basis in an annual session and winter and spring sessions every year. In addition, there are also several committees that hold regular meetings as well. To ensure that the member-states uphold all commitments, the Assembly makes decisions on official resolutions and recommendations on issues related to political and security affairs, economic and environmental issues, and democracy and human rights. In addition, the Assembly is engaged in diplomatic missions and has an extensive program for monitoring elections around the world. In fact, through the Warsaw office, it has fulfilled more than 150 electoral missions around the world (OSCE, 2014c). Worth mentioning is that in regards to the OSCE's internal organization there was not any specific institution established which could handle issues such as humanitarian interventions or R2P. Most of the discussions about Syria have taken place in the OSCE's Parliamentary Assembly.

At the Lisbon summit (OSCE, 1996) in 1996, the heads of government of the OSCE, after the organization had been renamed, signed a declaration for how to proceed with a new security model to meet the future challenges ahead. The new approach was further established in 1999 at the Istanbul summit when the Charter for European Security (1999) was adopted. In this charter, it was stated that:

> [The OSCE's member states] are committed to preventing the outbreak of violent conflicts wherever possible. The steps we have agreed to take in this Charter will strengthen the OSCE's ability in this respect as well as its capacity to settle conflicts and to rehabilitate societies ravaged by war and destruction.
>
> (OSCE, 1999)

Once more, it was reaffirmed that the OSCE must act in accordance with the United Nations Charter as well as that the UN's Security Council has the primary responsibility to maintain international peace and security. This has implications for the crisis in Syria, since it requires a UN-mandate for any actions by the OSCE. At this summit, the modern structure of the organization and its scope for the broader security dimensions became essential parts of the organization. In the section of the OSCE charter about "our common challenges," (OSCE, 1999, pp. 3–4) the message was that the old Europe during the Cold War was gone but that still conflicts between and within states could occur, and the OSCE is determined to prevent this from happening. In addition, new security challenges were raised, such as those regarding international terrorism, violent extremism, organized crime and drug trafficking. However, humanitarian intervention or the principle of R2P was not integrated as an explicit part of the OSCE's new concept of security, but there are several dimensions that could be suitable, as we will see, to the crisis in Syria.

Furthermore, new socio-economic issues were seen as major security challenges, including, for example, acute economic problems and environmental degradation. Finally, nowadays the OSCE recognizes the importance of security in the nearby areas in the Mediterranean, as instability there might create possible security challenges for OSCE states, as well, particularly with the new partners of Jordan, Israel and Egypt. Syria was not part of this approach with new partnership, but several of its neighbors are partners with the OSCE, and Turkey at the northern border is a member-state. In accordance with the broader concept of "the human dimension," "the politico-military dimension," and "the economic and environmental dimension," the OSCE charter also states that the OSCE recognizes its ability to deploy civilian expertise to be effective in missions of conflict prevention, crisis management, and post-conflict management (OSCE, 1999, pp. 3–4; Brichambaut, 2012, pp. 31–44). As a result, the OSCE also offers its assistance to provide a rapid peacekeeping operation in a case when participating states accept it. In its charter, the OSCE also recognizes its best and most effective role in field operations connected to post-conflict operations, democratization and human rights. For the crisis of Syria, these fields would be useful as some of many aspects to improve the situation in the country. Finally, it is stated that the OSCE can only take such an approach, with consensus, on a case-by-case under the rights and obligations of the United Nations. It means that all member-states have to agree on any mission in Syria, and it has to be a UN-mandate.

In 2003, at the Ministerial Council meeting in Maastricht, the new strategy was further developed when the "OSCE strategy to address threats to security and stability in the Twenty-First Century" (OSCE, 2003) was adopted. There were several reasons behind this development. OSCE admitted itself that the organization had been instrumental in paving the way for security and stability across the OSCE region towards the end of the twentieth century, and has contributed to important democratic transformation in the OSCE area (OSCE, 2003, p. 3).

Further:

> Threats to security and stability in the OSCE region are today more likely to arise as negative, destabilizing consequences of developments that cut across the politico-military, economic and environmental and human dimensions, than from any major armed conflict.
>
> (OSCE, 2003, p. 1)

At this point, still, the conflicts in the Balkan countries were alive, and particularly the southeastern part of Europe had weak governance. The states had failed to establish and improve stable democratic institutions; meanwhile, the socio-economic conditions were seen as a threat to security as well as to the stability of the region and, in the long run, the entirety of Europe.

In addition, it was stated that the OSCE is a broad organization with member-states from Europe, North America and parts of Asia, and that it would be committed to a free and democratic OSCE area. In addition, as before, it should respect international law in accordance with the Charter of United Nations. Furthermore, the OSCE stated that it has to be more flexible and cooperate with other international organizations, such as the United Nations, NATO, the European Union and the Council of Europe (which deals with human rights issues) and that its main effort is still to contribute to security, albeit now in a much broader sense. For a major and complicated crisis as in Syria, this means that the OSCE understands itself as only one of many other important actors, such as the Arab League.

Within the security concept, the politico-military, economic, environmental and human dimensions became important, including several aspects of how to meet new challenges, such as terrorism, migration, environment, organized crime, discrimination and intolerance and inter-state and intra-state conflicts. In addition, the new strategy stated that human rights, democracy, and rule of law now were essentials part of the security concept, and that internal conflicts posed the most dangerous risk for the neighboring states (OSCE, 2003, pp. 1–2). Still, however, the concept of R2P did not become an essential part of OSCE's security concept. What was meant with neighboring areas and if it meant that OSCE from now on could intervene in such areas, for example, in Syria, was not either officially specified or discussed.

Officially, the OSCE has three dimensions of cooperation areas to enhance security: the politico-military, the economic and environmental, and the human (OSCE, 1999, pp. 2–3; OSCE, 2014d). However, no matter the issue, the OSCE has a non-binding or non-legal status. This means that it is up to the member-states to make decisions in every single matter, as they are political commitments between the states, i.e., the governments. Though the OSCE has a comprehensive view of the concept of security, which contains actions from "hard" security issues, such as conflict management, to "soft" issues dealing with human rights, there is still not any specific declaration about humanitarian intervention or R2P, which directly could be applicable to the crisis in Syria.

The first dimension includes activities for conflict prevention and resolution, such as arms control, border management, combating terrorism, conflict prevention and resolution, military or defense reforms, and cooperation and policing (OSCE, 1999, §28–30, pp. 2–3). Arms control means that the OSCE has helped to avoid the spread of illegal weapons around the world since the end of the Cold War and provided necessary documents, such as codes of conduct and practices to deal with the issues. Border management involves activities such as training border control officers, ensuring cross-border cooperation, and providing guidelines and manuals to enhance safe border security and legitimate travel and commerce, rather than issues related to trafficking and negative human rights behavior. OSCE's effort to combat terrorism involves both intelligence and expertise in related areas, such as conflict management and conducting reports and manuals about different topics related to terrorism. Conflict preventions and management means that the OSCE also works to stop potential conflicts, facilitate different settlements to prevent a conflict or war from happening, and work with the post-conflict setting to move beyond future conflicts. On a weekly basis, the OSCE holds meetings or dialogues in Vienna, in which the OSCE helps states to reform the military. The OSCE has field operations and a conflict prevention center, which can give help regarding military conduct, confidence- and security-building measures, downsizing armies and training personnel on human rights law.

The second dimension involves issues related to economic and environmental prosperity and includes activities to tackle economic growth, migration management, transport and energy security, and ecologic threats and sustainable development (OSCE, 1999, §31–33, pp. 2–3; OSCE, 2014d). Third and finally, the human dimension contains a wide range of activities related to issues such as good democratic governance, democratization, free and fair elections, education, gender equality, human rights, media freedom, rule of law, combating trafficking, and issues of tolerance and non-discrimination (OSCE, 1999, §19–27).

Besides these dimensions of security, the OSCE has also adopted some basic norms or standards for behavior in relation to the four areas of democratic control of military forces, border management, policing, and rule of law-based governance (Ghebali, 2007; cf. OSCE, 2014d). The control of military forces includes norms such as effective democratic control over the military, which means, for example, that the military forces have to respect international law and human rights and can only, for instance, intervene in domestic security affairs if they follow the rule of the democratic constitution.

However, in regards to R2P, this has not thus far been incorporated as an explicit part of any agreements between the member-states of OSCE or any agenda of OSCE policies or practices, and in these cases the OSCE simply relies on the UN-system, which is intended to take care of such issues.

Existing capabilities for the implementation of R2P

Since R2P is not an explicit part of the OSCE-agenda, it means that there is no agreement between the member-states on how OSCE will act in such a situation, whether it happens in any of the member-states or in any other states, such as in the case of the neighboring Syria. However, in a broader sense, the OSCE can act in such a situation, albeit in accordance with the following prerequisites.

First, in regards to the OSCE's broader mission, it is within its scope to act in accordance with the politico-military dimension, where the OSCE has an aim to both prevent conflict from happening and handle post-conflict situations. In addition, the OSCE's human dimension also involves human rights issues. OSCE has the possibility to work as a mediator through diplomacy with issues such as R2P, preventing potential conflicts from happening, establishing settlements to solve the conflict, and working with what lies ahead beyond a conflict. For the Syrian case this would have been possible, and this goes hand in hand with the OSCE's general agenda. The OSCE could also contribute to solving some of the early consequences of the crisis related to border management and migration issues, which have been discussed by the OSCE's Parliamentary Assembly.

Second, though the OSCE's general mission is to secure its own member-states, the organization also has opened up a broader approach. The OSCE has partner states around the Mediterranean, such as Jordan, Israel, Egypt and the member-state of Turkey. During the last decade, the OSCE has also emphasized the need to address and tackle security issues in the regions around the OSCE countries, which means that there are possibilities to act in neighboring countries, such as Syria, if it means protecting the OSCE in a wider sense, as well. Third, the OSCE can only act in any mission if it has a clear UN mandate or if it is the will of another state, which means that the OSCE cannot act by itself, no matter what the situation is. Still, the UN has not agreed on any major intervention in the

Syrian crisis, and the OSCE has therefore not received any mission. Fourth, all missions require the support of all countries, or at least, they require that not any single government oppose it. Any mission requires an affirmative consensus, i.e., any government can veto if they do not like the mission for any reason. In this case, Russia has not been eager to involve other states in this crisis since it believes it is about domestic affairs. Finally, however, if the OCSE will act, it has the greatest capacity to act in a diplomatic mission to either prevent R2P for happening or to prevent it while it is happening. The OSCE has the capacity to contribute by handling issues related to diplomacy, border management and migration as well as issues that arise in the post-conflict phase, such as disarmament or if new democratic institutions replace traditional ones, particularly electoral missions.

Actual abilities to address R2P challenges

Though the OSCE might have some capacity to contribute to establish at least partially the norms of R2P, this has not always been the case—for example, in Syria. The OSCE is the largest regional security organization, but it has no military capacity at all, and it is rather an intergovernmental organization focusing on peace settlements and management through missions, such as diplomacy and monitoring of elections, when the member-states can agree to act, such in the case of over hundreds of electoral missions or as a mediator during the Ukraine crisis in 2014. Because some of the member-states are liberal democracies, such as most states in the European Union (EU), and some have authoritarian rule (Russia is the best example) while others are in between (such as Georgia and Ukraine), the OSCE cannot work as a normative power that stands for democracy and human rights, as one of the most important security aspects (Manners, 2002, pp. 235–258; Pace, 2007, pp. 1041–1065). Though one can argue whether the European Union is an effective normative power, its entire foreign policy, foreign aid, external trade and enlargement procedure includes the dimension of promoting democracy, human rights, rule of law and market economy. In addition, these dimensions are also supranational EU law, and all member-states have to follow it according to the legally binding treaties. But with the OSCE, there is really no sharing of a democratic community with common norms and values, and this also has implications on how to act on missions in Europe and perhaps also in other possible human security situations, such as the conflict in Syria.

Based on previous OSCE missions and work since the 1990s, there are also lessons to be learned with ongoing crises, such as the one in Ukraine or in Syria. The OSCE's actions regarding Syria have mainly involved giving a few statements to address the refugee crisis. For example, in OSCE's Parliamentary Assembly's winter meeting in February 2013, an independent OSCE report was presented, and a discussion took place on the humanitarian crisis in Syria (OSCE's Parliamentary Assembly, 2013a). The report identified key areas on how the member-states could act together to contribute to handle issues related to asylum applications and visa issues for Syrians, specifically for workers, students, women and children (OSCE's International Secretariat, 2013). Later on, in June 2013, there was a co-sponsored Turkish resolution in the Parliamentary Assembly by 58 parliamentarians from 17 countries urging that the international community, particularly the UN Security Council, should take action to stop the civil war and support a political transition to democracy (OSCE's Parliamentary Assembly 2013—Parliamentarians to vote on approach to crisis in Syria, 2013b). At this Istanbul annual session (2013), a resolution about the crisis in Syria was taken, in which the OSCE Parliamentary Assembly stated that it:

> Urges the end to brute force against civilians and systematic violations of international law, particularly the use of ballistic missiles and other heavy weaponry.
>
> Reminds the OSCE participating States of their responsibility to uphold human rights, fundamental freedoms, democracy and the rule of law, and therefore urges participating States to unequivocally condemn in the strongest terms the crimes against humanity committed in Syria…
>
> Urges the international community, and the UN Security Council in particular, to take decisive and urgent action with a view to fulfilling its primary responsibilities in terms of safeguarding international and regional peace, security and stability.
>
> (OSCE's Parliamentary Assembly, 2013c)

Furthermore, in October 2013, the autumn meeting of the Parliamentary Assembly discussed the crisis in Syria in relation to the Mediterranean forum of the OSCE. President Mignon of the Parliamentary Assembly of the European Council was invited and urged for a dialogue:

> We must all take responsibility to meet the challenges before us: the situation of refugees who arrive en masse and in very precarious conditions on the shores of the Mediterranean, the humanitarian consequences of the war in Syria, democratic transformations in the southern Mediterranean and the Middle East. The PACE Partner for Democracy status is a powerful tool for progress on these topics. Rights have no borders and I hope that our two assemblies will full use of all the tools of dialogue and parliamentary diplomacy to find appropriate solutions.
>
> (OSCE's Parliamentary Assembly, 2013d)

In early 2014, the United Nations High Commissioner for refugees, Antonio Guterres stated in front of the OSCE's Permanent Council that the conflict of the humanitarian crisis in Syria is a major threat to global security and has created over 2.5 million refugees, which affect the OSCE-countries, in particular Turkey. As a consequence, he urged the OSCE countries to have their border open for refugees and to take on a collective burden to solve the crisis.

In conclusion, beyond the parliamentary discussions and a few statements about the crisis in Syria and some policy recommendations for the member-states in regards to immigration issues, nothing more concrete has been done to solve the situation. This has to do with the lack of abilities for the OSCE to act in cases such as Syria, and there are several contributing explanations for why OSCE has not really intervened in Syria.

The world scene has changed the OSCE's role as an important actor

One explanation is that the OSCE might not always be important to its member-states, which means that any issue or mission will be discussed somewhere else (Brichambaut, 2012, p. 31; Togt, 2007). Nowadays, only the US and Russia have enough delegates in Vienna to follow any single topic of the OSCE, and they tend to follow all issues but with different approaches. The US tends to use the OSCE mainly as a tool to promote democratic development in eastern and southern Europe, while Russia understands the OSCE as one of few forums in which it has an equal status with its former adversaries from the West. However, Russia does not want to have any kind of strategies or missions that will have negative consequences for Russia, and it has, from time to time, accused the OSCE of being a tool for the West to impose its policies and interest. This was the case with the Orange Revolution in 2004 in Ukraine, and the same procedure occurred during the latest Ukrainian crisis in 2014. In addition, the OSCE's statement about irregularities during most elections in Belarus is another example. Vladimir Putin has officially made this very clear:

> They [unnamed Western States] are trying to transform the OSCE into a vulgar instrument designed to promote the foreign policy interests of one or a group of countries. And this task is also being accomplished by the OSCE's bureaucratic apparatus, which is absolutely not connected with the state founders in any way. Decision-making procedures and the involvement of so-called non-governmental organizations are tailored for this task. These organizations are formally independent but they are purposefully financed and therefore under control.
>
> (Pravda, 2007)

But besides the US and Russian approaches, other member-states, such as those within the EU, and Canada and Norway, tend to be more selective in regards to the internal OSCE work (Brichambaut, 2012, p. 31). Mostly, the agendas serve the national interest or a single issue that the state has the capacity to work with. In conclusion, the OSCE serves as a permanent security structure in Europe, but for most states, it is marginal compared with other important actors. The "big picture" (Bailes and Lachowski, 2010, pp. 9–11) has changed in Europe since the end of the Cold War, and nowadays, the EU, NATO, Russia and the US use it for other purposes. Though the OSCE has widened its scope of the security concept and its geographical presence since the Cold War ended, the budget has not increased, and it is very modest in relation to its overall ambition. But for smaller states that are not members of either the EU or NATO, it could be seen as a window of opportunity to raise and act on an issue, but it only relates to a few of the states in the East and in the Balkans. For Syria it means that most member-states see international organizations other than OSCE as more important to handle the crisis.

Mission beyond the border of OSCE?

Though the OSCE's aim is to establish security for its member-states across the Northern Hemisphere, it also has the ambition to connect other states and regions to promote democracy, human rights and security. Nowadays, the OSCE has partnerships with countries such as Japan, Afghanistan, South Korea, Thailand and Australia, as well as with countries around the Mediterranean, but not with Syria. However, there is an internal debate about whether this means that the OSCE should engage in missions outside of the member-states or not. The Final Act and all other official OSCE documents mainly call for interventions in the OSCE countries, but at the same time, the political development in world politics and in Europe during the 2000s opened up the potential for some outside engagement with a UN mandate or if all states (including the one where the mission is taking place) agree to act. Beyond that, it leaves a lot to discuss about missions in surrounding areas. So far, when the Arab Spring occurred, the OSCE offered to provide help to non-governmental organizations by providing assistance and training programs with elections and human rights issues (Pavlyuk and Vinnikov, 2012, pp. 171–174). However, the Arab Spring also made it obvious that there is a need for a stronger commitment by the Mediterranean partners for the cooperation to be more effective (Marascalchi, 2012, pp. 175–183). However, Syria is not a part of the partnership with the Mediterranean countries, which means that it is definitely outside of the territory of the OSCE; regardless, it is a neighbor and raises concerns about issues such as migration and security around its borders.

The principle of consensus and lack of performance

A third explanation has to do with the internal decision-making and the principle of consensus (or veto) and how it makes it almost impossible for major actions in most cases, such as an intervention in any domestic affair. Though there is a principle called the "consensus minus-one," the OSCE can act in cases if there is a clear violation of relevant commitments if all states except the "absent state" agree (Pourchot, 2011, pp. 179–195). However, beyond that, every single decision and action at all of the OSCE levels and branches can be vetoed by a member-state. In reality, this means that the OSCE has a long road to even adopt its own principles and manners of respect for human rights and democracy, particularly regarding post-Soviet territories (Pourchot, 2011, pp. 175–195). This also applies for handling conflicts involving domestic movements for independence such as in the former Yugoslavia (Kosovo), or Russia (Chechnya), Georgia (South Ossetia and Abkhazia), or between states such as Armenia and Azerbaijan (over Nagorno-Karabakh). The bottom line is that there are different views among the member-states on how to relate to the OSCE basic norms and values, but this impact on whether the OSCE could intervene in domestic affairs (Brichambaut, 2012, pp. 35–36).

In the case of Syria, however, because any such potential mission requires a UN mandate, it stops with that because Russia, except for some control of chemical weapons, has opposed every major effort from other countries for any effective resolution in the Security Council and any other actions that could be seen as a major international intervention on domestic affairs in Syria. Further, even if there were a UN mandate, Russia would oppose any such actions within the OSCE, as Russia has taken the position that all actions within the organization always have to be confirmed at the highest level, which means that the government of Russia will oppose any actions that are against its interests. (Bailes and Lachowski, 2010, pp. 9–11). According to Kropatcheva (2012), in the OSCE, Russia has acted as a realistic actor, and its cooperation has been limited to issues that are in its interest and that do not contravene Russia's long-term security agenda in post-Soviet states (Kropatcheva, 2012, pp. 370–394). Syria has always had strong relations with Russia (and the Soviet Union during the Cold War), and this seems still to matter. Besides this, any such action in a domestic conflict could lead to demands to solve a similar crisis in the future in Russia or in the post-Soviet territory. As a consequence, the principle of consensus is an obstacle if one has the ambition to be able to handle human security issues in Syria.

Does the OSCE have an adequate toolbox?

Though the OSCE has a centralized procedure of decision-making requiring consensus, the OSCE has developed a decentralized organization when it comes to handling concrete missions (Brichambaut, 2012, p. 31). Once a decision has been made, each field operation works very autonomously, at least as long as there remains a general support from the member-states. In particular, the OSCE has local officers and connections at the local level, which few other organizations have across Europe. In particular, the OSCE has a well-established toolbox to work with border management, monitoring elections, and being a mediator through diplomacy in a conflict situation before, during and after it happens. However, beyond that, the OSCE has no toolbox to generally deal with issues such as the one in Syria, including the military required to prevent a human disaster from happening or to deal with human security issues in a broader sense, including all sorts of military and civil actions. In the long run, at best, the OSCE can act as a socializing agency if a member-state decides to follow its own norms and rules (Pourchot, 2011, pp. 179–195). This means that the OSCE, in the long run, can interact with other international organizations to enlarge European values for other regions and states and thereby be able to handle similar situations, such as the one in Syria. But at some point, though the OSCE does not have the right toolbox for a military intervention, it does have experience as a mediator in non-international conflicts. In fact, sometimes, the OSCE is one of few organizations that has a toolbox for this. The OSCE also has the capacity to deal with border management to handle migration issues related to Syria.

Conclusion

The OSCE has the ambition to be a major and important regional organization for security. During the Cold War, it was a forum for dialogue between the West and East, and to some extent, it could therefore be seen as a successful organization, as it was one among other actors to contribute to avoiding the escalation of the Cold War into a real military war in Europe. It also promoted issues such as human rights in a time period during which Eastern Europe had dictatorships. But the new OSCE that was born in the aftermath of the end of the old Cold War in the 1990s, with a more democratic Europe than ever before, is widening its ambition also to establish economic and human security.

However, it seems that the OSCE does not have the capacity for such ambitions and missions as in Syria. The 57 member-states do not share the same norms or values; this is obvious in regards to democratic rule and human rights issues. Though the OSCE has been engaged in several electoral-monitoring missions among its member-states and in other parts of the world and despite the fact that it has several border management missions in Caucasus countries and has been a mediator in crises such as in Ukraine in recent years, still it lacks the ability to act in cases like Syria. There is no consensus among member-states on how to accomplish the wider scope of security. Most states only concentrate their efforts on a few security issues, and the European Union members tend to speak with one voice if they can agree. The United States understands it mainly as a tool to promote democracy and human rights in the post-Soviet sphere and in the remaining parts of Eastern Europe, while Russia tends to see it as the only organization in which it is an equal partner to the Western countries; this means that Russia blocks every initiative that might have a negative effect on its own security agenda in the Eastern sphere, such as in regards to democracy, elections, human rights, or intervention in any domestic affairs. Because the OSCE now also has other major competitive organizations, such as NATO and EU, it is a low priority for most states. The requirements of consensus in the decision-making process also make it difficult to conduct drastic missions, such as major interventions in any domestic affairs, as would be needed in the civil war in Syria, as some states like Russia will most likely veto any such mission.

Though the OSCE has not officially endorsed R2P as a core responsibility, it still fits within the organization's broader security agenda, but the OSCE still requires a mandate from the UN Security Council. However, the OSCE has the ability to act as a mediator to stop the conflict in Syria or to organize control of the borders, which would improve the situation for ordinary people and refugees, among others, but there are several obstacles to overcome before this yet could happen. As a consequence, so far the OSCE has played a minor role in the Syrian crisis, mostly urging its member-states to handle the refugee crisis in a constructive way.

References

Bailes, A. and Lachowski, Z. (2010). Collective Security and the politico-military role of the OSCE. *Security and Human Rights*, 2, 9–11.

Brichambaut, Perrin de M. (2012). The OSCE in perspective, six years of service, six questions and a few answers. *Security and Human Rights*, 1, 31–44.

Ghebali, Y. V. (2007). The OSCE involvement in security sector reform: Normative commitments and operational activities without an integrated approach. In D. Warner (ed.). *The OSCE at a turning point: OSCE Chairmanship and other challenges*. Geneva: PSIO Occasional Paper 2007.

Gueterres, A. (2014, February 21). *UN refugee head calls on OSCE to share the burden of Syria conflict – Statement by the UN High Commissioner for Refugees, Anadolu Agency*. Retrieved from: www.aa.com.tr/en/politics/291025-un-refugee-head-calls-on-osce-to-share-the-burden-of-syria-conflict (accessed August 20, 2014).

Helsinki Act (1975). *Conference on Security and Co-operation in Europe – Final Act*. Helsinki 1975. Retrieved from: www.osce.org/mc/39501?download=true (accessed August 20, 2014).

Kropatcheva, E. (2012). Russia and the role of the OSCE in European security: A 'Forum' for dialog or a 'Battlefield' of interest?' *European Security*, 21, 370–394.

Marascalchi, R. (2012). The OSCE response to the Arab Spring and the implications for the OSCE Mediterranean Partnership. *Security & Human Rights*, 23, 175–183.

Lynch, D. (2007). The OSCE as an Organization. In D. Warner (ed.). *The OSCE at a turning point: OSCE Chairmanship and other challenges*. Geneva: PSIO Occasional Paper 2007.

Manners, I. 2002. Normative power europe: A contradiction in terms? *Journal of Common Market Studies*, 40, 235–258.

Nailes, A. and Lachowski, Z. (2010). Collective Security and the politico-military role of the OSCE, *Security and Human Rights*, 1, 5–11.

OSCE (1990). *The Charter of Paris for a new Europe*. Retrieved from: www.osce.org/node/39516 (accessed August 20, 2014).

OSCE (1996). *Lisbon-summit Declaration – Lisbon-document*. Retrieved from: www.osce.org/mc/39539?download=true (accessed August 26, 2014).

OSCE (1999). *Charter for European Security*. Retrieved from: www.osce.org/mc/17502 (accessed August 26, 2014).

OSCE (2003). *OSCE strategy to address threats to security and stability in the twenty-first century*. Retrieved from: www.osce.org/mc/17504.

OSCE (2010). *Astana commemorative declaration towards a security community – Astana Summit meeting*. Retrieved from: www.osce.org/cio/74985?download=true (accessed May 10, 2014).

OSCE (2014a). *Budget and finances*. Retrieved from: www.osce.org/who/108228 (accessed August 20, 2014).

OSCE (2014b). *Who we are/Fact sheets – What is the OSCE?* Retrieved from: www.osce.org/odihr (accessed August 20, 2014).

OSCE (2014c). *OSCE Office for Democratic Institutions and Human Rights*. Retrieved from: www.osce.org/odihr.

OSCE (2014d). *What we do*. Retrieved from: www.osce.org/what (accessed August 20, 2014).

OSCE's International Secretariat of the OSCE Parliamentary Assembly (2013). *Humanitarian crisis in Syria: A special report on the impact of Syrian refugees in the OSCE region.* February 12, 2013. Retrieved from: www.oscepa.org/news-a-media/press-releases/2013/1195-updated-report-on-the-impact-of-the-syrian-refugee-crisis-in-the-osce-region (accessed August 20, 2014).

OSCE's Parliamentary Assembly (2013a). *Updated report on the impact of the Syrian refugee crisis in OSCE.* Retrieved from: htpp://www.oscepa.org/news-a-media-press-releases/2013/1195 (accessed August 20, 2014).

OSCE's Parliamentary Assembly (2013b). *Parliamentarians to vote on approach to crisis in Syria,* June 18, 2013. Retrieved from: www.osce.org/pa/102836 (accessed August 20, 2014).

OSCE's Parliamentary Assembly (2013c). *Istanbul Final Declaration – Resolution on the Humanitarian Crisis in Syria.* Retrieved from: www.oscepa.org/meetings/annual-sessions/2013-istanbul-annual-session/2013-istanbul-final-declaration/1646-09 (accessed August 20, 2014).

OSCE's Parliamentary Assembly (2013d). *PA Autumn Meeting begins with focus on trans-national threats, challenges of the Mediterranean region and the crisis in Syria.* October 14, 2013. Retrieved from: www.oscepa.org/news-a-media/press-releases/2013/1402-osce-pa-autumn-meeting-begins-with-focus-on-transnational-threats-challenges-of-the-mediterranean-region-and-the-crisis-in-syria (accessed August 20, 2014).

Pace, M. (2007). The construction of EU normative power, *Journal of Common Market Studies*, 45, 1041–1064.

Pavlyuk, O. and Vinnikov, A. (2012). The OSCE and the Arab Spring: Two years after. *Security & Human Rights, 23*, 171–174.

Pourchot, G. (2011). The OSCE: A Pan-European Society in the Making?. *European Integration*, 33, 179–195.

Pravda (2014). *Putin's speech at the Munich-Security conference 2007 – OSCE to sabotage Russia's presidential election.* Retrieved from: http://english.pravda.ru/russia/politics/01-02-2008/103818-osce_russia-0/ (accessed April 28, 2014).

Togt, der A. (2007). The OSCE and the EU. In D. Warner (ed.). *The OSCE at a turning point: OSCE Chairmanship and other challenges.* Geneva: PSIO Occasional Paper 2007.

12 Summary

Daniel Silander and Don Wallace

This study approached, in Chapter 1 (*Introduction*, developed by Daniel Silander and Don Wallace), the ongoing civil war in Syria by focusing on the UN and international organizations on the Responsibility to Protect (R2P) and human security. It was argued that the UN General Assembly (UNGA) and the UN Security Council (UNSC) have endorsed the legal and moral obligations of the international community to safeguard civilians from genocide and atrocities. UN member-states and regional organizations are, according to the UN Charter, required to protect and promote universal human rights and in 2005, the UN World Summit approved R2P. Despite UN legality and legitimacy to protect international peace and security and to promote human security, the UN has at numerous of times failed to uphold the basic principles set out in the UN Charter. The late twentieth century history shows how the UN at too many times acted too little and too late leaving state regimes able to conduct genocide and atrocities against men, women and children. In late 2013, an armed humanitarian intervention in Syria seemed to be inevitable as Arab and Western regional organizations with member-states called for R2P and the removal of President Bashar al-Assad. More than a year later, no such intervention had occurred leaving the Syrian government and President Assad untouched and with an ongoing humanitarian catastrophe for the Syrian population. Since the civil war began in 2011, the UN and other organizations have presented statistics on rising numbers of murdered and displaced civilians. In late 2014, more than 200,000 people were estimated to have been killed in the civil war and about half of the Syrian population being refugees in surrounding states or displaced within Syria. The UN High Commissioner for Human Rights accused President Assad of Syria of war crimes and crimes against humanity and called for the international community to send President Assad to the International Criminal Court.

This book has sought to discuss the responsibility to protect civilians and prevent humanitarian catastrophes from happening by discussing the capabilities and abilities of international organizations to address R2P. The main objective of the study has been to explore how different multinational organizations around the world have engaged in the implementation of R2P in general, but more importantly in Syria. As the UNSC has continued to be paralyzed to uphold its duty to provide for peace, security and human rights in Syria, due to disagreements among member-states, this study has focused on the capabilities and abilities of multinational organizations to promote the principles in the UN Charter and of R2P as an alternative path towards improved human security. R2P was endorsed by the UN Security Council in Darfur and Libya, stressing that state sovereignty is not a shield for state abuse against civilians. On the contrary, state sovereignty embeds the obligation to safeguard civilians and provide for domestic security, but if such obligation is not met, R2P legally and morally endorses the international community to justify humanitarian intervention to protect human security.

Chapter 2, *The United Nations, international organizations and responsibility to protect*, developed by Don Wallace and Daniel Silander, addresses in short the political history of R2P by discussing the 2001 report by the International Commission on Intervention and States Sovereignty (ICISS) and the international debate on human versus state security. The ICISS explicitly stressed the responsibility of the international community to safeguard human security within states that were unwilling or failed to provide security for their people. Such international obligation was not only linked to individual states, but also other legal bodies in international, regional and non-governmental organizations. We have argued that a too often forgotten dimension of the ICISS report was the acknowledgement of international organizations to implement R2P when necessary and how multinational organizations could be key players within the international community to turn a principle into a norm and action. The important role of international organizations was also acknowledged in the 2005 UNGA World Summit Outcome Document, with guidance from the UN Charter and Chapter VIII on activities of regional organizations to promote the purposes and principles of the UN. In addition, we emphasized how Article 52 of the UN Charter addresses the responsibility of regional actors to help the UN to provide for regional and local peace and security before becoming a UN Security Council issue. Article 52 stresses not only the importance of regional actors to deal with regional insecurity, but also to do so before referring them to the Security Council, opening up for multinational organizations to provide for peace and security in Syria. Contrary to the ICISS Report, the UN Outcome Document of 2005, however, stressed the necessity of UN Security Council authority before international organizations activities on R2P. The capabilities and abilities of international organizations to act upon R2P gained great attention due to their various actions in Libya of 2010. The declarations on R2P against the Libyan regime and Colonel Gaddafi by the African Union (AU), the League of Arab States (LAS), the European Union (EU) and the North Atlantic Treaty Organization (NATO) highlighted the important role international organizations can have against brutal regimes and how these organizations also may provide capabilities to the UN to provide for peace and human rights. The analysis of multinational organizations and R2P in the case of Syria has had two dimensions; first exploring the capacity of each organization by focusing on military, economic, political and technological resources and second exploring the actual ability of each organization in the possibility and/or willingness to act.

Chapter 2 also set out what the UNSC, the UNGA and the UN Human Rights Council have done and not done to provide for peace, security and human rights in Syria. Syria is another example of what scholarly debate has labeled the failing states syndrome. It is argued that state sovereignty is derived from the people and entails international respect for state security and domestically respect for human rights and security of its people. The failing states syndrome in Syria has become an international challenge to state security and human security within Syria and the region at large, requiring R2P action from the international community.

In Chapter 3, *Contextualizing conflict: trends and challenges in the Syrian Civil War*, Stephen Marr provides a discussion on the scope and timeline of the escalation of violence of 2011 leading up to the humanitarian catastrophe of today. Stephen Marr looks back on the Arab uprisings of the early 2011 and how Syria was perceived by state leaders and in media as unlikely to be touched by these regional events. President Assad himself announced how the Syrian people legitimately accepted regime policies. In August of 2013, President Assad was accused of using chemical weapons against civilians as the ultimate horrifying symbol of a repressive and cruel regime faced by a full-scale civil war. The state-sanctioned violence against civilians began with the crackdown on the popular demonstrations against the regime in spring 2011. As the demonstrations intensified in number of protesters and in geographical scope, the Syrian regime stepped up its violence. Soon, the Syrian regime was challenged by armed rebellions demanding an end to the Syrian regime. As the civil war developed into 2014, the number of those killed was estimated at above 200,000 and with about half of the Syrian population being refuges in neighboring states or displaced in a war-torn Syria. The author posits that there are several causes to the survival of the Syrian regime and the ongoing civil war. One is the strength of the Syrian regime and its ability to gain military loyalty despite military defeats and lost territories to anti-government forces. Stephen Marr also addresses the weakness and factionalization of the anti-government forces and opposition movements and the improved regime and military capabilities to deal with these military and political challenges. Some of the immediate security challenges to be handled by the international community to stop the civil war are laid out in the chapter. The author stresses how the international community at the beginning disagreed on how to portray and whom to blame for the human insecurity in Syria undermining any international efforts to prevent the situation from deteriorating. The international community also disagreed on whether a military intervention in the name of R2P would be successful and what would happen if such intervention led to regime change given the fragmented opposition consisting of about 1,000 armed militias, including jihadist groups.

The existence of the *ICC*, according to Don Wallace in Chapter 4, affirms the international legal obligation that those individuals who commit mass atrocity crimes must be held accountable. The ICC is limited to providing a tribunal as an alternative to national courts for holding individuals rather than nation-states accountable for crimes. Though only individuals may be held legally accountable under the ICC, in the context of R2P, where nations are required to protect their populations, these individuals would likely be government officials in positions of authority, such as President al-Assad of Syria. Should these criminal acts become factually attributable to a state, demonstrating its failures to abide by its R2P obligations, the state will lose legitimacy and its exclusive sovereign rights over its population. In this regard the ICC shares the perspective of R2P that it is the responsibility of both national governments and the international community to prevent atrocity crimes. However, implementing this perspective is problematic where the state of the suspect or the location of the mass atrocity is not a party to the Rome Statute, though there can be a referral by the UNSC to the ICC, the very ability of the ICC for facilitating the principles of R2P is dependent on the political agendas of the permanent members of the UNSC. Chapter 4 finds that the investigation and prosecution by the ICC of atrocity crimes committed in the ceaseless humanitarian crisis in Syria should be a substantive part of the R2P response by the international community. The ICC could play a significant role in the operationalization of the Responsibility to Protect (R2P) for Syria in that it could contribute to the third pillar of the approach to R2P outlined by the Report of the UN Secretary-General, for advancing the agenda of the 2005 World Summit Outcome Document. The reliance upon the UNSC, not upon the ICC, for the determination of the threshold question of whether a situation involves a violation of R2P principles faces a challenge from the conflicting agendas of the permanent members. Despite a global outcry against the Syrian conflict and calls for a referral by the UNSC to the ICC, the issue of UNSC intervention remains intensely contested among permanent Council members, with Russia and China vetoing UNSC resolutions. However, it is the intractable political position of these veto-holding members in the UNSC and the ICC's dependence on the UNSC to exercise its authority over non-States Parties that impede any successful role for the ICC with the situation in Syria. Because its jurisdiction over chemical weapons is limited to their use in international conflicts, the ICC, even with a referral from the UNSC, might not be able to consider the criminal liability of Syrian officials for the specific use of such weapons. Further, the isolated and sporadic chemical attacks in Syria might not be classified as widespread or systematic, and no individual or group has been clearly defined as the instigators of the attacks, preventing the situation from being assessed as a crime against humanity.

John Janzekovic in Chapter 5 discusses the role of the *OPCW* and its involvement in the Syrian crisis. It was the lack of a historical, firm legal framework dealing with the use of chemical weapons that prompted the development of the Chemical Weapons Convention (CWC) that entered into force in 1997. Syria was not a party to the CWC prior to 2013 therefore it was not legally committed to CWC prohibitions against the development, production or use of chemical weapons. The OPCW-UN investigators have confirmed that a large-scale sarin attack had been delivered by rockets hitting the Ghouta area in Damascus, killing 1,400 people. Further, since the OPCW is not structured to pursue responsibility, the Assad regime has not been clearly identified as the perpetrator of the August

21, 2013 chemical attack. Thus, without an investigation into individual responsibility any possible further international response to the use of chemical weapons is in doubt. John Janzekovic observes that an important R2P principle is the responsibility to prevent the need for direct and immediate protection. In the case of Syria, the preventive approach regarding the further use of chemical weapons was successful. With the OPCW Director-General reporting that identification and removal of chemical and nerve agents in Syria was completed on June 23, 2014. This marks a significant achievement for the R2P preventive pillar. John Janzekovic cautions that though the OPCW-UN mission in Syria is an example of how the international community responding effectively to a very serious situation that potentially saved many lives, this international response demonstrates that it takes an extreme and very specific danger before a practical and effective response is forthcoming.

Though the *OIC* has not explicitly endorsed the responsibility to protect, it was a staunch defender of coercive intervention in Libya and has supported non-military international involvement in Syria. According to Melinda Negrón-Gonzales in Chapter 6 there are two institutional limitations that preclude the OIC from significantly advancing R2P principles. The first is its firm commitment to state sovereignty and non-interference in the internal affairs of its members. The second limitation stems from its lack of institutional instruments to *monitor* and *enforce* compliance with the R2P-related principles of its charter. With a mandate that includes the promotion of good governance and human rights and a more active role in conflict resolution, the OIC can serve as a major global player in the advancement of R2P. Yet, the OIC's swift response to the crisis in Libya in 2011 stands in sharp contrast to its dithering on Syria. From the time peaceful protests were met with Syrian state violence, the OIC has issued statements condemning violence by both rebels and state forces, and has called for negotiations to reach a political settlement that respects Syria's sovereignty and territorial integrity. Although the OIC has condemned both sides for human rights violations, it has echoed R2P's first pillar by singling out the Syrian state as the party that bears primary responsibility for maintaining law and order and protecting civilians. Nevertheless, there is a marked difference between the organization's responses to atrocities in Libya and Syria. Of course, the OIC's unprecedented authorization of military intervention in Libya can be attributed in part to Gaddafi's international isolation. Unlike Libya, however, Syria was not seen as an international pariah and generally enjoyed good relations with its neighbors, importantly of which Iran is a member of the OIC, which resulted in a much longer wait-and-see period after violence escalated. In contrast to the Libyan case, the OIC has never advocated for R2P third pillar military intervention, and has in fact repeatedly argued against it. The OIC has worked diligently alongside the UN and other international partners to address the humanitarian dimension of the civil war, actions that fall under R2P's third pillar, on timely and decisive response to atrocities. Further, it has supported dialogue and a political solution, but lacking the tools to serve as interlocutor to facilitate an end to the atrocities, it has publicly supported the mediation efforts of other international actors, such as the Arab League and United Nations.

Chapter 7, on the *LAS*, often referred to as the Arab League, co-authored by Alan Patterson and Craig McLean, explores why the organization have been relatively inefficient at dealing with the Syrian regime. Although the Syrian regime was suspended from the organization in November 2011, due to regime brutality against demonstrators, it is argued that despite that the Arab League has capabilities to act upon R2P in Syria, member-states have had diverging foreign policies towards President Assad, undermining the organization's ability to speak with one voice. The analysis indicates a limited ability to make use of regional capabilities due to the lack of integration in high politics. The different nature of regimes in addition to the intergovernmental nature of the organization, where integration in areas of foreign and defense policy has been limited, has left the League with little impact on Syria. The League did, at an early stage of the civil war, call for an Arab-UN peacekeeping force, but was rejected by the Syrian regime. In late 2011, the League and the Syrian regime approved a peace plan, but violence continued to escalate, undermining any further peace talks and leading to economic sanctions by the League on Syria. Despite efforts by the League to find diplomatic solutions to the conflict, in sending peace monitors to Syria, and to push for UNSC resolutions on Syria, the disagreements within the UNSC have become a major obstacle to the League. There have also been obvious disagreements between major states, such as Egypt and Saudi Arabia, on how to deal with Syria, and different approaches to Syria based on the long-term tensions between Shia and Sunni sects within the political regimes.

In Chapter 8, Daniel Silander highlights the harsh rhetoric of the *GCC* on the Syrian regime. The six member-states agreed, at an early stage of the Syrian civil war, that the Syrian regime under the leadership of President Assad was to be blamed for the ongoing atrocities. The GCC argued that the escalation of violence against civilians within Syria required the removal of President Assad. Due to the mass atrocities, the six GCC member-states called for UN Security Council action to find a final solution to the ongoing violence. Although the Syrian Foreign Minister accused the GCC of intervening in Syrian domestic politics, all six GCC member-states continued to argue that Syria required regime change. Although the GCC was originally a regional organization of economic nature, the idea of political and military integration has been raised by the member-states. While a few GCC member-states have continued to stress economic integration as main objective, other member-states have had interests in promoting political and military integration. Such interests have, however, met obstacles with member-states having different relationships to other non-GCC powers in Iran and Hezbollah in Lebanon. The analysis on the GCC indicates that the six member-states have agreed on promoting R2P towards the Syrian regime. However, the relatively low number of member-states, the limited political and military capabilities and the challenged abilities to act upon R2P in coordinating joint forces, to develop a joint security and defense policy, and to decide on how to relate to Iran, have left the GCC too weak to successfully push for international actions on Syria in the name of R2P.

NATO is explored in Chapter 9 by Daniel Silander. It is argued that NATO has fundamentally transformed, from an organization deterring communism to become an entity of 28 member-states focusing on a wide range of security challenges, including human security and issues of humanitarian intervention. In addition, NATO has changed from a security organization focused on the transatlantic region to engagement in Afghanistan, Darfur, Kosovo, Libya and Sudan, among many other non-transatlantic areas. NATO has identified the strategic need to find partnerships with other regional organizations to promote its objectives globally. In Libya, NATO and the League found an agreement to work for R2P against the Libyan regime. The conducted analysis of NATO on R2P in Syria highlights the normative nature of NATO, with its democratic member-states having the objective to safeguard freedoms in political rights and civil liberties. Although NATO member-states have not formally endorsed the R2P, key member-states of NATO have addressed the importance of promoting R2P in failed states. The actions on R2P in Kosovo and Libya also opened for a debate to endorse R2P based on the normative foundations of the organization. The analysis on NATO identifies, however, that despite the objective to safeguard the principles of democracy, individual liberty and the rule of law, challenges within NATO exist on R2P. Despite the fact that NATO member-states have seen worsened diplomatic relations with Russia, due to different positions on Syria and the escalation of diplomatic tension over Ukraine, NATO has also, besides a paralyzed UN Security Council, faced internal debates on when, how and why NATO should act in Syria. The broadened security concept and geographical context have led to internal disputes on whether R2P is to be followed outside NATO member-states territory. Since Syria is out of NATO's geographical territory, the 28 member-states have had different opinions on what to do with Syria, if doing anything at all. The debate has also highlighted the imbalance on burden-sharing between the US and European allies, the American war-fatigue and the European unwillingness to spend more money on strategic military developments in technology and infrastructure to become an essential military player on R2P challenges.

Historically the role played by the *G7/G8* in dealing with situations such as the contemporary situation in Syria is shaped by the very nature of this institution. As Niall Michelsen in Chapter 10 observes, the focus of the G7/G8 has evolved from being overwhelmingly economic to increasingly political, to significantly security in focus. The G7/G8 is embedded in a complex international institutional network, and in matters involving international security and state sovereignty, when the G7/G8 chooses to act it has two broad options. One is to work as a coordinator of the actions taken by others (states and MGOs primarily) as in the Kosovo crisis. The second is to work through its members directly in crisis management, which is more characteristic of its behavior in the Syrian civil war. With the crisis in Syria, the G8 moved as quickly as is possible for an institution that has no secretariat or any active presence between its annual summits. More recently in its first meeting after the expulsion of Russia in Brussels, Belgium in June 2014, the G8–1 continued its condemnation of the Syrian government. Further it condemned the vetoes of Russia and China of UN Security Council (UNSC) Resolution drafts that would have authorized a referral to the ICC. In its new form the G8–1 called for a shift in budgetary focus to humanitarian actors that can reach those most in need. The G8/G8–1 has never overtly called for military action, although it referenced future actions by the UNSC, which could entail military intervention in Syria. Niall Michelsen observes that the G8 stands as an institution that has consistently addressed the situation and directed international attention on the humanitarian dimensions of the problem. Although it has frequently spoken with admirable clarity, the Syrian crisis is a case where the words might not have made a major impact on the ground. Ultimately the responsibility for the lack of international action must reside with nation-states and other international organizations, though the G8 has been unsuccessful in swaying other international institutions to adopt its position. The G8–1 has a serious legitimacy deficit due to its limited membership. The larger G20 addresses this legitimacy deficit but also lacks the institutional capacity to effect long-term policies. If the international community seeks to fully and consistently implement R2P it is likely that these existing institutional arrangements are inadequate.

With its 57 members across the Northern Hemisphere from Europe, Asia and North America, the *OSCE* can be seen as the largest regional security organization around the world. Officially, the OSCE has three dimensions of cooperation areas to enhance security: the politico-military, the economic and environmental, and the human. Chapter 11, by Martin Nilsson, observes that though the OSCE has a comprehensive view of the concept of security, which contains actions from "hard" security issues, such as conflict management, to "soft" issues dealing with human rights, there is still not any specific declaration about humanitarian intervention or R2P, which directly could be applicable to the crisis in Syria. R2P is not an explicit part of the OSCE-agenda, thus there is no agreement between the member-states on how OSCE will act in such a situation, whether it happens in any of the member-states or in any other states, such as in the case of the neighboring Syria. Though the OSCE might have some capacity to contribute to establish at least partially the norms of R2P, this has not always been the case—for example, in Syria. The OSCE has no military capacity at all, and it is rather an intergovernmental organization focusing on peace settlements and management through missions, such as diplomacy and monitoring of elections. The OSCE's actions regarding Syria have mainly involved giving a few statements to address the refugee crisis. Beyond the parliamentary discussions and a few statements about the crisis in Syria and some policy recommendations for the member-states in regards to immigration issues, nothing more concrete has been done to solve the situation. This has to do with the lack of abilities for the OSCE to act in cases such as Syria, and there are several contributing explanations for why OSCE has not really intervened in Syria. Though the OSCE has widened its scope of the security concept and its geographical presence since the

Cold War ended, the budget has not increased, and it is very modest in relation to its overall ambition. However, it seems that the OSCE does not have the capacity for such ambitions and missions as in Syria. The diverse membership does not share the same values in regards to democratic rule and human rights issues. Though the OSCE has not officially endorsed R2P as a core responsibility, it still fits within the organization's broader security agenda. The OSCE has the ability to act as a mediator to stop the conflict in Syria or to organize control of the borders, which would improve the situation for ordinary people and refugees, among others, but there are several institutional and budgetary obstacles to overcome before this yet could happen. As a consequence, so far the OSCE has played a minor role in the Syrian crisis, mostly urging its member-states to handle the refugee crisis in a construct.

These chapters highlight in their ways the many challenges facing the concept of the Responsibility to Protect both generally and with regard to Syria. The lessons from Syria indicate a world that sees few benefits deriving from the exercise of R2P and only a challenge to state sovereignty. The history of the use of R2P does not bode well for future endeavors, especially when the example of Libya is considered. The sheer isolation of Gaddafi's regime, which provided space for the OIC, the Arab League, and the GCC to endorse the international exercise of R2P in Libya does not exist with Syria. The differing approaches between the League and the OIC stem largely from the differing membership of these two IOs where an important nation, Iran, is not represented in the latter and serves as an ally to the Syrian regime. The OIC continues to offer cautions about state sovereignty should intervention in Syria be contemplated. Yet the endorsement by the Arab League, the OIC and the GCC for R2P intervention by the international community into Libya was seen as being critical to involvement by the more Western-oriented IOs such as NATO. The evolving membership of the G8, now G8–1, has allowed a full-throated endorsement of UNSC resolutions calling for referral to the ICC, but this only underscores its increased lack of representativeness of the world stage. The singular success of the OPCW in having chemical weapons removed from Syria raises questions about its seeming lack of generalizability to other efforts. By comparison to the unused capacity of the ICC, the OPCW was not permitted to identify culpable individuals, only the corpus delicti of serious violations of international law. This omission underscores the growing sense of frustration at developing an institution that can identify and punish individuals for violations of international criminal law, but the ICC cannot, in this most egregious of situations, be utilized. Several of the chapters highlight the involvement of the MNO of topic in the exercise of R2P with Libya only to find in several situations that there was a tremendous cost in the almost surreptitious mission creep following the UNSC authorizing vote that quickly evolved from protection of civilians to regime change. The negative reaction from both Russia and China to what they perceive as an abuse of UNSC authority has had consequences for any possibility for the use of the ICC to prosecute and for the devolution of the G8 to the G8–1. The preference given by the 2005 UN World Summit to approval by the UNSC prior to the exercise of certainly military intervention appears to have been extended to other types of interventions by the IOs examined here; the complete absence of recent efforts by the UNSC to resolve the Syrian crisis has led to a similar absence by IOs, despite ample capacity for several of these IOs to take on many R2P tasks.

As a consequence of the years of civil strife—the extreme sectarian violence being experienced by the country, its shattered economy, and its vast displaced population—discussion of implementing the three pillars of R2P principles can only appear to be a cruel joke to the Syrian people. At some point in the post-conflict reconstruction of what remains of this country, the international community may have another opportunity at R2P. Such potential international actions on R2P in Syria would again, however, come too late adding Syria to a long list of previous international failures on human security such as in Rwanda, Ethiopia, Sudan and the Balkans among other places. Although there has been an important, gradual change in international rhetoric of principles to favor of human security, Syria is another example of the political unwillingness to protect civilians when state security interests are at stake. Sovereign states are, according to the UN Charter and numerous of conventions, declarations, and summits, legally and morally expected to safeguard human rights. If this does not happen, the international community is expected to take humanitarian actions. The international inaction towards Syria is but a cruel void for the Syrian people of how previous pronouncements on R2P have not been followed by meaningful action to protect them from its oppressive regime.

If "we" believe in a better world in which individuals must never be killed or tortured by an authoritarian and highly illegitimate regime, we must take action. Who is this "we" then? We are the ones who see the Syrian regime, under the motivating standards of R2P, as a pariah. We are also the ones who believe that it is everyone's human right to live secure from mass atrocities. In the case of Syria and President Assad, we are the international community that strongly believes that all individuals are entitled to secured human rights and that the Syrian regime must be held accountable for hundreds of thousands of killed and millions of refugees and displaced persons. Finally, we are also the ones who witness the failure of the UNSC to provide for humanitarian protection in Syria due to individual state security interests among some of the UN permanent members.

Although we most surely agree that the "we" should be the underlying principles of the UN, based on its established authority for promoting and protecting human rights, the historical record of the UN for undertaking the basic principles of R2P is seriously flawed. In addition, although "we" also most surely agree that humanitarian actions under the auspices of the UN are highly legitimate and something for which to strive, the inertia of the UN when mass atrocities become obvious cannot excuse the "we" from not taking action. Since "we" have a historical record of failures on human rights issues, with complete collapses in moral behavior in too many places in the world, "we" need to assess how we will be ready, perhaps through international organizations that do not see themselves waiting for UNSC permission to act, to save the next generation of Syrian civilians from the present conflict and despair. Should "we" relent and submit to a situation of a UN that is paralyzed, and become mere spectators to this atrocity, should we acquiesce to a conception that the human rights the West takes for granted are simply not universal, then, contemporary challenges to Syrian human rights will most surely be followed by tomorrow's challenges to our human rights in the Western democracies.

Index

Page numbers in **bold** denote figures.

For Product Safety Concerns and Information please contact our EU representative GPSR@taylorandfrancis.com
Taylor & Francis Verlag GmbH, Kaufingerstraße 24, 80331 München, Germany

www.ingramcontent.com/pod-product-compliance
Ingram Content Group UK Ltd.
Pitfield, Milton Keynes, MK11 3LW, UK
UKHW022129190926
475702UK00013B/1702